THE HARPERCOLLINS B[...]
of
ENGLISH POETRY
1950 — 2010

Sudeep Sen [www.sudeepsen.net] is widely recognized as a major new generation voice in world literature and 'one of the finest younger English-language poets in the international literary scene' (*BBC Radio*). He is 'fascinated not just by language but the possibilities of language' (*Scotland on Sunday*). He read English Literature at the University of Delhi and as an Inlaks Scholar received an MS from the Journalism School at Columbia University (New York). His awards, fellowships & residencies include: Hawthornden Fellowship (UK), Pushcart Prize nomination (USA), BreadLoaf (USA), Pleiades (Macedonia), NLPVF Dutch Foundation for Literature (Amsterdam), Ledig House (New York), Sanskriti (New Delhi), Wolfsberg UBS Pro Helvetia (Switzerland), Tyrone Guthrie Centre (Ireland), and Shanghai Writers Programme (China). He was international writer-in-residence at the Scottish Poetry Library (Edinburgh) and visiting scholar at Harvard University.

Sen's critically acclaimed books include *The Lunar Visitations*, *New York Times*, *Dali's Twisted Hands*, *Postmarked India: New & Selected Poems* (HarperCollins), *Distracted Geographies*, *Prayer Flag*, *Rain*, *Aria* (A K Ramanujan Translation Award), *Ladakh* and *Letters of Glass*. *Blue Nude: New & Selected Poems | Translations 1979–2014* (Jorge Zalamea International Poetry Prize) is forthcoming. He has also edited several important anthologies, including *The HarperCollins Book of English Poetry, Poetry Foundation Indian Poetry Portfolio, Poetry Review Centrefold of Indian Poems, The Literary Review Indian Poetry, World Literature Today Writing from Modern India, The Yellow Nib Contemporary English Poetry by Indians, Midnight's Grandchildren: Post-Independence English Poetry from India, Wasafiri New Writing from India, South Asia & the Diaspora*, and, *Lines Review Twelve Modern Young Indian Poets.*

His poems, translated into twenty-five languages, have featured in international anthologies by Penguin, HarperCollins, Bloomsbury, Routledge, Norton, Knopf, Everyman, Random House, Macmillan, and Granta. His words have appeared in the *Times Literary Supplement, Newsweek, Guardian, Observer, Independent, Telegraph, Financial Times, Herald, London Magazine, Poetry Review, Literary Review, Harvard Review, Hindu, Hindustan Times, Times of India, Indian Express, Outlook, India Today*, and broadcast on BBC, PBS, CNN IBN, NDTV, AIR & *Doordarshan*. Sen's newer work appears in *New Writing 15* (Granta), *Language for a New Century* (Norton), *Leela: An Erotic Play of Verse and Art* (Collins), *Indian Love Poems* (Knopf/Random House/Everyman), *Out of Bounds* (Bloodaxe), and *Initiate: Oxford New Writing* (Blackwell). He is the editorial director of AARK ARTS and the editor of *Atlas*. [www.atlasaarkarts.net]

Works by Sudeep Sen

POETRY | FICTION | NON-FICTION
[Books | Chapbooks | CDs | E-books]

Leaning Against the Lamppost; The Man in the Hut; The Lunar Visitations; Kali in Ottava Rima; New York Times; Parallel: Selected Poems; South African Woodcut; Mount Vesuvius in Eight Frames; Dali's Twisted Hands; Postmarked India: New & Selected Poems; BodyText; Retracing American Contours; Almanac; Lines of Desire; A Blank Letter; Perpetual Diary; Postcards from Bangladesh; Monsoon; The Single Malt; Prayer Flag; Distracted Geographies: An Archipelago of Intent; Rain; Rainbow; Heat; Winter; Stills from Sanskriti; Ladakh; Dreaming of Cezanne; Letters of Glass; Whispering Anklets; Blue Nude: New & Selected Poems | Translations 1979–2014 (forthcoming)

DRAMA
[Radio | Stage]

Vesuvius *(London: BBC Radio)*, Vesuvius *(London: Border Crossing)*, BodyText *(London: Border Crossing)*, Rain *(New Delhi: British Council & Mumbai: Kala Ghoda Arts Festival)*, Wo|Man *(New Delhi: India International Centre)*, T³ *(New Delhi: The Attic)*, Rain *(New Delhi & Los Angeles)*

FILM
[Short Feature | Documentary]

Rhythm, White Shoe Story, Woman of a Thousand Fires, Babylon is Dying: Diary of Third Street, Flying Home & others

TRANSLATION
[Books | Chapbooks]

In Another Tongue; Hayat Saif: Selected Poems; Love & Other Poems by Aminur Rahman; Spellbound & Other Poems by Fazal Shahabuddin; Love Poems by Shamsur Rahman; Selected Poems of Anamika; Aria | Anika

EDITOR | CO-EDITOR
[Books | Journals | E-zine]

Lines Review Twelve Modern Young Indian Poets; Wasafiri Contemporary Writings from India, South Asia & the Diaspora; Index on Censorship Songs [Poems] of Partition; Biblio Portfolio of South Asian Poetry; The British Council Book of Emerging English Poets from Bangladesh; Dash: Four New German Writers; Sestet; Modern English Poetry from Bangladesh; Midnight's Grandchildren: Post-Independence English Poetry from India; The Literary Review Indian Poetry, The Yellow Nib Contemporary English Poetry by Indians, World Literature Today Writing from Modern India, Poetry Foundation Indian Poetry Portfolio, Poetry Review Centrefold of Indian Poems, The HarperCollins Book of English Poetry, Atlas

edited by

SUDEEP SEN

HarperCollins *Publishers*

First published in India by
HarperCollins *Publishers* in 2012

HarperCollins Publishers India, Cyber City, Building 10-A, Gurugram,
Haryana-122002, India
www.harpercollins.co.in

6 8 10 9 7 5

P-ISBN 978-93-5029-041-5
E-ISBN 978-93-5029-517-5

Cover & Book design by Sudeep Sen

Typeset in Adobe Caslon Pro, Arial & Arial Narrow 10/12 pts.
InoSoft Systems

Printed and bound at
MicroPrints India, New Delhi

This product is made of FSC®-certified and other controlled material.

HarperCollins Publishers, Macken House, 39/40 Mayor Street Upper, Dublin 1, D01 C9W8, Ireland

for
ARIA

&

BABA
1930 — 2011

CONTENTS

SUDEEP SEN

CON | TEXT / FOREWORD

Ink runs from the corners of my mouth.
There is no happiness like mine.
I have been eating poetry.
— MARK STRAND, 'Eating Poetry'

Contemporary English fiction by Indians is now well known and widely established as part of the mainstream national and international literature with authors like V S Naipaul, Anita Desai, Salman Rushdie, Vikram Seth, Amitav Ghosh, Arundhati Roy, Amit Chaudhuri, Shashi Tharoor, Pico Iyer, Jhumpa Lahiri, Kiran Desai, Vikram Chandra, Aravind Adiga, and many others. They have won a range of prestigious prizes and awards including the Nobel, Booker, Commonwealth, Pulitzer, Sahitya Akademi, among others.

"Indian poetry in English has a longer and more distinguished tradition than Indian fiction in English," asserts literary critic and novelist Pankaj Mishra in *The Times Literary Supplement* (December 3, 2004). A leading UK poetry publisher, in a catalogue item states, "Many Indian poets were mining the rich vein of 'chutnified' (Salman Rushdie's word) Indian English long before novelists like Rushdie and Upamanyu Chatterjee started using it in their fiction."

Both these observations may well be true, but the ground reality of the story of Indian poetry in English is completely different. In the wider cultural arena, very little is known about Indian poetry and poets, within and more so outside India. Only a handful of contemporary English-language Indian poets command an international and national status. And the others who are visible happen to be known within very tight and narrow confines of the poetry circles, university reading circuits, and literary festivals. Beyond the initiated groups, not many follow or read contemporary English poetry, though ironically a great number write it.

There are not enough discerning anthologies of contemporary Indian poetry published in India and even less abroad—and the few that exist [and not very easily available] have tended to be rather narrow, inward-looking, and unsatisfactory. The lack of comprehensive poetry anthologies is something of a major surprise considering the vast cultural power of the world's largest democracy, and India's position as the third-largest English-language publisher in the world.

Anthologies of new writing serve as perfect vehicles and repository that showcase and highlight the best in current literatures. They also capture the pulse of literary culture, and act as good sources for archival material for future generations. Many fine single-author individual volumes by Indian poets have appeared in India and elsewhere, but their scattered appearances (and the aforementioned lack of a worthy library of comprehensive poetry anthologies) do not add up to what one would think of as a body of contemporary works that reflects a movement in new English poetry by Indians. This anthology hopes to redress some of the shortfall or near absence.

I have chosen to focus on poetry written in English, as a wider selection that includes India's many official languages would make this volume too voluminous and unwieldy. This is just the start and hopefully there shall be more such anthologies representing Indian poetry, including those in translation which in itself is an extensive and huge area.

A unique feature of this anthology is the fact that the overwhelming bulk of the poems are new and unpublished in individual author volumes. Over ninety per cent of the eighty-five poets have specially contributed new work for this book. Therefore the contents of this book give the reader a fine idea and a fresh taste of the vibrant contemporary Indian poetry and cultural scene. Carrying new and unpublished work is a major departure from other available anthologies, where some editors of these volumes have shown a tendency to mostly pick work from already published books or from existing older anthologies.

The history of contemporary English poetry by Indians is well over sixty years old — it has been over sixty years since India became a Republic in 1950. And to celebrate this occasion, the contemporary poets included in this book are all born post-1950, and all use English — one of India's many official languages.

The range of style, preoccupation, technique, is vast, various and impressive — each poet stamping their own signature and subtly displaying their own vision. The poets who are presented in these pages live in India and the broader Indian diasporas such as the United States and Canada, United Kingdom and Europe, Africa and Asia, Australia and the Pacific.

This diversity and multicultural representation allow the poets to have an internal dialogue between themselves and the varied topographical cultural spaces they come from or are influenced by. Therefore the poems create an inherent syntactical and historical tension — one that ultimately celebrates the written word, imagination, artistry, intellect, and humanity.

The publisher, during our early discussions, hoped that I would write a suitable foreword so that this project has my imprimatur — I am happy to have done that. Ordinarily one would be expected to provide a long, historical, and academic introduction to a book-length project such as this — but having given it much thought I decided that I want the poems themselves to primarily create their own aesthetic and critical discourse without the aid of someone hand-holding the reader. I believe that eventually only the printed word and its success as a piece of creative text or artifact on the page matter — and no critical jargon, contextualization, footnotes, and explanations are really required. It is easy enough to find bibliographical sources, existing anthologies, critical essays, scholarly studies, and poetical histories of Indian poetry, if anyone is inclined to do so for research, background knowledge, and further interest.

I have arranged the poets alphabetically using their first names so that there is a further sense of intimacy and a community-feel among fellow poets. This will hopefully break traditional barriers that come with formal arrangements when using last names or age as hierarchical arcs. What matters in this book are the well-crafted passionately felt poems themselves and their unique, intelligent and artistic qualities — and not reputation of the poets per se. So you will find the stars and established poets sharing the same platform with relatively newer promising writers in a large room without walls where both individual and collective echoes are equally eloquent and important.

The subject matter of the poems and their poetic concerns are staggeringly large and wide-ranging. There is introspection and gregariousness, politics and pedagogy, history and science, illness and fantasy, love and erotica, sex and death — the list is centrifugal, efferent, and expansive.

There is free verse and an astonishing penchant for formal verse — so you are likely to encounter a pantoum next to an acrostic poem, a triolet juxtaposed against a ghazal, lyric narratives and prose poetry, Sapphic fragments and Bhartrhari-style shataka, mosaic pastiché, ekphrastic verse, sonnet, rubai, poem songs, prayer chants, documentary feeds, rap, reggae, creole, canzone, tritina, sestina, ottava rima, rime royale and variations on waka: haiku, tanka, katauta, choka, bussokusekika, sedoka — the Indian poets are in full flight.

Taking into consideration the quality of the contents in this anthology, I would provocatively assert that the best English poetry written by Indians in the contemporary national and international literary arena is perhaps as good or superior to Indian fiction in English as a whole. There is bravura, experimentation, risk-taking, innovation, erudition, and delightfully uninhibited and fine use of language by the poets here. And for the best of them, this book is just a mere show window displaying only a small slice of the authors' individual oeuvre that is wide-ranging and impressive.

Importantly, this substantially generous selection of over 400 poems by eighty-five poets — spread over nearly 550 pages in this volume — significantly shifts, expands, remaps, and realigns the existing topography and tenor of contemporary English poetry by Indians.

My purpose as a practicing poet, translator, and literary editor, is to offer you a judiciously selected bouquet of modern poetry written by Indians in English, one that presents an unusual and original wordscape of a vastly multilingual, historic and artistic terrain of the variousness of India and the Indian diaspora.

Peruse and enjoy — in this book — the fine work that displays the poets' individual and collective palette, a palette that contains what is arguably the best post-1950s-born Indian poets in the contemporary English literary scene.

— S. S.
New Delhi | May 21, 2012

ADITI MACHADO

ADITI MACHADO (b. 1988) won the Srinivas Rayaprol Poetry Prize and the Toto Funds the Arts Award for Creative Writing in 2009. She is the poetry editor of *Asymptote*, a journal of translation. She has a BA from Mount Carmel College, Bangalore, and an MFA in poetry from Washington University, St. Louis, where she currently lives.

LEARNING A FOREIGN LANGUAGE

You are attempting to describe your body.

There are empty spaces where skin was, bone, muscle, fat.

You would call them *wounds* if you had the word.

Absent organs if you were a poet.

'There was a lover with a great knife. There was thunder.

He came and cut me. Then a count appeared, kissed,

healed me back to speech.'

Or:

You're standing on a rock with fast water about you.

The next rock is a leap too far and has the glint of scalpel.

The wind rushes at you, full-blooded.

All this ravenous water might consume you, leaf.

You're stuck in vocal paralysis till you're shot with drugs:
        a new word falling like a log
so you can cross over, learn to say *I love you / have some tea?*

SELF-PORTRAIT

The world flickered in and out of x-ray. There had been a click.
Now I am handed an image, as if a map, as if it could lead.
The scale is awry; geography immeasurable. There are stars

and eyes, a government of electricity in the machine-sky.
It is so still the skins of bats hung on trees freeze
into lanterns in the mine-dark night. I am in the corner

of the photograph, below the trees, its whitish leaves
not quite fallen – stalactites – and my hand is raised.
It is a wedding of some kind. All this breathing,

conjugating mass of people are my family. The batlights
in the trees regiment a glow on my face. It spreads. I turn
salt-pillar.

SURREALIST FILM-MAKING

The train is running off track, the air oneiric and chill.
We cut across the forest like thieves. All that derails
is one thread of your scarf – I am dizzy with its unravelling.
How linear it is. Almost absurd, this logic of movement.
The train breaks; the trolley man falls back, burns
his face with coffee. Outside trees commit acrobatics
in the elastic wind. I shoot three scenes with you
by the window. We have blackened out your eyes,
but a strange science is at work: here your pupils
are visible; here your hair flies in with the draught (action-
reaction); and there your skin is so pale we see blood
channel through. I shake my black box. It rattles.
It too works with theorems and will they come apart
if opened?

REHAB: A CONFESSION

My first time I was so young and at the beach.
I'd been buried for half a day. I came out
with new skin, an hour-glass of sand in my hair.

My mother bought me a clay doll.
I would shave its leg, as if to get it clean,
then sniff the discard.

Two years ago it was an earth goddess class.
I'd pictured myself worming through thick airless
mud, coming up for oxygen like a marathon swimmer.

Instead, there were mantras and coloured fabric
streaming, hip movements, exercise: *harness*
your energy, she said. It made me think of oxen

and cornrowed farmland, those sleek lines
of loam, railroad tracks for me to hurtle down,
and *god I'm awake now,* this morning, I thought

as I got out cold into the garden – I couldn't
resist – my toes turning the soil over, soft spades,
the sun opening out like a great kiln.

Could I bake there? I watched my skin
turn terracotta, my body pose like a sculpture.
Friends, I almost didn't get here.

AIMEE NEZHUKUMATATHIL

AIMEE NEZHUKUMATATHIL (b. 1974) is the author of *Lucky Fish*, *At the Drive-In Volcano*, winner of the Balcones Prize, and *Miracle Fruit*, which received the Tupelo Press Prize, the ForeWord Magazine Book of the Year Award in poetry, and the Global Filipino Award. Other awards for her writing include a National Endowment for the Arts fellowship in poetry and The Pushcart Prize. Her poetry and essays have been widely anthologized and have appeared in *180 More: Extraordinary Poems for Everyday* (New York: Random House), *Language for a New Century* (New York: W.W. Norton), and *The Literary Review Indian Poetry* (New Jersey: Fairleigh Dickinson University, edited by Sudeep Sen). She is associate professor of English at the State University of New York at Fredonia where she was awarded a Chancellor's Medal of Excellence, and lives with her husband and sons in Western New York.

ORANGE POPSICLE

Five weeks and you still feel the tang
of the knife at your side –
the stitch of summer sewn
back into your belly.
In the dark, the baby
blinks his eyes at you.

❧

Of course you cannot sleep. Thirty-two hours

of labour and all you want to do is eat.
The nurses allow you only
meat broths thinned with water, but for dessert:

an orange popsicle. You learn to love
this lonely time of night. The frozen crush

in your mouth slams you into a driveway
and suddenly, you are nine again. Your dad bursts

onto the scene with a box
of double stick-delights:
cherry, lime, grape. Your friends juice

into frightful clowns with coloured swollen lips.

❧

You, too, are a clown. Baggy pants and a ruffle
of spit around your neck. Your trick is to carry
a bucket. Pretend it is full of water. How did
you get to be a mother? *Pretend.*
You will do lots of pretending. Anything to make
the audience think they are about to be splashed.

HOW TO BE A POET

Breath[1]

Spider[2]

Boxes[3]

Eyeliner[4]

Thirst[5]

---

1. Even though the mudskipper can breathe through his tail, I wouldn't recommend picking one up with your bare hands. At the very least, use gloves.
2. Of course, some cultures throw onions at a newly-wed couple instead.
3. Not every box of Cracker Jack has a prize. In fact, as many as twelve per cent of the boxes are distributed to stores across the country prize-less.
4. Eye paint was used in ancient Egypt as a sort of insect repellent throughout the summer months especially. You can imagine insects were much larger then: locust, scarab, giant crickets.
5. Eight glasses of water is recommended, but not required.

BIBLIOMANCY

The old practice of using books to determine you will marry

Begin with a thick book splayed open
on a kitchen counter and watch the way

the girl stabs and stabs at it with her eyes
closed. The little teeth bites on the page stand

for a screaming, the way peacocks screech
with disgust whenever they catch sight

of their own clawed feet. Each word pokes out
a new promise, a fortune, better than any cookie:

she will meet a boy who keeps smooth rocks
in his pocket. She knows what to listen for.

LETTER FOUND AT THE TOWER OF SILENCE

In ancient Mumbai, bodies of the dead were placed atop a tower of silence, exposed to the silence, exposed to the sun and to birds of prey.

Dear Feather of Sly Bird Who Nibbles on My Arm –

Dear Small Wind Inside Cardamom Pod –

Dear Mushroom Blooming from My Side –

Your body, rested, in the sun is the ultimate act of charity
for birds and mice.

Sometimes a peacock saunters at the base of the Tower, a
shot of blue to nip you.

There is no need for melon slice, no need for a bite

of talk, absolutely no need to write me back –

A J THOMAS

A J THOMAS (b. 1952) writes poetry and fiction in English; as well as translates poetry, fiction and drama from Malayalam into English. He has several published books to his credit. He did his PhD in English (Translation Studies), and is a recipient of the Katha Award, the AKMG Prize, and the Hutch Crossword Award in 2007 for translating M. Mukundan's novel, *Kesavante Vilaapangal (Kesavan's Lamentations).* He voluntarily retired in August 2010 as Editor of *Indian Literature*, the bimonthly English journal of the Sahitya Akademi (National Academy of Letters) in New Delhi, and continues as its Guest Editor. Anthology appearances (among others) include *The Literary Review Indian Poetry* (New Jersey: Fairleigh Dickinson University), edited by Sudeep Sen. Currently, he is teaching English at the Benghazi University, Libya, in its Ajdabiya branch.

FADING

My mother's leathery face and
Caved in lips, sans teeth or denture
The broken arm in plaster rubbing
The side of the left breast once fed me
But now turned septic. Her three months
In the hospital had got her life back
To be snatched away anytime;
Death was on the prowl we knew.

She who was so full of life and hope
Suddenly turned to me one day and said:
'Why should I live on? My time is gone.
Let me go now. Don't worry about me.'
There was a blank listlessness about her
Eyes and lips.

In her last stint in the hospital
When she went in and out of
Cubicles of consciousness
Her roving eyes could not see
The reassurance her son sought
To bring, the security of well-being –
Only blankness, blankness.

RUSTIC VIGNETTES

The wind is the same
As ever, over the centuries
Blowing in stiff, straight draughts
Keeping the tree-leaves akimbo
And the black-tipped clouds in great, straight streams
The sky looks clean-washed and dipped in indigo
Hung out to dry
The sunshine seems to shimmer more
As if it has a life all its own
The rural spirit
Superimposed with
The aspirations of a fast-globalizing world...
Young women flash away on Kinetic Hondas
Older women on mopeds slug away
With funny caps on their heads!

FROM SILENCE

Begin your utterance
From silence.
Let it be
The first ripple on the surface.
Let the profundity of your self
Lie hidden beneath.

AMIT CHAUDHURI

Amit Chaudhuri (b. 1962) is the author of five novels, the latest of which is *The Immortals*, which was a *New Yorker* and *San Francisco Chronicle* Book of the Year, and Critics' Choice, Best Books of 2009, in *the Boston Globe* and *the Irish Times*. Among the many prizes he has won for his fiction are the Commonwealth Literature Prize, the Betty Trask award, the Encore Prize, the *Los Angeles Times* Book Prize, and the Indian government's Sahitya Akademi Award. He is a Fellow of the Royal Society of Literature, and was a judge of the Man Booker International Prize. In 2008, a *Guardian* editorial about him appeared in the newspaper's famous 'In Praise of...' series, the first time an Indian writer was so honoured. His first novel, *A Strange and Sublime Address*, is included in Colm Toibin and Carmen Callil's *Two Hundred Best Novels of the Last Fifty Years*. His second novel, *Afternoon Raag*, was on Anne Enright's list of 10 Best Short Novels in the *Guardian*. He is Professor of Contemporary Literature at the University of East Anglia, and has two highly regarded critical works to his name: *DH Lawrence and 'Difference'* and *Clearing a Space: Essays on India, Literature, and Culture*. He is editor of the *Picador Book of Modern Indian Literature*, and his essays on Tagore have appeared in a short book, *On Tagore*. He has one book of poetry, *St Cyril Road and Other Poems* (Penguin), and an earlier chapbook, *Insomniac* (Aark Arts). He is a musician, a singer in the North Indian classical tradition, with two HMV India recordings, as well as being a composer and performer in experimental music. His second CD in this genre, *Found Music* (EMI; Babel), was an allaboutjazz.com Critic's Choice of 2010.

INSOMNIAC

There is that crack of light
which becomes clearer after a few moments.
Though you shut your eyes
that clarity neither develops nor changes.
Then you move in and out
with your breathing.
And, not sleep, but a whole universe comes to you,
newsprint, an unfair observation,
the twilight of characters.
Until even that fades
and you are left with the spaces it occupied,
the false, heavy calm of waiting,
and, that crack of light,
now become mortal, become vulnerable,
announces to you the safety and comfort of what is to come.

DEATH OF A BUST

written on hearing news of Chintamoni Kar's death

This child came of age years ago;
her eyes, once unseeing, became bright
as irises; they looked at the world.
A smile moistened the lips.
The plaits fell behind her, a motionless pair.
They were what was most dead about her
but even they had a bright, obedient newness.
She was sixteen; she looked with a sixteen-year-
old's composure on the world.
She transcended the small town she came from, but
always remained of it, rooted to its maze.
Then, one day, for no discernible reason, life
left her; she stayed where she was, transfixed, but
was clay only; had turned into clay –
the lips were the same the expression too,
but we saw how easy it was to reduce, how soft
the substance was. Let it take place
somewhere outside our vision. She, whom we'd glanced at
sometimes, was removed from our midst. She was clay;
so we opened the earth and returned her there.

EDUCATION

As soon as I could dangle my legs
and sit at table
I learnt to use a fork and a spoon at lunchtime
in the proper way.
They hung from my hands
like limp pincers.
Cornflakes, toast, milk;
the shape of these words
on my palate.
And the mud-like stain on the toilet
paper I'd scrape my backside with
and consult daily: dark yellow,
unlike the pale shit I'd seen left
in the toilets by the English boys.

THE WRITERS

on constantly mishearing 'rioting' as 'writing' on the BBC

There has been writing for ten days now,
unabated. People are anxious, fed up.
There is writing in Paris, in disaffected suburbs,
but also in small towns, and old ones like Lyon.
The writers have been burning cars; they've thrown
homemade Molotov cocktails at policemen.
Contrary to initial reports, the writers
belong to several communities: Algerian
and Caribbean, certainly, but also Romanian,
Polish, and even French. Some are incredibly
young: the youngest is thirteen.
They stand edgily on street-corners, hardly
looking at each other. Long-standing neglect
and an absence of both authority and employment
have led to what are now ten nights of writing.

CORDLESS

for Sunetra Gupta

Here, in this new house in Old Headington,
with its aroma of new fittings,
it slips from your mind, it is easy to forget
where you have kept
it; in the cellar, down the stairs,
in the small, main corridor,
in the sitting room or the floor of the garden?
Small polished object, in a small house in a clean street so far from home,
in your second life,
it begins to ring, makes that muffled but insistent cry,
and, for a period, you are searching for it
in the cellar, going down the stairs in the electric lights,
or discover it in the bathroom,
purring, whining,
or find that you had misplaced it, that it is nearer you in this place
than you had imagined.

THE FALL OF BAGHDAD

Strangely, there was a gale that night
which started as wind – the usual
Nor'wester. We went to sleep, watching
the news, our lives in our stomachs.
We slept badly; the French windows shook
and she and I woke from a dream, thinking they
had come, and our city was taken. The door
banged shut; I walked to the balcony to see
if anything was broken. The familiar rooftops
of daytime, hours after midnight, were unwoken.

MORAL EDUCATION

a song[*]

When you are waking up
You must first wash face at tap
And do all necessary ablutions.
Then after you are having shower
You must sit for half an hour
Preparing quietly for the day's tuition.

Always be meek and mild
Never be loud and wild
Once a morning bow your head and pray
Eat your breakfast happily
To your grandparents say 'Ha ji'
To your parents do namaste.

Chorus:
Your destiny is our concern
And cause for trepidation.
But hear this song, you can't go wrong
With a moral education.

Once in school, study meekly
Don't look at girls except once weekly
Listen to what your teacher tells you to
Eat a pear at break time, shun
Boys who smoke and having fun
Never lie and always speak what's true

Help old lady cross the street
When you're home drink milk and eat
Then do your homework and go to play
But just for one hour, and then
You come back to mother again
Because by now it is the end of day.

---

[*] *A song that is based on, and refers to, the illustrated English-language charts sold on pavements and sometimes hung up in classrooms in municipal schools for the instruction of children. The song attempts to be true to the content, the intent, and the grammatical peculiarities of the charts.*

Chorus:
Rise early tomorrow, give no one sorrow
O child of the nation
The rays bring light, your future's bright
With a moral education. *(repeat once)*

Guitar solo, 4 bars, then chorus, repeat twice

TRUCKER

a song

Buri nazar wale tera muh kala
Bhali nazar wale tera hai ujala

OK ta ta bye bye
This is how we live and die

Buri nazar wale …

AMITAVA KUMAR

AMITAVA KUMAR (b. 1963) is a writer and journalist born in Ara, Bihar; he grew up in the nearby town of Patna, famous for its corruption, crushing poverty and delicious mangoes. Kumar is the author of *Evidence of Suspicion: A Writer's Report on the War on Terror* (Picador India, 2010), *Home Products: A Novel* (Picador India, 2007), *Husband of a Fanatic* (Penguin India, 2004), *Bombay-London-New York* (Penguin India, 2002), *Passport Photos* (Penguin India, 2000), and a book of poems, *No Tears for the N.R.I.* (Writers Workshop, 1996). In addition, he was the scriptwriter for two documentary films, *Pure Chutney* (1997) and *Dirty Laundry* (2005). Anthology appearances (among others) include *The Yellow Nib Contemporary English Poetry by Indians* (Belfast: Queens University), and *World Literature Today Writing from Modern India* (Norman: University of Oklahoma), both edited by Sudeep Sen. Currently, he is Professor of English at Vassar College. He lives in upstate New York with his wife and two children.

USE SCISSORS TO CUT THE MAP INTO FOUR SCENES

1. GOOD MORALE

The Colonel dreamed that when it rained like this snakes crawled inside the tent. Their length, and the mesmerizing torpor, filled him with disquiet. He killed one by slicing it with an old sword that used to hang on the wall above the mantelpiece in his father's home. His great-grandfather was a cavalryman in the Second World War and the sheath displayed the regimental colors, a faded ribbon that once might have been blue striped with black and orange.

The snake's death was so easy that it filled him with regret and vanished only when his bearer brought breakfast. The Colonel was sensitive to the changes in his mood; it made him alert to what could be happening to his men.

On sunny days, the soldiers played volleyball during the afternoon. One day he had found one of them taking part in the game instead of standing guard. The man was older than him, with five or six kids in a village near Samastipur. Like a schoolboy, the soldier took excited, bouncing steps on court; he was playing with the Kalashnikov pressed on his left like a crippled hand.

The Colonel felt the surge of sudden anger. He asked the soldier to take off his jacket and sit in a crouch on the ground while holding his ears. The platoon was called to attention near the court, the sagging net hanging like a shroud between two tall chinars. The wind cut into them from the surrounding mountains.

If they were careless when they stepped near the perimeter, a sniper using the same rifle that the soldier had held useless at his side could kill them from a distance of 1,350 meters. The militants waited for fools to wander into the open to take a piss, their dicks in hand. The lecture went on. 'I'll have to write the letter of condolence to your wife or your parents, behanchod, and I have no interest in doing that. Don't turn your back on your duty or you'll soon be lying dead on the ground, your feet up in the air like a woman who enjoys getting fucked.'

But for the most part the men didn't disappoint him. They followed all the rules. The Colonel had never thought it was some crap about their love for the country that earned his men's loyalty, although there could be a bit of that too. It was only the strict adherence to discipline that kept them alive. There was no doubt in his mind about that basic truth. His own task was to ensure that his men remained faithful to their training and never lost their morale.

His great-grandfather had fought in Europe, in the British Army, exchanging the wheat-fields of Uttar Pradesh for the fruit orchards in France. The food was strange but plentiful. The women in skirts and scarves were enticing and their children looked like little angels. But the men were homesick and terrified of combat and by the prospect of dying on foreign shores. Several of them used knives to make terrible cuts in their foot that they then filled with copper. The doctor knew what was happening, but was helpless, and signed the papers for discharge.

In this camp, the men could forget that they were not fighting in another country. When the convoys roared out of the gates, they could see painted on the bridge right outside the words 'Go back, Indian dogs'. He ordered the words painted over but, each time, they reappeared in the morning. In one of the letters that had once been preserved in his family, the Colonel's ancestor had written about pears being offered to soldiers by the children in France. It was different here. Every day, the kids shouted slogans in the streets and were capable of quite cheerfully tossing a grenade into the camp.

The rains meant that there was no volleyball today. At two, there was shouting outside the gates. The wooden bridge upstream had lost a plank and a boy had fallen in the swollen river. The boy's mother wanted them to find her child's body. In the middle, the current was strong but the water was only waist-high in most places. Twenty of his men, in their uniforms but wearing caps instead of helmets, spread from bank to bank. They held a thick rope in their hands, advancing in a slow line, haltingly, like students at their first dance lesson.

Three months ago, there had been the incident of a young woman who had been hit by a truck at night. The people in the area believed that her death had another cause, that she had been raped and killed in his camp. But the inquiry commission had done its work. It had declared that the rumours were not true and yet there was little that he could do to kill them. The hostility against his men and the attacks outside had risen dramatically. It had been a nightmare, and morale had suffered.

The Colonel was standing with the toes of his waterproofs resting on a tussock. He surveyed the crowd that had gathered to watch the operation. The men from the village shouted suggestions, and even encouragement, to the soldiers. The skies were still grey. It would soon be evening. The Colonel saw that his fingers were turning raw in the cold but he felt his spirits lift. He was going to order his bearer to give each of his men who were in the water a bottle of rum from his account. He could already see, as if in a dream, what would happen tomorrow or soon thereafter. The dead boy's father would appear at his door. He would speak of his older, surviving son, who had lost an arm in an accident, when he stepped on a mine. The Colonel would listen patiently.

'He is strong and his heart is of gold,' the father was going to say, with maybe spittle or real tears collecting on the side of his mouth, 'please save us and give him a job at your camp.' The Colonel would take his time but he would, of course, say yes and make everyone happy.

2. POSTMORTEM

The nurse left work at five o'clock.

She had seen the dead woman's husband sitting, near the entrance, under the yellow sign that Doctor Ahmed had hung some months ago. 'While You Wait, Meditate.' He was sitting with his arms crossed, elbows cupped in the palms of his hands, and hadn't looked up when she passed him on her way out.

Just after lunch, a convoy had come from the Army camp. Two uniformed soldiers carried in the body on a stretcher. One soldier, a small rifle in his left hand, threw open the office door and announced the Colonel. Doctor Ahmed had automatically stood up.

The Colonel was plump. He looked calm and extremely clean, the way bullfrogs do, gleaming green and gold in the mud. He put his baton on the table and asked the nurse to leave the office.

When Doctor Ahmed rang his bell, the nurse went back in and was told to get his wife, Zakia, from their home on the top floor. Usually, he just called her on the phone. The nurse hurried up, guessing that she was also to give the news about the Colonel.

Doctor Zakia was a pediatrician but she immediately understood why she was to do the postmortem. The soldiers put the stretcher in the operating room and left. The doctor removed the white sheet and then, choking, recited the Fatiha. It was difficult for her to continue the examination—she had a grown-up daughter.

Then the nurse was alone with the young woman for over four hours, cleaning her of the blood and the filth, and then stitching her up. The abdomen and thighs had turned green, but this was expected. There was a pronounced swelling of the tongue and lips.

The nurse wondered whether the body would last till the funeral. If there was a protest, it would take the entire day in the sun for the procession to reach the cemetery.

A year ago, a doctor in the north had announced that the corpse brought to him was of a woman who had been gang-raped. This was a mistake. The Army put out the story that the woman used to come to the camp for customers and that her husband found out and had probably got her killed.

In the warm and stuffy room, the nurse realized that her teeth were chattering. She stopped and for a long while stared at the back of her gloved hands. Then she turned them over, as if she were praying, and studied the film of dark coagulated matter on her fingers.

There was no slippage and still it was hard work. Doctor Zakia would probably tell the family that the body had been washed thrice. The women would nevertheless insist on doing what was proper. How was she to save them? No one teaches you in nursing school to cover cigarette burns on the privates or to stitch torn nipples.

When she finally stepped out of the room she was startled to see a dozen soldiers in the hallway. She met the eye of the one closest to her and flinched, but he was quiet, even shy, like a dog that has brought in a squirrel and dropped it on the carpet.

At six, she was sitting in front of the television in her tiny living room. And there she was, the young woman in her wedding photograph. The newsreader said the body had been found in a ditch after the woman had gone missing for twenty-six hours. She had been struck sometime at night by a speeding vehicle.

3. MILK IS GOOD FOR YOU

The boy is barely seven. He tells his teacher that if he looks long enough at the sun, he can make his sight go black. His teacher slaps him on the head, not with force, but still it stings, and the boy smiles.

He is a good boy. The teacher has known him since he was a baby. The boy's father is the teacher's first cousin; he is also older than the teacher by at least ten years, and has been the village-tailor for as long as he can remember.

Once, when the boy was four, he was peeing in the teacher's front yard and announced that he was going to start drinking more milk because his pee was coming out yellow.

Milk?

'Yes,' the boy said, 'milk is good for you and can make your pee white again.'

A little over two years later, the teacher had started the geography class in the afternoon when someone brought the news of the explosion. They raced to the hospital on his bicycle, the boy sitting behind him on the carriage, the small hands clutching his teacher's shirt. In the waiting room, he noticed that the child had peed in his pants.

The boy's elder brother was inside. He had stepped into a millet field three miles north, where the Army had planted mines and marked with a red strip of cloth and a painted sign. Doctor Ahmed tried his best. He stitched the injured leg but was unable to save an arm.

Before the summer was over, the older boy dropped out and began to work in the tea-shop at the bus-station. He was a hard worker. You can see him there at all hours of the day, working with his one good arm, boiling the milky mixture till the dark tea-leaves rise to the top looking like dead ants.

The younger one still comes to school. He is clever. Just the other day in class he collected the snow from the windowsill and asked if they could sell it in packets in other parts of the country where it is hot.

The teacher later repeated this story at the tea-shop. A customer joked, 'Maybe the Army can help with that. Their trucks can take the snow back to the plains.' The one-armed boy looked up from the kerosene stove. He said, 'Or the snow could be used in the coffins in which we could send back all the soldiers.'

4. FORTY TAKES

A white sheet, only slightly unclean, was spread out on a table that had been placed beside a pomegranate tree. On the table, thermoses filled with tea and also a tray of small, surprisingly elegant, sandwiches from the hotel where the film-crew was staying. Near the top of a distant hill, the hotel's bright white façade and orange flag were visible from the ramshackle building where the shooting was in progress.

The young actor who was playing the villain, a one-armed terrorist, had his right arm wrapped under his shirt. His right sleeve hung loose. He was impatient, full of irritation, a cigarette dangling from his full lips. He said to no one in particular that forty takes of a single shot, however important, should be left to people in Hollywood. People laughed when he added, 'After so many takes, it really does begin to feel like acting.'

For an earlier generation of actors, this valley was the place to shoot romantic songs. But all that had changed in the last twenty years. The film crews had returned to make films here about terrorism. You could still shoot a love-story here but it at least needed a bomb blast. That is what the viewers now expected when they saw the snow-capped mountains on the screen.

The actor playing the terrorist wanted to know how he could pretend he was murdering someone if each time the victim had picked himself up and wandered away to talk on his mobile or take a leak. Forty takes!

From the middle distance came an assistant's voice, asking for silence, but the actor who had been complaining paid no heed. He said, 'I can feel my false beard growing longer while I wait here.' He looked at the new actress from Delhi who was also said to be an ace tennis player. She didn't act as if she had heard the joke. She had been given the role of a nurse in the movie.

The actors had begun to arrive over the last few days. Before then, the director had been shooting crowd scenes. A funeral procession for a young woman was fired upon by the Army because it feared that unless the crowd was dispersed a riot would start. The firing, and the riot that resulted, were important parts of the script. Each day now scenes requiring smaller number of people, mostly professional actors in important roles, were being blocked and shot.

Today they were shooting a scene in a rundown school for children. A young man who had lost an arm and become a terrorist had come to get help from his old teacher. The two talked, and argued. At last, the teacher would shoot the youth, first aiming badly and hitting him in his good arm, and then right between his eyes. This scene would appear at the film's end.

Swaroop, the director, was from a city near the southern tip of India. He had been trained at the film-school New York University and then served as assistant to a Mexican man whose film's name had been mistranslated in English as 'Love's a Bitch'. Swaroop had developed the script from a report he had read in the news about a young woman's body found in a ditch near an Army camp. He had contemplated a love-story for a while and then given up on the idea. The script now turned on the relationship between two men, an older mentor who was the teacher, and a younger, damaged man who becomes a terrorist. The film's cinematographer was a Chinese man from Hong Kong. A stuntman who was good with fight scenes and bright explosions had come from Australia and was to be found sitting expressionless all night in the hotel bar.

At last, it was time for the young man playing the villain. As he walked towards the school with the assistant who was holding the clapboard, he practised by saying to no one in particular, 'The priest, the policeman, anyone with any power, wants to know your name, your religion. But a bomb doesn't care what–.' He stopped in mid-delivery and asked the assistant, "Do you know what I'd kill for right now.'

ANAND THAKORE

ANAND THAKORE (b. 1971) was born in Mumbai, spent a part of his childhood in the UK, and has lived in India since then. A trained Hindustani classical vocalist, he has been a disciple of Pandit Satyasheel Deshpande and has performed Hindustani vocal music in many parts of the country. He was educated at Solihull Public School, UK, and at Cathedral School, Mumbai. He earned a BA in English at Elphinstone College, where he also studied Sanskrit Literature. He subsequently earned An MA in English Literature from the University of Poona, Pune. Thakore's poems and critical essays on music and poetry have appeared in various national and international journals and anthologies. He is the author of three collections of verse: *Waking in December* (Harbour Line, 2001), *Elephant Bathing* (Poetrywala, 2012) and *Mughal Sequence* (Poetrywala 2012). Thakore is the founder of 'Harbour Line', a Mumbai-based writers' collective which he co-founded and runs. He is also the chief co-ordinator of 'Kshitij', an interactive forum for Hindustani musicians. He is the recipient of a national scholarship for music and a grant from the Charles Wallace trust for experimental work in the UK. Thakore describes his work as a poet and a musician, as 'having arisen from a fortuitous confluence of seemingly disparate cultural Histories'. *Guldasta-e-Khayal*, his most recent Hindustani classical CD, appeared in 2011; *Sabadpiya Ki Khoj*, a pamphlet of Hindi lyrics, composed by him, in 2007. He lives in Mumbai, where he teaches music privately, in the *guru-shishya* tradition, and gives frequent performances of his music and poetry.

MY FATHER'S OLD MAN

Summer that year had come to an early close.
Rain beguiled us with its cryptic promise of renewal
And the jackfruit tree still clung to its ripened fruit,
When he gave me his watch and his bunch of keys,
And his dead wife's file of verse and prose.

For the first slow fortnight after she died, he was too worn-out
Even to bathe; but then he took to watching television,
And studying the morning paper when he could.
At first we took turns, my father and I,
Helping him with his list of things to be bought

To keep the house running, wading through absence,
Looking out beyond hope for the oarless raft of his grief.
We wreathed her photograph with lilies and marigold,
And talked of cricket, politics and the state of the stockmarket,
Hoping that our chatter would drown out her silence;

But as the months drew on we drew back in fear,
From those mordant, phantasm-peopled spaces
That homed in on his pain; and once a week, when he shaved,
We feared the bitter conundrums his tilted mirror posed:
That voice thrumming at the back of his head – was it him or her?

Was the flesh his guest or his ailing host?
We had no answers and dared not guess, or seek
To tune our deadened nerves to the pitch of his loss,
Till a month before the end, we left him alone,
With a hired night-nurse and his wife's mute ghost,

An old wooden bed and a God to thank,
And locked ourselves in separate adjacent rooms,
Our whiskey consanguineous, a febrile sealing
Of troubled veins and bonds, and a sealing-off:
We let the man die while we dreamed and drank.

STEAM BATH

I cannot tell if he is someone I know:
The naked man in the corner, whose face this steam obscures,
Colluding with crushed hemp and an ancient ache,
And unfurling its billows to form, as it froths and pours,

The face of a man whose angst I have touched,
Whose lust I have clutched and harboured like a clone;
His bleak misgivings now nearly mine,
His lips of steam closing in on my own,

To claim their insistent predatory kiss.
I am wise to his way of assuming congruence.
I smile at the furrow in his narrowing brows.
He cannot become me when I breathe like this –

But will I leave here, undaunted by his fears,
Redeemed by heat when I reach for this door;
Or will he follow me softly across this floor:
The man I have longed to sweat out for years?

GHAZAL

Shall I hold my tongue, Lord, or call tonight?
Contain myself, or start another brawl tonight?

My dead mentor returns. Shall I silence him with words,
Or wrap his image in a shawl tonight?

I am lured by the dark I longed to outgrow.
I long to crawl back into that caul tonight;

And the words of the saints fade like bad dreams.
Their voices will not fill this hall tonight.

Leave me, Lord, leave me alone with my song,
For I shall not be your thrall tonight;

And leave the door open, behind you, when you leave.
I have another guest to enthrall tonight:

Come, my heart, let us be friends again,
And celebrate the ancient fall tonight.

DUET ON THE DEATH OF A CAT

Two monks were fighting over a cat. The master appeared, drew his long sword, and sliced the cat into two halves. 'Here,' he said, 'is your cat, and here, is yours.' The words of the koan must not be interpreted, only received.
—Ritesh Reddy, second-degree blackbelt, private lecture.

We've left here before but this time we're through:
The master's a hustler, a monster, a fake;
And he's sliced our pretty little cat in two.

Surrender's our motto, but this simply won't do.
Have we nothing but a pair of selves at stake?
We've been here before but this time we're through.

Who rends this mesh, ends this myth of me and you?
The long tail reaches back for the mouth of its snake;
And the master has sliced our cat in two.

No sign to decipher, no vision. No clue:
If death is not real, whom does death unmake?
We've been through this before but this time we're through.

Someone could tell us what this means, but who?
Who puts us to sleep, who shakes us awake?
The master has sliced our cat in two.

Time for this ship to abandon its crew –
But we're *thinking* again, the ancient mistake –
We've left here before but this time we're through.
The master has sliced our cat in two.

THE SCHOOLBOY ON THE PONT ALEXANDRE TROIS

Paris 87

Looking out across the darkening water,
but finding no sign of the 'great, graceful arch'
his Michelin Guide has promised him he will see,
he begins once again to feel like a bridge.

Here, at last, is what he was born to do:
to span the sad rift
between the gifted and the tone-deaf,
the sober and the merry,
the keepers of accounts
and the votaries of love;

and to sprawl unquestioningly
across strong currents of turbulence,
so his mother can cross home
into the south she dreams of,
his father move out into the sheltering north,
listening unmoved
while he bears their weight,
and they exchange strange words upon their way.

Before him, below him, the river flows on unconcerned.
A mild yellow haze comes over Les Invalides,
and on the way home the quays and markets,
the streets and public squares
seem suddenly full of ways to be.
Night comes companionably upon the Opera Comique,
and it doesn't occur to him until the next morning,
that the bridge he looked out from
was the one he was looking for.

ANANYA S GUHA

ANANYA S GUHA (b. 1957) grew up in Shillong, Meghalaya. He has been working for the last nineteen years at the Indira Gandhi National Open University as an academic administrator. He is currently 'Officer on Special Duty' in the IGNOU Institute for Vocational Education and Training in Shillong. He has been at the IGNOU for the last eighteen years, prior to that a lecturer, senior lecturer and the head of the department of English at St. Edmund's College, Shillong. He has a doctoral degree on the novels of William Golding. He has published three collections of poetry: *What Else is Alive?*, *Poems*, and *Dusk Descends*. Anthology appearances (among others) include *Dancing Earth: An Anthology of Poetry from the Northeast* (New Delhi: Penguin India / co-edited by Kynpham Sing Nongkynrih and Robin S. Ngangom), and *The Literary Review Indian Poetry* (New Jersey: Fairleigh Dickinson University / edited by Sudeep Sen). His individual poems have been published in magazines, e-zines and websites, in India and abroad, including *Chandrabhaga*, *Kavya Bharati*, *Indian PEN*, *The Telegraph*, *The Statesman*, *The Sunday Mail*, *Poeisis*, *The New Welsh Review*, *Greens Magazine*, *Gloom Cupboard*, *Glasgow Review*, *Winterspin*, and *Other Voices*. He has also published articles and papers related to education in journals and magazines such as *Social Responsibility Journal*, *University News*, and others. He lives in Shillong.

LAMENT

In this night's tide
ghoulish barking
even time is a spent
force, abandoning
the withering of silence
stray cars roam streets
the loquacious drunk reminisces
loudly, and the brazen night
wakes up into throes of poetry
my love your space is timeless
your streets smile sleepily,
and tom toms rend the sky
what if you are perverse?
what if you enkindle mammoth
fires, to whip reality
what if passers-by ravage
your lonesome streets
into a half-sung elegy?

YOU

You knock at the heart's
call, and past seeps
through the uncovered
mind, you bring back a whiff
that sends rapture of hope
you create that energy
which was once upon us
You are time's stranger
yet no enemy of the past
which you refurbish in
your myriad ways, images
recline as in stupor
Your incantations are no myth
as your mind discovers arcane
moments, of still small memories
You are you, and the schism is me.

IN OBLIVION

I negotiate with
crowds sullenly as
if entombed in
nights catcall or
thralled in horrific
skies;

I stutter, stammer
in crowds of procession
who stampede evening's
silence by a raucousness
they understand,
and arraign in
the midst of thunder
I negotiate them
with fear muted
in uncanny moods,
I negotiate them
with flaunting
prudery, saying
I know you
I like you
I love you
for you are merely
crowd among crowds
one in the lonely many;
hibiscus of yearning
to tear city scrapes
and achieve millions

In oblivion.

ANINDITA SENGUPTA

ANINDITA SENGUPTA'S (b. 1978) collection of poetry, *City of Water*, was published by Sahitya Akademi in 2010. Her work has also appeared in several journals and anthologies including *Not A Muse* (Haven Books, 2009), *Writing Love* (Rupa, 2010) and *Poetry with Prakriti* (Prakriti Foundation, 2010). In 2008, she received the Toto Funds the Arts Award for Creative Writing and in 2010, the Charles Wallace Writers Fellowship at University of Kent, England. In 2012, she received the Muse India Young Writer award for City of Water. She works as an independent journalist and editorial consultant in Mumbai and is founder-editor of *Ultra Violet* (http://ultraviolet.in), a site for contemporary feminism in India.

BRINK

The meaning of quiet – those corridors
knew it well. *Softly girls. The building is old,*

Mother C lisped up stairs, her wimple
flaring like a halo. At table tennis, we twirled spins

like neat habits. A single smash could dismantle
our world. Outside school, a man with a cleft lip

spiced slices of raw mango. Red chilli
burst into our mouth like explosions of sea water.

The heat moved us to shower. We limp-toed
into womanhood in spotless socks,

a generation afraid of bringing things down.
A backyard of bramble and weed was where

we found noise. It wandered knock-kneed
and had a tongue full of pins.

LIFT

Glancing past the slum at noon, they shift quick,
lift faces to sun like stones. Blue tarpaulin

gaudies houses in squalor. Inside, children celled
in dust and smells – fish blood, gutter water, rain –

chanting A for apple, B for bear like prayers
for promised land. They plug their ears, glide up.

Everything's relative, ma says. Her smile
browns at edges like meat roasting on low flame.

Fingermarks, like forks, crisscross her back
in red. They close their mouths at dusk

so nothing escapes, not even anger.
Behind closed doors, they fling their bags down,

stamp and kick them with hard feet
as if they're living bodies, aching and silent.

BHEESHMA

Fog roils by the riverside,
stooping and white-bearded

as an ancient curse. Two girls
in red leggings sit on the ledge,

swing their legs. One turns her face
to the wind, freezes into a moue.

The other falls into blind alleys
of water. There is a third who waits,

smoking a cigarette in the corner
where even sailors don't dare.

A ship hulks in, mooing.
He wakes. The digital blinks 4.

He limps to the loo, fumbles strings,
drizzles drops, thinks *there must be*

a better way. The night thumps
his pillow, an impatient hand,

and his head is a basin of dark water.
He plunges in, finds again

the same revolve of time, a picture
of days to come, each day exactly

like the one before. His eyes
are pinned to the window

with waiting. On the walls,
shadows hunch like whales.

ANITA NAIR

ANITA NAIR (b. 1966) was born in Shoranur, Kerala. She grew up in Chennai and later moved to Kerala where she did her BA in English language and literature. She worked as an advertising writer before opting to write full time in 2001. Nair is the author of five works of fiction: *Satyr of the Subway & Eleven Other Stories, The Better Man, Ladies Coupé, Mistress* and *Lessons in Forgetting*; a collection of essays: *Goodnight & God Bless*; a collection of poems: *Malabar Mind;* and has edited *Where the Rain is Born: Writings about Kerala.* Nair has also written four books for children and two plays *Nine Faces of Being* and *A Twist of Lime*. Anthology appearances (among others) include *The Yellow Nib Contemporary English Poetry by Indians* (Belfast: Queens University), and *World Literature Today Writing from Modern India* (Norman: University of Oklahoma), both edited by Sudeep Sen, also in *The Toronto Review* and *The Notre Dame Review*. She was awarded the 'FLO FICCI Women Achievers Awards 2008 for Literature'. *Mistress* was on the 2008 Orange Prize long list in the UK, was named a finalist for the 2007 PEN/Beyond Margins Award in the USA and for the 2007 LiBeraturpreis in Germany. Most recently she was felicitated by Montblanc as part of their Signature for Good initiative with UNICEF. Anita Nair writes regularly for several publications and lives in Bangalore.

MINISTRY OF DECEIT

Was it a Sunday evening
When you left a window carelessly open
You rang first that gong of betrayal?

Was it one high noon
When you thoughtlessly fed her bones of the lamb
You sang first that litany of duplicity?

Was it under a moonlit sky
When your face flowered in surreptitious joy
You knew first that triumph of transgression?

Was it under a kitchen light
As you lay bare fish bones of guilt
You exorcised first imprudent trust?

A Saturday, a Monday,
Pearly light, yellow light, in the dark
Eighty-six thousand four hundred ways exist.

To baptize the fool
Smug in the knowledge
She will never be deceived.

Halleluiah

THIS HOUSE MINE

I saw in the rock
my father's lower lip
unable to hide the pout of countless sweepings
of wind, water and all that is time.

It trembles, see how it trembles
I saw in the rock my father.

So I called men to carve me steps
ordered the sun to splash it ochre.
Build for me a sandal plane of repose
Still the tremble and his fear
I saw in the rock my father

From the hill, a butterfly lifted
my mother's soul, yellow green
unable to pause in its yearnings
to drink deep of honey and all that is here

It flutters, see how it flutters
I saw in the butterfly my mother.

So I called men to trap the light
ordered the clouds to halt in its path.
Rain in here all you have
For her to drink her fill of content
I saw in the butterfly my mother

Now there is me
a coil of scales, one upon one
diamonds unfurl as it slithers
and seek to bury itself alive.

It shies, see how it shies
I saw in the serpent, I

So I called men to build me a burrow
ordered the earth to lend its hue.
Spread wide your green hearts, palm tree

sing for me, bamboo
weave your dreams spiders, I urged.

Thus I laid to rest doubts, dissipation, and
relentless wanderings of the vagrant heart.

AN OSTRICH'S LOVE SONG

Fight your own battles.
If you win, I'll rejoice
With you in your triumph and glory.

If you lose,
You have the solace,
Of hiding your head between two pillows.

TRANSGRESSIONS

This is for real
the weight of this hand
that gathers me to the curve of a hip
and so as I lie
in this nest of bed clothes and slumbering flesh
I tell myself
this warmth is content.
The rest –
the foolish leaping of a vagrant heart
at a look exchanged
across a room crowded
with people and objects;
the feel of fleeting skin;
the ripening of hunger
will not transgress into tomorrow.

This must
be it then:
the derangement
of all senses...
when you breathe
the Giorgio
pulsing my pulse points
and I am drunk
on the whisky
you sip
between mouthfuls
of espresso.

Words crawl
And hiss
between us.
What
we dare not...
our syllables do:
with abandon

with naked joy,
they arch their necks
a ritual
to consummate
this intensity
so much more
than mere
desire.

❦

I give you
my hand
to clasp.
I give you
my cheek
to kiss.
I give you
my dreams
to remember me by.

ANJUM HASAN

ANJUM HASAN's (b. 1972) latest book is a collection of stories called *Difficult Pleasures* (Penguin-Viking). Her first novel, *Lunatic in my Head* (Zubaan-Penguin India), was short-listed for the Crossword Fiction Award, and her second, *Neti, Neti* (IndiaInk), long-listed for the Man Asia Literary Prize 2008 and the DSC Prize for South Asian Literature 2010, and short-listed for the Hindu Best Fiction Award. She published a collection of poems, *Street on the Hill* (Sahitya Akademi), in 2006. Anjum's poems have appeared in national and international magazines including *Atlas, Fulcrum, Critical Quarterly, Heat Magazine, Indian Literature* and others. Anthology appearances include *The Bloodaxe Book of Contemporary Indian Poetry* (Bloodaxe), *Language for a New Century: Contemporary Poetry from the Middle East, Asia and Beyond* (Norton), *Anthology of Contemporary Poetry from the Northeast* (NEHU), *The Literary Review Indian Poetry* (New Jersey: Fairleigh Dickinson University), *The Yellow Nib Contemporary English Poetry by Indians* (Belfast: Queens University), *World Literature Today Writing from Modern India* (Norman: University of Oklahoma), the last three edited by Sudeep Sen. She has also published short fiction, travel essays and book reviews. Anjum Hasan was Charles Wallace writer-in-residence at the University of Kent in Canterbury (UK). She works as Book Editor for *The Caravan*, and lives in Bangalore.

NO SENTENCE

No sentence is as long as the waking moment of the night.
Every lunchtime butter garlic fries, the boys water
the lawn. No elegy equals blood and glass.
The bazaar girls spread their turquoise rings, their owls
and their dolphins. No one's earned the right.
I watch a butterfly swing by the frangipani.
No human is just human. Even the mosquitoes
here dream as they bite. We discuss where
to go for dinner. No memory sheathes its object tight.
The sun drops low then fades out, the lanterns sway.
No one can say – now, the world's suffering adds up.
The waxing moon, the banana flower, the gin on ice.
No joy is without gaudiness, no murderer lacks a name.
I dream my mother's missing. Nothing could make time
go by without newspapers and screams
and yet I can always find a way to say:
I mourn for it because it used to be my life.

WHEN I GROW UP

I would like to be the hanger-on at the edge of a photograph
in which a politician has just won an election and someone
is trying to kill him with too many yellow sweets.

I would like to be a vendor of nylon garlands on a winter morning,
walking with a glowing basket full of something not pretending
to be flowers and succeeding.

I would like to be a honey-coloured cat licking itself on a wall,
unaware that the day will pass and tomorrow it will
still be a honey-coloured cat licking itself but all over again.

I would not like to be:

the school boy who is whacked so hard he just drops his head
into his hands and goes round and round in circles, his pain
trying to lead him to that place where there is no pain.

THE WORLD AS MY ILLNESS

January fever like the musk of a Bangalore evening when winter's
going, could be gone tomorrow with more shiny blue paracetamol strips,
blank, blank, blank where the words and hot traffic noises were,
leaving just a candle dripping inside you when you shift, just the
too nearness of the vendor of greens, the thirsty distances to water.

Brave tender daffodils cold, dripping like frost from the seven o' clock
windows, and then my heart with pleasure sings because they're not
gilded or radiant and I'm not dying: just a gently masochist English cold
that burns up my nose, and the daffodils' wet yellow madness poking
out of winter, saying – this has happened, this has happened before.

Northumberland boil on the sole of the foot, in a pink and white room
pain hardening like a breakfast egg when walking is the language
of everything here, when this language of grass and sheep hardly ever
needs the punctuation of mile-castle, turnstile, tree, when walking is
means without end, and then my foot understands and ashamedly heals.

Summer swollen with salt and blood, stiff coil of a cramp, the scent
in the lane of some flowering tree, everything tightening slowly then
melting in circles like love or a fan in the heat, teenagers dancing
to the same circular beat – harey Ram, harey Ram, harey Krishna,
harey Ram, painkiller waking me up, painkiller putting me to sleep.

THE DAY NO ONE DIED

after Frank O' Hara

It's a day to drink a large soda
in Bangalore, gulmohar flowers livid on the left
and there on the right. I take the creaking 278,
a woman with one cataract eye's handing a bag
of bananas to the conductor at Mekhri circle.
She knows it too, today's the day

no one dies. The soda bottle's

hissing a bit like laughter in my hand when
I pass through Cantonment railway station
without a platform ticket, the policeman watching but
maybe too hot to move. I'm predicting the overbridge
will collapse soon but I walk on it every time.
My doctor's back from Bombay, yawning, henna
on her hands. Ma planned to boycott the wedding
but didn't, she says as she watches
the inside of me on her screen

and then I'm in a rickshaw to Lavelle Road
to see photographs of empty lots in the gallery,
alone with them, not sure why they're all sunny lots.
Someone in the guestbook has written, 'We were fooled.'
I like it that I can sit and eat peach melba,
read till the waiter brings back the afternoon menu.
Then I'm out again, drizzled on by the big wet men
sculpture on Mallya Road, turning

onto Kasturba Road and there in the May dusk and 6 o' clock
traffic, the black leaves of a rain tree are, I'm not exaggerating,
like a thousand small quivering birds about to take off.

THIS BIOGRAPHY

My heart beat fast or did not beat at all;
I could not say all that I thought and thought
till words deserted me. I loved too abstractly.
I dreaded how all there was to give was me —
like water, this biography. I unravelled far too easily
then fled to selfish deserts and slept on the hardest rocks.
I couldn't make what others made and broke and broke
and made, that sweet choreography. I went alone
and missed the world continually. I misread smiles;
I stuttered before open arms, but time passed too fast
for disappointment's imprint on the glass of memory.
I sought the future even when the blood swirled now,
I let the past decide too greedily. I kept searching out
the window, I tried to stay half hidden from the light.

ANUPAMA RAJU

ANUPAMA RAJU'S (b. 1975) work features in several anthologies: *Ten: The New Indian Poets* (edited by Jayanta Mahapatra), *Mosaic: An Anthology of Poems* (2008), and *Poetry with Prakriti* (2007–2008). Her poems have been published in *The Caravan, The Little Magazine, Mint Lounge, Indian Literature,* and *Pratilipi.* She is the writer for a collaborative Indo-French Poetry and Photography Project (2012). Anupama has also been translating the Malayalam author Paul Zacharia's short stories into English. As a journalist, her book reviews and interviews regularly appear in *The Hindu Literary Review.* Anupama Raju lives in Trivandrum, where she works as a corporate trainer and freelance writer.

MONSTER POEM

Let me wake you up, creature of silence
breathe into your waiting body, feed you drops
of night blood so that you will survive the day.

You will survive, dearest spirit, in words
lying in cemeteries poets built long ago
to remember dead muses for centuries to come.

Your muse remembers you, beloved child of darkness,
as a brooding bundle of images, recalls how your five
limbs crawled into pages waiting to be stitched up.

I see you crawl now into this page, your ears alert
to the cries of a new born metaphor, your eyes
watching its fragile fingers curl into meanings.

But you are not fragile. A swift move and four stanzas
later, you swallow the unsuspecting ideas. Deed done,
greed fulfilled, you live again. While I die.

ECLIPSE

I shall not think of you these damned days
but let longing wet silences thrive in rain
like moss-eaten lines brewing on my face.
I shall not think of you these damned days
but let lusty moons swallow January sunrays
when diamonds of night shine, quite insane.
I shall not think of you these damned days
but let longing wet silences thrive – rain.

NAME, PLACE, ANIMAL, THING

Letters stuck. Meanings
born. Identities emerge.
What isn't in a name?

Journeys begin, new soil
invites, aromas swim.
Take me to that place.

Have everything it doesn't have:
Literacy, language, bank accounts.
Still, not as happy as an animal.

Touch, hold, smell, taste.
Made of memories and desires.
The thing is: I need.

TREE

That night the heart grew into a giant tree
building its nest on birds fleeing a tree.

Dreams lost their way climbing your body
born of a banyan seed buried under my tree.

Nightmares ate up the grass in my garden
freed demons beneath the haunted tree.

Snakes crept back into secret skeletons
hanging like bats from what was a tree.

Rain rose from the ground, sending rivers
skyward, washing away homes on the tree.

Limbs floated in night sky searching for life –
gift from gods who killed, fighting for a tree.

Your eyes sprouted wings, beat on my breasts.
That night, my heart became the giant tree.

ARUNDHATHI SUBRAMANIAM

ARUNDHATHI SUBRAMANIAM (b. 1967) is a poet and writer on spirituality and culture. She has worked over the years as poetry editor, curator, and journalist on literature, classical dance and theatre. She is the author of three books of poems, most recently *Where I Live: New and Selected Poems* (Bloodaxe, UK, 2009). Her prose works include the biography of a contemporary mystic (*Sadhguru: More Than a Life*, Penguin) and a book on the Buddha (*The Book of Buddha*, Penguin). As editor, she has worked on a Penguin anthology of essays on sacred journeys in the country (*Pilgrim's India*), and co-edited a Penguin anthology of contemporary Indian love poems in English (*Confronting Love*). Her poetry has been widely anthologized in India and abroad and translated into several languages. She has received the Raza Award for Poetry (2009), the Charles Wallace Fellowship (2003); the Visiting Arts Fellowship for a UK poetry tour (2006); and the Homi Bhabha Fellowship in 2012. She has been editor of the India domain of the Poetry International Web [http://india.poetryinternational.org] since its inception. She divides her time between Mumbai and a yoga centre in Coimbatore.

THE WAY YOU ARRIVE

The way your words reach me,
phantom-walking
through all those tensile,
suspicious membranes of self.

The way you unclog
these streets and bylanes
so I can surge
through starshine and aqueduct,
the luminous canals of a world
turned Venetian.

The way you enter a room
and the day's events scatter
like islands in the sea.

The way you arrive.

TEXTILE

Some days
nothing in your wardrobe satisfies

not the heat-maddened ikats, the secular pastels

There's no season you can call your own.

Like everyone else
you wait
in queues
for the drought to end

although you know everything
there is to know
about the guile and the gristle
of the heart –
its handloom desires
                                its spandex fantasies
its polycot, its wear-and-tear
polytheism.

And you know
that when it finally
happens,

the whoosh

            of textile, versatile,
            block-printed by sun

it will feel big enough
to put an end
to all the throbbing questions
forever.

But the winters –
they get colder each time

And so you return
reluctantly

to digging
through the seam
and stretch and protest
of tattered muscle

deeper
into the world's oldest fabric

into the
darkening,
widening
meritocracy
of the heart.

MY FRIENDS

They're sodden, the lot of them,
leafy, with more than a whiff
of damage
mottled with history
dark with grime.

God knows I've wanted them different
less bizarre, more jaunty,
less handle-with-care

more airbrushed
less prone
to dreams of rancidity

a little more willing
to soak in the sun.

They don't measure up.
They're unpunctual.
They turn suddenly tuberous.

But I keep them
for those days.

For their crooked smiles
their sudden pauses –

signs that they know
about the sound of mulch

and how green stems twist
and thicken
as they vanish
into the dark

finding their way
through sticky
vernacular tissues
of mud

improvising
hardening
improvising –

HOW SOME HINDUS FIND THEIR PERSONAL GODS

for AS who wonders about ishta devtas

It's about learning to trust
the tug
that draws you to a shadowed alcove
in your life
undisturbed by footfall
and butter lamps

a blue dark coolness
where you find him
waiting patiently
that perfect minor deity –

shy, crumbly,
oven-fresh, just a little
wry, content to play a cameo
in everyone's life but your own.

A god who looks
like he could understand
errors in translation
blizzards on the screen
lapses in memory

who might even learn by rote
the fury
the wheeze
the Pali
the pidgin
the gnashing mixer-grinder
the awkward Remington stutter
of your heart,
who could make them his own.

After that you can settle for none other.

CATNAP

This shoebox started out
a stiff-upper-lipped quadrilateral,
Upholder of Symmetry, Proportion, Principle,
sanctuary to an upright couple
of pedigree leather moccasins.

This week
shoebox learns
to sigh
de-
    cant,
contemplate

gravity.

Old idealist softens,
grows whiskers,
paw,
drowsing chin,
slumped tail,
Arctic eye.

Form is emptiness
Emptiness is form, Shariputra.

Shoebox abdicates
shape
and Gucci worship,

secedes from
nostalgia.

Pukka sahib
learns
to purr.

EPIGRAMS FOR LIFE AFTER FORTY

Between the doorbell
and the death knell
is the tax exemption certificate.

There are fewer capital letters
than we supposed.

Other people's stories will do.
Sticky nougatine green-and-pink stories.
Other people's stories.

Untenanting is more difficult
than unbelonging.

The body? The same alignment
of flesh, bone, the scent of soap, yesterday's
headlines, a soupcon of opera.

But there *are* choices
other than cringing vassal state
and walled medieval town.

And there is a language
of aftermath,
a language of ocean and fluttering sail,
of fishing villages malabared
by palm, and dreams laced
with arrack and moonlight.

And it can even be
enough.

ARYANIL MUKHERJEE

ARYANIL MUKHERJEE (b. 1964) is a bilingual poet, translator, and editor who grew up in Kolkata, India, and later emmigrated to the United States. He has authored ten books of poetry and essays in two languages. Widely published in both Indian (Bengali) and American poetry circles, his work has been featured in many anthologies, including the Indian Poetry issue of *TLR*, *Indivisible*, an anthology of South Asian American poetry, and *Pared de Agua*, an anthology of contemporary Bengali poetry Olifante Press, Madrid, Spain. He edits *Kaurab*, a much-celebrated Bangla literary magazine of experimental poetry and literature published since 1970. His poetry has been translated into Hindi and Spanish. A PhD in aerospace engineering, Aryanil works as an engineering mathematician and lives in Cincinnati.

the big room isn't a kissing set. not mortality.
not cloning.

butterflies entering graveyard
yearning for a bloody penetration beyond flesh & lard
talk of blood berries caught in thickstrewn foliage
and their angelic blossoms
the portion of reality that plays with memory
as much the sky with feathers
vines and their berries
the vase and its lid finally touching
butterflies in the graveyard
sacred thread sticking to a brahmin torso
electrocutes –
the mantra arrives

why so much color for a civil war theme?
the manufacturer controls its politics of memory
but amnesia makes thumb the shortest digit
the bruised hound spares us in our dream

HONEYCOMB SCRIPTURES :: NEW CONSTRUCT

the sea ends somewhere near our collective
excessive and public decay turns its immensity into sand
where the nostalgic egg is hidden
by that unable bird
natural inventor of the art of flight, yet flightless
broken feathers force us to think about a bird's past
as if it did not have a today somewhere
someplace we don't know

think of Kolkata. a city without abstract sculptures
think of self-erosion as the dredger disappears in the rain
everything is like something else
the first name in the rollcall helps raise the rest of hands
March is either too close to April or too far

the birds stayed close to where the blind girl knitted. not too far *Lalgola Passenger* cuts through redwood forest. *Falaknama* transports clam scent from *Amazon*. at the same time, we heard the storm warning on 103.4. primarily addressing coastal fishermen. leave your solitary home on the meadow to the twister. and run....

the new thrush found collectibles in the deserted nest
used fiber   new construct

HONEYCOMB SCRIPTURES :: SEA UNDER MICROSCOPE

it's the sea under the microscope
amoeba turning into a murderous whale
to remind us of our self-devouring affiliations

there are places where pain is statured as the mother of poetry
who is constantly smearing on us
its tender poultice of mud
and *life goes on*   *and that is progress*

there is a bridge in the painting
arched over white lilies
we think of them with such intensity
that new memories can form
and the vase can discharge its red lilacs
its an ancient bridge rusty
painted according to ancient principles
with a color that is now detritus
dust to dust ashes to ashes

the little chicken bore a littler chic
an egg buoys up in between
upon which i stand
and separate son from mother

some point out other hideouts. below the dense foliage of eyelashes. lines on the underleaf. memory lives on the edge of this moment. a moment that didn't attend. a time if that was ripe, the mood right, thirst precise, a suitable afternoon, boodbathed like the afternoon, if that was its momentary grain....

no wonder the corner clings on to its occupant. hunt the inquisition and drag it along. to the origin of a traceback. shameless insouciant inspection of its private parts. nonetheless a fly buzzing somewhere. verbose stammer in a mouthful of speech. stomach growls.

in the end all relations are predator – prey
on red sand roams a monitor lizard. Bengal monitor
family *Varanidae*. genus *Varanus*
touches sand & rock in one movement and body part
the split tongue – fetches both scent & touch
of the prey

and a detailed sensory map of its red sand geography
planted in the lizard's brain

more ground is covered
and a map is made in the brain out of a need
to chronicle this relationship
this hunger
that chases our favorite thought to that edge of landscape
where the trap is set

BHANU KAPIL

BHANU KAPIL (b. 1968) was born in England, to Indian parents, and grew up in Greater London. She came to the US in 1990 and currently lives in Loveland, Colorado, and teaches at Naropa University, Boulder, and Goddard College, Vermont. A writer forged by this history of migration who has come to understand the border as a site of both transformation and loss, Kapil's work crosses genre and subject borders. Her books include *Autobiography of a Cyborg* (2000), *The Vertical Interrogation of Strangers* (2001), *Incubation: A Space for Monsters* (2006) and Schizophrene (2011). Anthology appearances (among others) include *The Yellow Nib Modern English Poetry by Indians* (Belfast: Queens University) edited by Sudeep Sen. She has completed in 2009 a long prose work, *Humanimal: A Project for Future Children*, a creative non-fiction account of the Wolfgirls of Midnapure, two children found living with wolves in 1920s' Bengal.

1. SCHIZOPHRENE

I threw the book into the dark garden. The account begun mid-ocean, in a storm.

Immigrant. Nothing happens. *Immigrant.*

Below the aeroplane is the river.

Someone who could weight me down, whether physically or with language, in all the ports of call: Athens in January, Munich in February, London in March! Immigrant, there's nothing erotic about the ten rupees in your pocket. The account begins mid-ocean, where even your boarding pass is knotted in a handkerchief in your broken-down suitcase in the hold. Dazzling you, I select your suitcase. You watch it float over the railing and into the air. Yellow lightning in the silver sky, and the three sheets of rain, so bamboo, so cream. Stupid man, you watch your suitcase sink, burning up its requisite energy simply by breathing. Everything breathes, even you. Breathe, immigrant. Fly, immigrant. Sail, immigrant. Blue.

When I opened the door, there was a weird blue light coming off the snow.
    I threw
the book into the snow.

The ship left Bombay at dawn, a pink smear, the sunlight both a position and an entity.

The ship docked. The ferry left Calais at dawn, a green sky, I kept drawing the horizon, the static line somehow disc-like.

Near seven, I saw an intense set of orange, red and gold lines above the place where the sun would be.

The ship docked, and I found my home in the grid system: the damp wooden stool in the bath, a slice of bread with cheese on it, and so on. All my life, I've been trying to adhere to the surface of your city, your three grey rectangles split into four parts; a red dot; the axis rotated seventy-six degrees, and so on.

But then I threw the book into the grid. It was a wet grid.

The snow wet the book then froze it like a passive sun. These notes are directed towards the region I wanted to perceive, but could not. Notes for a schizophrene night, a schizophrene day, a rapid sketch.

The book before writing, arcing once more through the crisp dark air. And the line the book makes is an axis, a hunk of electromagnetic fur torn from the side of something still living and thrown, like a wire, threaded, a spark towards the grass.

A line for someone on their first voyage, a non-contemporary subject, the woman, or even the man, the person with an articulate gender, a flux where the body always is, who asks what's forbidden and what's expected in the annular zone. In the airport. On the earth.

A veil. A harness. A rope.

Do psychiatrists register the complex and rich vibrations produced by their dreaming subjects? The indigo or emerald-green *crown* that coats the hair and shoulders of an *interviewee*, erasing distinctions between what is outside, the sky, and what's beneath it? That digs into the head?

The 'emanating structures appear in the light that comes from the body, and it is these structures that perform a rudimentary narrative'. A *memory or two*?

Writing, I notice that the schizophrenic narrative is not split, for which an antidote is commercially produced in quantities that exceed populations.

Rather, it cannot process the dynamic elements of an image, any image, whether pleasant, enriching or already so bad it can't be tendered in the lexicon of poses available to it.

I need a new pen.

An idea for a novel before it's shattered, there on the bench next to the fountain, which is frozen, deconstructed, in the air.

I walk the long way to the Tate from the Pimlico tube, a fact more intense each time I repeat it in my mind. An erotics. A mad progression that exceeds a central frame, like seeing something then falling down.

I break my walk at the fountain, as I've done since childhood, which is chromatography. The white panels, then a livid black.

It's already late. A black world coming down from the heavens. Black with stars.

They're walking into that, the darkness pouring into their mouths when they reach the hills. Coming down over the two of them: a man of about sixty, that red afternoon into evening, the dirt of that place a kind of orange-brown, and his granddaughter, eight years old that July. A Londoner, she's wearing a blue and yellow dress with a daisy print. As for the man, he's dressed in a white cotton dhoti and a kurta, with an almond-cake pale shawl, embroidered along its narrow border with maroon and turquoise paisley swirls.

The upwelling of philosophy attends to we can't see. A light tent over the text.

Nevertheless, re-reading these words, I can't have them in my house. And so I open the door, flinching from the blue fire of the individual blades of grass, the bonds of the plant material that release a colour when they are crushed. I saw something flare when the book hit the ground. That sub-red spike without a source.

❧

'I was born in a country that no longer exists.'

❧

When India broke, the wings of the golden eagle torn from her body by their roots, he broke too. When he arrived at his brother's house in Delhi, he collapsed, screaming, insensate to the arrival of his wife a week later, her sari covered with blood. Straining and bucking in a makeshift cage. *We kept him in a cellar for a year.*

❧

A rose. Its stem wrapped in a blue and white checkered tea towel of the sort used to wrap the earthenware pot of unset yoghurt, again and again. Arriving. The rose. Like a colour, just ahead of them, a kind of stick, or torch, she thinks, held there and upright, in her grandfather's grasp.

❧

When they reach the jungle, the luminous stands of bamboo sway in the rain, creaking and popping at their touch, at the brush of their arms. Darkness has truly fallen now, obliterating the city below. Its population.

❧

A man comes to the gate where they stop. He walks into the fragrant gloom of the garden and snaps the stem, a green still visible at seven. And I reach out my hand.

❧

'*Tea?*' And when the chessboard appears, diamond-shaped from where she's sitting, and copper-edged in the Russian fashion, the girl drifts. I don't see her, I feel her.

Then, as if he, too, can feel the mountains pulsing through the walls of the house, her grandfather gets up. She gets up. And they go.

❧

3. A HEALING NARRATIVE

Fragments attract each other, a swarm of iron filings, black with golden flecks but without a soul. I stroke them with my finger so they scatter then relax.

In correspondence.

In the involuntary response to being touched.

On a plate.

Against the tree, a woman is pinned, upright and strung with lights or gunpowder flares and nodes. Who stuck her there?

Her body is covered with mud and at the same time it possesses the invisible force of an architectural element encountered in a post-war structure. Did I literally give her life?

I wrote about her body, the vertical grave she created in my mind, and in the minds of anyone who heard about her, this anonymous and delicate 'box'. This imprint. This metal animal. This veil of charcoal and vermillion powder, smudged to form a curtain of hair falling over the face. Like an animal almost in flight, but possessed, restricted to the band of earth that precedes the border or follows it, depending on which way you cross; the woman stares, focusing on a point. Someone else is staring too.

Can you smell her burning fur?

4. ABIOGENESIS

Abiogenesis: to flux, to squat: a conjunction of living and non-living matter: [3]: from *Schizophrene*, a book without purpose/with a dead start. But with the body displaying signs of early spring: *pink bits* sensitive to being touched, like a Jain woman crossing the street in her linen mask and with her pole.

And in *blanked-out jungle space*, where all I could do was stare. From the verandah, the view warped. The river flowed out of its given shape and into my eyes. Even the sky was a volatile, all-powerful parent. I fantasized about having larger breasts than I do. Just beneath the mesh, on a divan, *in the sun*, I fell asleep even as ashram life unfolded behind me, the rustle of the women's saris as they cleaned the bell. Each god was dressed with marigolds and a fresh trap of white cloth, folded and creased like a chrysalis around the eight blue limbs.

On a crisp Easter morning in London, I stripped down. Over the years, I received my society's support. In the States, I worked hard at waitressing. I read *Ava*. I sold things off when the time came and though, if I'd waited, I would have made an even greater profit, I'm glad I did. Without any real feelings, I returned to the United Kingdom, where it was all 'Fish and Chips, then?' 'Let's go to Blockbusters and get a video.' 'What do you want to watch? *Die Hard* 3?' 'What? With what's his name? Nah, hate him. What about Spooks? We can watch it from the beginning.' 'No, I fancy staying in. Do you?'

I *denuded the garden* of its branches. I chewed them up. *You put me down*. My ashes found their spot on the mantel and no-one moved them. In some sense, I was still your *friend*. My body kept yours safe on the long nights when your body drowned itself in the habit of the dream. Its green.

Abiogenesis: to flux and squat in an inhabited place, risking something. What? I loved that scene next to the car in *The Piano Teacher*. When I was a child, I used to strip down and beat myself with a stick. Is this, *a root distinguished from its branching plant*, kept in a jar on a shelf to grow, watered, schizophrenic?

Is it a right thing or a mad thing not to want to re-connect, to avoid reading or writing because of what those will bring?

Dreamed I forgot my coat on the aeroplane.

Once again, I give you a tiny cyborg as a kind of fluid immigrant appearing in many places at different times and as such: a somatic structure with the ability to process many different kinds of memory at once.

5. ELECTROBION

Partial Solar Eclipse, India, August 1, 2008 . 5.02 pm. On my bedside table, 'electrobion' appears on the plastic, orange mat of the sort used to protect the table-cloth from the cup; there's a word for this, I can't recall…

Turmeric plants, lemon tree, amrooth tree, pomegranate tree, mint, tulsi, and some ragged flowering herbs: green chilli, gold…gold flower? But they can't translate, and do not know the word in Hindi. A girl, and two boys, the daughter and grandsons of the priest in the garage, with whom we share this kitchen garden. At the end of the street is a Shiva temple. Its massive Shivling towers above the Le Corbusier vibe of this Asian city; a black geo-oblong with three white stripes on what I suddenly understand to be a 'forehead'. *Ye kya hai*? It's the unseen face of god. Sometimes, the English I get back is crisp, more accurate and emotional than the English I would use.

These electrobion notes, which are not really notes but dreamed up, basic observations which belie the facts, the following fact, which in turn destroys a content as yet unwritten: *I don't exist.*

We shift our chairs to avoid the sunlight, eclipse light, which could damage us forever.

The diagonal shadow in the lemon tree, diamond-edged by five, is a product of moonlight as much as sunlight.

The priest's brother, visiting from the village, comes out of the garage to pray, a plastic blue mat rolled up beneath his arm. He slips off his shoes and finds a spot by the basil to sit down. We offer him tea and oranges but he waves them off, closes his eyes and sings:

I'm waiting for you beneath this tree. Why don't you come?

In the neighbour's garden is a palm with torn metallic paper peeling from its radial trunk. A girl of about fifteen sweeps the patio, as she does each morning at seven and each late afternoon. I quell, in my body, the knowledge of what she's paid to do this. She gestures with her rough broom to the marble stretch beneath our chairs, and so we move into the house, which is netted, barred and where the danger increases, if you're paranoid, and diminishes, when you sleep.

I lie down beneath the lemon tree then stand up, leaving an outline in the soft pink earth. I re-fill my silhouette with glossy, bi-colour leaves creased down the middle, their seams bulky with dust; tiny lemons from the lowest branches; bunched garlands of marigolds from the sloped shelf next to the Shiva temple, emptied from a white plastic bag; and *divas* from the shrine, still flickering, like cakes. And hemp. The hemp is pre-biotic, activated and repelled by the smoky flame.

What wets it down?
What makes it clean?

6. VERTIGO

A ghost mutates through intensity, gathering enough energy to touch you through your thin blouse, or your leggings, or your scarf.

A ghost damages the triptych of ancestors composed of descending, passive and synthetic scraps.

But what if the ghost is empty because it's making a space for you?

Vertigo is a symptom of profound attraction. An excess of desire.

Once, after a long shift at KFC, during which we ran out of baked beans and the manager sent me across the Birmingham New Street plaza with a twenty-pound note, to Marks and Spencer's, for a family-size tin, I didn't go back to the flat in Selby where my boyfriend lived. I went to the cinema in my red and white striped shirt and watched *Au Revoir Les Enfants*. A Londoner, I blinked in the rainy quiet darkness that had fallen by the time I left. I ducked into a bright room. There, I was picked up by a Muslim man with a thick Yorkshire accent, who bought me a Malibu and orange. I was conscious of having wasted my entire summer on a boyfriend. My parents thought I was interning as a trainee journalist on a regional broadsheet. I'd told the KFC manager my mother was dying, and that I had to take every weekend off to be with her in the hospital. On Saturday mornings, my boyfriend would drive us to the sea in his refurbished Nash Metropolitan. Once, he drove us to France. I drank coffee on the ferry, staring into the blazing pink sun while he slept, his head on my lap. But that night, a Thursday night, I ended up in a graveyard with the man from the bar, and his friend, who had arrived as we were leaving. A ghost is a duplicate, a tall and handsome man who contracts then dilates so swiftly, you can't refuse. In fact, you don't say a word when a ghost, when two ghosts, lead you by your upper arm into an empty place, verdant with cypress and elm.

75. 'We walk through the rusted bracken to the lido, to the place where the Park Woods give way to a cultivated beach. The darkness beneath the trees is a treatment, something a person might seek out to modify other sensations. It's a thick balm made from summer herbs and cooked in a pan. Comfrey turns the skin green where it sits. And if London, in turn, is packed inside the remnants of this forest, I can describe it only because I lived there and recall these themes, which are not themes. Returning, I change at Baker Street and take the Metropolitan line north. Where it ends I get off. Start walking.'

— Ban, who lived for the first nine years of her life at 76 Lansbury Drive, Hayes, Middlesex and so cuts back one, revving, slipping on the wet grass, to begin. Will you give a hand to Ban? Do you have a sentiment, do you have class? Let me tell you before you extend yourself that Ban is disgusting. Let me tell you that Ban is a difficult person to love, full of transience. I could tell you things about Ban.

76. 'Back at the house, there were some sugar crystals on the carpet. I knew I should hoover them up before they got ground in. My husband slamming doors, etc, banging around, you should do this, you should do that. My son threw in some white bin-liners. I was like – thanks? But later, when it was time to make something to eat, I'd lost track. I didn't know whether to defrost the meat.'

— Ban's friend at KFC, during lunch on a plaza bench. Ban is pure sympathy, still in uniform, one of the girls. That's something that's come clear to me over the years that I've known of her, through others and finally, though it was too late, in person: Ban wants desperately to carve out her body from her body, to conceive herself with a human life in mind. Whatever. I can't bring myself to do much more than tell what happened. Ban on a bench, passing, nodding, brushing the crumbs from the burger off her rough red skirt.

77. 'We wanted to look for bottles, the tiny bottles we had heard were left in the roots of oak trees by elves. My dad said: 'Be back by four.' And we leaped from the car into the rain. It was raining, but only lightly and we had anoraks on. I recalled the haystacks I'd once seen, at the very end of the park, where a gate was, and a white house with a thousand glittering windows. Once, in the private meadow edging the park, I saw riders in their scarlet coats. Their horses had coats. I'd shouted: 'Oi! Over here! Yoo hoo!,'

longing to touch the dark brown fur and feel the warm breath on my face. So I said to Thippy, come on. Thippy was a Sikh boy with hair down to his waist. Out of view of my father, he took off his pint-sized turban and let it fall. We said we'd say we were sisters, if someone asked, as we sometimes did at Balfours when we went to buy sherbert with ten pence stolen from the kitchen jar. It took two hours, that afternoon, to reach the haystacks and during our walk, we understood, in our hearts, that returning to the car would be just as bad as going back later. It was all the same. When we reached the gate, it was pouring and our hands were blue on the backs of them from the cold. A creamy mist had risen from the grass. From this mist appeared a horse, a completely white horse with mud-packed legs, and the rider tugged it so it came to where we screamed: 'Horsey! Over here, horsey!' And let us pet it, forever, chatting, a man. When we got back to the car, we were terribly wet. We got into the car, a blue Ford Cortina dented silver from my father's many accidents. We got into the car and in slow motion my father twisted from the chest up, from the driver's seat, to hit my face so hard the side of my head hit the window. At this moment, I became Ban. When Thippy grew up, and his own father dragged him home from the school disco at Villier's High School, and beat him on his legs and back, he became a Sikh fundamentalist. He'd grown a beard by seventeen, and refused to meet my eyes on the rare occasions his parents forced him to come to our house for a Friday night dinner. He wore a black turban with a saffron headband and when he completely grew up he bought the house next to his parents and they built a corridor between the two. But what I've left out is his brother, a boy I knew in childhood who also made me Ban. Not because he accompanied me; on the contrary, because he, too, made me weep. He wasn't a boy. When we were eight, he was eighteen. When we were ten, he was twenty.'

— A story of Ban's childhood. Has Ban described the countryside well, as it extends from the immigrant township built on the slope beneath the Nestle factory, but above the canal, where children swam in summer? Has Ban described the pink azaleas against the dark silver background of the labyrinth, fragrant with juniper and other rotting things? Answer: No. Ban fails narrative. Ban fails portraiture. Ban fails life, which is colour. It is 'costume and valence'. It is something more than this.

78. 'It's getting dusky over the Makhatini flats. Last night, I told P. I did not want to continue seeing him when I returned to New York. I believe, in breaking up with him, I compared myself to a Safeway rotisserie chicken. I said I didn't want to be one. Then I put down the phone and went back to drinking my roobios tea. Yes and no. I should have asked her to make some coffee instead.'

— In the mid 90s, Ban went to the Zulu Homeland, to visit a childhood friend from Hayes, a suburban girl of mixed race who married an Afrikaaner she met in Capetown. I can't name that girl, or say why she left the suburbs, as Ban, in her phone call to another friend, the person I ultimately interviewed, didn't go into details. In the notes I took, Ban comes across as a person with a soft heart, but what I slice off is the 'she'. Who, in this day and age, refers to a person for the first time as 'her'? Who is this 'her'? Is Ban, a 'black' person, using a mode of address she would not dare to in the United Kingdom? Is Ban black? Though now she is black. And flecked with silver. At the bottom of a river. 'I have excellent clothes,' Ban once wrote to her friend, a letter I kept when it was given to me, not wanting to be rude.

79. 'Mother of my soul.'

— Towards the end of her life, in her early forties, still very beautiful despite her age, dark brown hair knotted with paintbrushes in a tatty bun above C7, the last bone of the spine as it goes down through the neck, Ban returned to India, where her ancestors were from, and lay down, as close as she could get, next to the border with Pakistan. A few feet away, under the gaze of a military presence, two guards a few feet away from the Wagah checkpoint, she simply did this (lie down), then stood up and with a long stick torn from a nearby tree, though the area is desolate, marked the outline. Then she re-filled it with orange and red marigolds purchased, earlier that day, from the Shiva temple of a village further in. It must have been a Monday. Then she sat down next to this body and placed a hand on the place where its chest would be, and another upon on her own. When I discovered this, I began to write on Ban. It was this writing that led me further in, to the place I did not want to be, Ban's soul. 'Mother of my soul,' she wrote in an early notebook, what in England is still called a Diary, 'You're so very bright.' What did Ban mean? My question was innocent. I was innocent. But Ban, in a sense, was waiting for me, in the darkness of the border, no longer proximal but centred, arms waving in a blur, waiting with everything that was wrong.

BIBHU PADHI

BIBHU PADHI (b. 1951) was born in the medieval town of Cuttack in Orissa, and has lived there ever since. His seventh book, *Migratory Days*, was published last year. His poetry has appeared in distinguished magazines throughout the English-speaking world. His poems have been included in several anthologies and school and college textbooks in India, UK and USA, two of the most recent being *Language for a New Century* (New York: Norton, 2008), *Midnight's Grandchildren: Post Independence Poetry from India* (Macedonia: Struga Poetry Evenings), edited by Sudeep Sen. He has a book on D.H. Lawrence and has co-written (with his wife, Minakshi Padhi) a reference book on Indian philosophy and religion. Before taking early retirement, he taught English at several colleges and universities in India.

BREATH, SLEEP

for Keith Sagar

Summer. Lie down on a cool,
marbled floor, and watch.

Perhaps, for the first time,
you'd be feeling how the vast space

of earth and sky has been
entering and exiting

your body, almost without
your knowledge, just as

the tree doesn't know how
so many breaths touch

its still, stagnant leaves –
the air it can't see,

breeze, the strong
wind from the hills,

the frenetic storm preceding
an unseasonal rain.

Since the time I began to
learn and follow

the basic vocabulary,
I've been told how

incredible a thing
breath is – in death, in life.

I fall back on myself
so that I might find which

other things might be
helping me to live.

And then, this discovery –
the world is within me!

Stunned, I take a deep
breath, and quietly fall into

a fine, memorable sleep.

A TIME, A PLACE, A NAME

At this hour, when
the edges of sleep
enclose the blurred edges

of history,
anything can
happen, anything

can choose to be here,
float in on night air,
occupy our homes.

Infants who have been given
numbers as names, looking
for their mothers;

shadowy figures that defy
all descriptions, playing
their ancient, mythic games

among the trees, below their
dark roots, with those hidden,
root-like treasures of our faith;

bodies that have remained
dead for centuries, because
we were not there at that

precise, ritual time, so that
we could've put them into
the wood-locked,

cleaning flames.
Now, among rumours
of death and sleep,

we wait for yet another day,
through the rest of the night,
our hearts hardening into

a pain that is too remote for us
for any name, but somehow deeply
here, like a history of stones.

TREES AT DHENKANAL

for Tess Gallagher

I owe you my long stay
here, at your green place.

I have watched you beside
my daily paths, breathing tall
and great, as if you were teaching me

what silence was, how to pray –

a surrender to
a sufficiently grown man's
safe distances from time

and space, cities
that merely cluster into

narrow roads, violent encounters,
divisions and differences.

But I have felt lonely too
with you. How you wait for

a touch that remembers
its earliest fingers, looks
forward to, waits!

Trees: Have you been here
since the time I was born
at the noisy Cuttack

some fifty years ago, taking care
of my intermediate growth

as if you knew me from another
life? I do. I have watched you.

Wait, wait a while before you
answer, take your own time.

Say yes. I have been here
because of you.

Ask your
numberless greens
(and what galaxies of shades!)

to use purposefully
sun-open days
of laughter and joy,

my black days
of retirement and retreat.

DESERT THOUGHT AND A PRAYER: 1991

for Richard Wilbur

There's a crowd of men taking charge
of the lonely deserts for the first time,
hunting in the bare sand for something
that lies quiet in the subterranean dark,
dreaming about the future, feeling sorry
for humanity's lurid modes of defense
and attack, hoping to be where it needs
its dark primeval security, quite itself.

There are other things happening too,
just above the planet's ancient body,
nearer its outer skin of eye-blinding whiteness,
simmering in the sun – a blindness of rage
overtaking old friendships, mocking at
all our ill-calculated designs for prosperity
and peace, smiling at our selfish pride;
a savage power that defies all words
of myth and history, overlooks our
children's dreams, their stunted lives.

Is there a way of return, a retreat
into the warmth of home, back to
an infant's dark privacy? Is there
a word that will take care of time,
what it urges us to forget, its wish
to forgive? The answers seem to lie
elsewhere, for from this page,
suspended in the anxious desert air.
Dear God: May someone locate them
there, feel their naked intimacy,
their hint of love and care.

SOMEONE HAS BEEN MISSING

for Minu

Something has been missing
from my sleep, something
that touched me for
first time long ago, when I
went about the town just as
the tropical rains came down.

A touch of reassurance
appearing quietly, when no one
was there to see, safely enclosed in
its circle of warmth – a consolation.
A touch I have been carrying for
twenty-one years, secretly.

Things have come and gone
in the meantime. The children of our
moments of wakefulness have grown,
declared their own dreams. For
all these years I've been looking
for the touch, once again, roaming
my lonely way when no one is seeing.

This night has been different.
Sleep has been rare, being away
at an intriguing distance of time.
I pray for it, wait, patience in
my eyes, impatience in my mind,
limp into my ill-deserved sleep.
I can feel the touch reappearing
in all its gentleness of dream.

I can see the remoter things –
angels descending on my skin,
shining, friends disappearing
in a hasty farewell into the darkest
quarters of the night. And there
she is, raining on my forehead and lips.
Woman of my dream: Why did you
have to wake me from my sleep?

A NAME THAT STAYS

How invisibly things come together,
without one's knowledge, replace others!

A name thresholding a heart,
lean through its isolation,

so quietly that one would think
it was there already, all these days?

A face that appears sad and distant, mutely
recognizing the distance on another face?

A night passes in an adjacent room
in its own retiring style, as if

it feared the blindness of other nights
of yesterday, of a moonless Tuesday night.

And then a thin, bruised feeling of remembrance
going far back to days and years.

I suppose the same feeling is returned to me
as I come out of my desolate hours.

As we sit together, talk of commonplace things,
a friendship of a lifetime is slowly taking its shape.

Let us keep it that way, carry it over
the brink, find us together on another, lonelier day.

Let the years change their dates, the tall trees shed
their browns year after year, quietly regain their greens.

All of these they've seen, haven't they? Come,
let us wait for our all forgetting, unending day.

C P SURENDRAN

C P SURENDRAN (b. 1959) was born in Kerala. He received his MA in English Literature from the University of Delhi, and taught briefly at a college in Calicut before becoming a journalist. He has published two novels: *An Iron Harvest* and *Lost and Found*; four books of poetry: *Gemini II, Posthumous Poems, Canaries on the Moon,* and *Portraits of the Space We Occupy*. His poetry and fiction have appeared in *Atlas, The Times of India, The Illustrated Weekly of India, Biblio, London Magazine,* and other newspapers and journals. Anthology appearances (among others) include *Twelve Modern Young Indian Poets* (Edinburgh: Lines Review), and *Wasafiri India South Asia & the Diaspora* (London: QMW University), both edited by Sudeep Sen. Surendran lives in Gurgaon and works as a journalist.

ENEMY

I had just fought this war and come back,
Minding my own business and drinking beer.

Then I met this girl at Joe's
Who wrote poems on the back
Of napkins with ketchup.

Show me your heart, she said.

Don't have one, I said.
She said hearts were what made her go.

Finally, I dug up the old, dark thing.

And she said, oh, but this is a grenade.

I told you, I said, and bit the pin.

BENEDICTION

Statues of gold by their hundreds

Their armoured breasts prow
The servile air, the sunlight cleft by their drawn swords
And crested helmets fall to lesser shades; towers of ivory and glass
Bow beneath their burden,
Affect airs of amnesty, reason
Beyond reckoning, exhortatory passion.

They point a glabrous hand up north where the orphaned heavens
Trundle along their splintered axis
Reveal in metal and stone
The multitude of my august selves, precious enough to spawn
Their own praetorian guard.

The day is a mirror
And I see myself everywhere.

LUMINOUS

Or consider the way we twine our hands
Under the wooded night air
So tight as if they might be chopped at wrist
By an up-sprung axe unshackled from the bleeding roots.

Or the way you search my face as you kiss
Deep enough to know what makes
The leopard's blood leap from spot to spot
And lean back, wounded cub, shaking at the thought
This was the rumoured future
We forfeited
At assigned gatherings and waiting halls
Arrivals and departures
Where the spirit balked
And braced without hope.

And we walk the back alleys

Of this accidental town,
Past darkened doorways
And burning windows,
Between parked cars
And empty little restaurants

From future and past
Return

By land, sea and air
By sleight of hand
And turn of phrase
To this wholly present

Moment of grace.

MALABARI: INSPIRATION

Space shot with yellow,
April and May burn Malabar,
Laburnum's last coast.
Enter June, on long stilts of rain,
Putting out the fire in floral eyes
By its watery breath. Brightness blinded.
Little ixora and jasmine
Nod their heads to the beating rain;
Tremble for the peace between two blows
Remembering laburnum,
The firmness of that flame.

MILK STILL BOILS

He lies in bed, one hand
Thrown across his eyes. This,
He figures, is more like it.
He no longer thinks about her,
Or him. Just them.
And the postures they struck
Just before the milkman came.
In a minute he will be up
To put the milk on the boil
And no one the wiser.

A COLD FEELING

Words are cold things, come after
Broken ties and wrong doors closing
In the middle of the night.
They form frost at the turning hour
When the mouth holds in a round stare
The loss that the dark piles behind the eyes
And no candle brings from the shade
All you've touched or read.

Sometimes I wake in this cold,
An icy sea winding over my head
Like a shroud. Words are old things
Come after much yearning,
When the body is dead and cold.

RENUNCIATION

First light on the kitchen table
Breakfast for one. Beer and wine.
Feline eyes kiss fallen tart.

Lunch is a conceit of three. My cat,
Your snapshot and me. Secret rum
In mint tea. Invalidation of the sun.

Last light comes to sup. Dinner is a feat
In rectitude. Water and whiskey.
Campaign of shadows on the wall. No despair.

A sliver of music around the ankles
In a dream's corridor.
Endless retreat of inaccessible feet.

CURIOS

It's three in the morning.
The house rings with alarms,
There's someone leaning
On the doorbell. It's her
After three years.
He lets her in,
Puts on some tea.
She lights a cigarette
With a match that might set
The house on fire.
She unpacks the weather
Which is New York.
They sit in silence.
The room turns into a museum of moods

PROSPECT

While you were looking away

A dog yawned in the sun

And in the distance

A train blindfolded
By a tunnel
Window by window
Regained vision.

I thought of all the things
That could happen
When we are looking away,

The universe we miss in a blink.

CHITRA BANERJEE DIVAKARUNI

CHITRA BANERJEE DIVAKARUNI (b. 1956) was born in Calcutta. She graduated from Calcutta University and Wright State University in Ohio, and received her PhD in English from the University of California at Berkeley. Her four volumes of poetry are *Dark Like the River, The Reason for Nasturtiums, Black Candle,* and *Leaving Yuba City: New & Selected Poems.* She has published eleven books of short stories and novels, including *Arranged Marriage, The Mistress of Spices, Sister of my Heart, The Vine of Desire* and *One Amazing Thing*; as well as edited *Multitude: Cross-Cultural Readings for Writers.* Anthology appearances (among others) include *Twelve Modern Young Indian Poets* (Edinburgh: Lines Review), *The Yellow Nib Contemporary English Poetry by Indians* (Belfast: Queens University), *World Literature Today Writing from Modern India* (Norman: University of Oklahoma), all edited by Sudeep Sen. She has won numerous awards for her writing. She teaches English and creative writing and lives in the USA.

AFTER DEATH: A LANDSCAPE

after Francesco Clemente's Indian Miniature—6

Fire on one side, wind on the other.
I stride over the hill's green
body. I have no legs.
At my touch the shy leaves open
into the shapes of eyes. I have
no mouth. At my breath
fruits ripen to crimson silk.
No hands. So the stars
float down like fireflies and pass
into me, the calm moon
hangs in frail fullness where
my face might once have been. I move
across the prickly-pear skin
of the earth. I bless
the fish, the stiff, silver-slender
cranes. They bring me
to the cupola, its dome
mother-of-pearl, its crest
gold as longing. Are there lotus blossoms
in the air? They bring me
to my newborn body. It is wrapped
in the red of beginning. Or is it
ending? I hold
in my right hand the pale kite
with its clear dark eye. The string
lifts me. I fly.

THE RIVER

after Francesco Clemente's Indian Miniature—12

I lie on the grass and listen
to the river inside me. It
pulses and churns, surges up
against the clenched rock
of my heart
until finally it spurts from my head
in a dark jet. Behind,
the clouds glide along
on paper wings, the palace walls
grow taller, brick by brick, till they rise beyond
the painting's edge. The river

is deep now and still, an opaque lake
filled with blue fish. The
ground is tilting, the green touch-me-not plants
angle away from my body. I
am falling. The lake cups its liquid fingers
for me, the fish glint
like light on ice. Evening,
and the cool river rocks gleaming

pink as new pearls. The water rises.
I am disappearing, my body
rippling into circles, legs, waist,
armpits. My hair floats upward, fine
as water-weeds. I give
my face to the river, the lines
of my forehead, my palms. When the last cell
of my body has dissolved, the last cry
of the lake-birds, I will, once more,
hear the river inside.

ARJUN

after Francesco Clemente's Indian Miniature—13

Wall. Rock. Field. Sky.
From the high balcony I watch the land
open and fall away
beneath my drawn bow. Pattern
of mosaic. Point of roof. Hieroglyph
of cloud. My arms are white as stone,
slender as the hope of love. My thighs
smooth as the peeled silver trunks
of eucalyptus. Brick on magenta brick. Flower
on crimson flower. I breathe in

the taut elastic smell
of the quivering bowstring. Aim
at the unrisen sun. The grass is splashed
with the memory of light. The palace
is dappled by the thought
of dawn. Wave. Spire. Hedge. Arrow. Eye.
I have split in three and recede
further and further from my original self. Now
I am minute as the circle-centre
of a target against a distant

haystack. The wind is visible and curls
whitely around my head. I lift my hand
to catch it. Smell of Jacaranda. Thorn
of the blackwood tree. I release
the string. And am flung
forward. Time parts for me as water.
Blood. Bone. Wet earth. Sunlight
on a speeding metal tip. When I reappear
it will be as lightning
into your innocent future.

THE WORLD TREE

after Francesco Clemente's Indian Miniature—14

The tree grows out of my navel. Black
as snakeskin, it slithers upward, away
from my voice. It spreads
across the entire morning, its leaves
tongues that drink the light. It has ground
its heel into my belly. I
can no longer tell its roots
from my dry, gnarled veins. And when it knows
I will never forget the pain
of birthing, it parts its branches

so I can see, far
in that ocean of green,
a figure, tiny and perfect, pale
as ivory, leaning
on his elbow. He looks down and I know
that mouth, those eyes. I
raise my arm. I am calling
loud as I can. He gazes
into the distance, the bright, rippling
air. It is clear
he sees, hears nothing. I continue
to call. The tree grows and grows
into the world between us.

Softened by her wearing, these white saris,
yet stiff with reproof. You? still here?
while in Bengal the jasmined widow moon
paces insomniac outside my bedroom sill,
and from chill ricestalks the jhi jhi chants
a prayer for the dead, or the old – the same thing.
White is the colour of futility, foam on flood waters
(did you know twenty thousand died this year?)
It is spittle dried on the lips of ghosts doomed
to tell and retell a story no one hears.
In childhood too you were disobedient. Once,
running from me you tumbled down the stairs,
had to be taken for stitches. I held you still –
your father never could stand blood.
Under the doctor's lamp your lips were
bruised oleanders. Now my eyes are going,
that shade returns to me more and more,
your outraged gaze. You wanted me
to save you, like I want (as though such things
are possible) you to save me. After she fell
Third Aunt was bed-prisoned seven months.
When they dressed her for cremation,
the sores were rash crimson, huge as
king hibiscus. Why is it that as lives fade
memory brightens its steep, stubborn tints?
White is what I pray for, a graceful erasure,
colour of the bel flower I've asked them
to dip in sandalwood and drape on my body
so that you, reaching a still house too late,
will be faced only with fragrance.

DALJIT NAGRA

DALJIT NAGRA (b. 1966) comes from a Punjabi background. He was born and raised in London then Sheffield. He has won several prestigious prizes for his poetry. In 2004, he won the Forward Prize for Best Individual Poem with *Look We Have Coming to Dover!* This was also the title of his first collection published by Faber & Faber in 2007. This won the Forward Prize for Best First Collection and The South Bank Show Decibel Award. His second collection, *Tippoo Sultan's Incredible White-Man Eating Tiger Toy-Machine!!!* was short-listed for the T.S. Eliot Prize. Daljit's poems have been published in *New Yorker, Atlantic Review, London Review of Books, Times Literary Supplement, Poetry Review, Poetry London, Poetry International, Ark, Rialto, The North,* and *Atlas.* He is a regular contributor to BBC radio and has written articles for *The Financial Times, The Guardian, The Observer* and *The Times of India.*

THIS BE THE PUKKA VERSE

Ah the Raj! Our mother-incarnate
Victoria Imperatrix rules the sceptred
sphere overseeing legions of maidens'
'fishing fleets' that break the waves
to net the love of a heaven Etonian!
Fetes on lawns with mansion whacking
banks or dances by moonlight
at *the Viceroy — the Viceroy's ball!*

The burra pegs of brandy pawnee
and pink gin in barrack rooms
that require the doolally scram on *Jaldi*
punkawallaahh! for six meal days
with tiffin with peacocks and humps
and tongue for the breeches for the topi-
of-khaki and swagger stick bobbery
shikar. *Tally ho!* for the boars in a hush

and by Amritsar what a 12-bore howdah
double on howdahs for *bang!bang!*
bagging the flamiest tiger! Panthers,
leopards, blackbucks and swanny
bustards, and Kipling or Tatler at Tollygunge.
Lock, stock and bobbing palanquins
for Hill Station gothic verandahs
where dawn Himalayas through Poobong

or Ooty mist, and the basso profundo
of evensong, housey-housey and hammocks
under the Milky Way…Then waking
to twirl those vintage sabre-curved
mustachios for zenanas behind bazaars
where the girls give a breathless nautch
whilst ayahs are snookered by sahib's
sport where the off-shoot half-breeds

are vagabonds and mad dogs in a jolly
good lingam-land, where the sun
never sets, overflowing with silk and spice
and all the gems of the earth! *Er*

darling, it's not quiiite the koh-i-noor...
Would you? On a train that's tickety-boo
hooting on time through a tunnel. *A*
diamond! Darling, I feel so whole.

TIPPOO SULTAN'S INCREDIBLE WHITE-MAN-EATING TIGER-TOY MACHINE!!!

To flesh a poem
you rifle through
your store of imperial
Word – dying
to blood that hoard
swotted since foreign
kid of the class
who chewed the fat
of the raw meat minty
tongue that English
is
nowadays your wrought-up
state where you won't
repose having thrashed out
some lines. Instead
you're awfully scary
once in your stripes
you're Tippoo's toy,
his tigery accessory,
clawing the mirror –
a man overcome
by the camps of history!
Thus
you whip up each score
for your game at speed
so you're galloping for that
top-hat sahib!
Just look at you pouncing
on beats, when that gentleman
screams your eyes
are ablaze, you're no longer
mankind! O God,
you've become a Sher
of Punjaaab on the wallahs of the
rrrrraaaaaaaaaaaajjj!!!

PHALLACY

How oft do mates bang on at length about
how well they're hung, they grab their crotch then slash
the air, then chuck an arm at will around
a chum while necking Stella till they're lashed.
To tell the truth, I'm really not well hung
and thus I hide from mates my prince's state,
this conk is king of my poor frame, no trunks
would lunchbox find to bank a lady's gaze.
And yet I hope the guys won't feel too down
when I recount my lover's hardly wimpish –
watch her stiffen over *corrrrrs!* from louts
who check her out too long (for she's that fit!).
    In bed, most nights she'll sigh: *O love, I love*
    the woman's way you work your subtle touch.

HAVE I GOT OLD NEWS FOR YOU

You've been mapping the best mortgage deals
for our first house, recalling the latest
tracker rate you hint we play it
safe with a five-year
fixed.

You're by the telly when Dubya flashes up,
he's safely in the past yet twitching a smirk
in his cowboy gear like he's verged
on a mind-blowing
thought.

I'm sorry Love, in the head to head, my head
had gone astray so you were second best,
it's just that I banked on a dead cert
gaffe to raise us
a laugh.

You don't hand me another Bud, but quiz my smiles
at this sniggery ad-lib game of gags
(that won your broken
laughter back then).
I'm thrown

to our courtship years when we lived in the clouds
of *Guantanamoww, Eyraaq,* and of course *Aff-*
ghanestaan freed by John Simpson
for the Crusades, way before
our daughters

trod the earth.

DAVID DABYDEEN

DAVID DABYDEEN (b. 1956), born of Indian parentage, emigrated from the Caribbean at an early age to England, where he won a scholarship for Cambridge University. He is now a professor of English literature at the University of Warwick. He lives and works alternately in England and Guyana, and he is his country's ambassador to UNESCO and China. Dabydeen has published three volumes of poetry: *Slave Song* (1984), *Coolie Odyssey* (1988), and the epic poem *Turner* (1993). He also published six novels and two studies on the British artist William Hogarth, notably Hogarth's representation of Africans. Dabydeen is himself a descendant of coolies, i.e., hired labourers recruited from India. Anthology appearances (among others) include *Wasafiri India South Asia & the Diaspora* (London: QMW University), and *The Yellow Nib Modern English Poetry by Indians* (Belfast: Queens University), both edited by Sudeep Sen.

from TURNER

I

Stillborn from all the signs. First a woman sobs
Above the creak of timbers and the cleaving
Of the sea, sobs from the depths of true
Hurt and grief, as you will never hear
But from woman giving birth, belly
Blown and flapping loose and torn like sails,
Rough sailors' hands jerking and tugging
At ropes of veins, to no avail. Blood vessels
Burst asunder, all below-deck are drowned.
Afterwards, stillness, but for the murmuring
Of women. The ship, anchored in compassion
And for profit's sake (what well-bred captain
Can resist the call of his helpless
Concubine, or the prospect of a natural
Increase in cargo?), sets sail again,
The part-born, sometimes with its mother,
Tossed overboard. Such was my bounty
Delivered so unexpectedly that at first
I could not believe this miracle of fate,
This longed-for gift of motherhood.
What was deemed mere food for sharks will become
My fable. I named it Turner
As I have given fresh names to birds and fish
And humankind, all things living but unknown,
Dimly recalled, or dead.

II

It plopped into the water and soon swelled
Like a brumplak seed that bursts buckshot
From its pod, falling into the pond
In the backdam of my mother's house, and fattening,
Where small boys like I was hold sticks to the water
For fish; branches stripped and shaped from the impala
Tree, no other, for we know – only the gods
Can tell how – that they bend so supple,
Almost a circle without snapping, yet strong
Enough to pull in a baby alligator.

Maybe by instinct, maybe the wisdom
Of our village elders passed down forever
(Until Turner came) which we suck in from birth
Like woodsmoke in my mother's kitchen,
Coconut shells stoking up a fire,
And I squat with my two sisters, small we are,
I don't know exactly how much in age –
Though since Turner's days I have learnt to count,
Weigh, measure, abstract, rationalize –
But we are small enough nearly to pass
Upright under the belly of the cow
Whilst our father pulls the teats and wheezes
Milk into a pakreet shell, swoosh, swoosh
Swoosh, the sound still haunts, survives the roar
And crash and endless wash and lap
Of waves, and we stoop under the belly
Of the cow and I can see I am just
Taller than its haunches, and when my sisters
Kneel their heads reach its knees. We play
Games as our father milks, crawling under
The belly like warriors, then springing up
At the other side to hurl spears at enemies
Hiding behind the chaltee tree in the cow-pen,
From which we pick twigs each morning, chew the ends,
Brush our teeth clean. The cow moves its head
To one side, watches us with covetous eyes
As if it wants to play, but my father
Will forbid it, for even when the milking is done,
He will not let us jump on the cow's back,
Nor decorate its heels with the blue and yellow
Bark of hemlik, nor put a chaktee straw
Into its nostrils until it sneezes
And snorts with laughter, but will lead it
Straight to pasture, and send us off to school,
To Manu, the magician, who will teach
Us how to squeeze, drain, blend, boil the juices
Of herbs for medicines, or bandage the sprained
Foot of a chicken. So the cow stands still,
But looks at us with a harlot's eye and winks,
And we can see the mischief in its face
Which our father can't because he's so far
Behind, concentrating on his fingers as if

Worshipping the gods, and it flicks its tail,
Beating off flies, but really to join in,
To lash and surprise us as we wait in ambush
Under its belly for the English
To come from another village, who will plunder
The crops, burn the huts, stampede the goats,
Drag girls away by ropes.

SLAVE SONG

Tie me haan up.
Juk out me eye.
Haal me teet out
So me na go bite.
Put chain rung me neck.
Lash me foot tight.
Set yu daag fo gyaad
Maan till nite –

Bu yu caan stap me cack floodin in de goldmine
Caan stap me cack splashin in de sunshine!

Whip me till me bleed
Till me beg.
Tell me how me hanimal
African orang-utan
Tell me how me cannibal
Fit fo slata fit fo hang.
Slice waan lip out
Waan ear an waan leg –

Bu yu caan stap me cack dippin in de honeypot
Drippin at de tip an happy as a hottentot!

Look how e'ya leap from bush to bush like a black crappau
Seeking out a watahole,
Blind by de sunflare, tongue like a dussbowl –
See how e'ya sip laang an full an slow!
Till e swell an heavy, stubban, chupit, full o sleep
Like camoudie swalla calf an stretch out in de grass, content,
Full o peace...
Hibiscus bloom, a cool breeze blow
An from a hill a wataflow
Canary singin saaf an low...

Is so when yu dun dream she pink tit,
Totempole she puss,
Leff yu teetmark like a tattoo in she troat!

She gi me taat
She gi me wife
So tear out me liver
Or stake me haat
Me still gat life!

FOR MA

Roll roti! roll roti! roll roti! roll roti!
Curry cookin in de karahee
Bora boilin wid de bagee
Woodsmoke sweet in me nose like agarbattee –
Ayuh wake up wake up ayuh pickni wake up ayuh man
Wid de sunshine in yu eye an de river a flow
An brung doves burstin from de trees an de kiskidees
An de whole savannah swimmin green an a glow!

Wata foh fetch battam-house foh daub fresh bucket foh mend clothes foh beat
Wake up ayuh pickni wuk na dun wuk foh duh
Cutlass foh shaap wood foh chap fence foh build dat bull bruk dung
Is wha da maan a stretch e haan an yaan foh!
Hear a cow baal in de yaad how dem swell wid milk-fraff
Goat a groan dem want go graze an sheep a caff-caff –
Ayuh wake up wake up time na deh foh cry time na deh foh laff
Hen a lay an cow a drap time na deh foh stap!

'Hear how a baai a taak
Like BBC!
Look how a baai a waak
Like white maan,
Caak-hat pun he head, wrist-watch pun he haan!
Yu dadee na Dabydeen, plant gyaden near Blackbush Pass?
He na cut wid sickle an dig wid faak?
He na sell maaket, plantain an caan?
An a who pickni yu rass?
Well me never see story like dis since me baan!

E bin Inglan two maaning, illegal,
Eye-up waan-two white hooman,
Bu is wha dem sweet watalily seed
Go want do wid hungrybelly Blackbush weed
Like yu, how yu teet yella like dhall
An yu tongue black like casrip!
Dem should a spit, vamit pun yu, beat yu rass wid whip!
Is lungara like yu spoil dem good white people country,
Choke an rab, bruk-an-enta, tief dem people prapaty!

So yu tink yu can come hey an play big-shat,
Fill we eye wid cigarette, iceapple an all dat?
Aweh po country people bu aweh ga pride:
Jess touch me gyal-pickni, me go buss yu back-side.'

DEBJANI CHATTERJEE

DEBJANI CHATTERJEE (b. 1952) was born in Delhi. She has written and edited over fifty books; and won many awards, including an honorary doctorate (from Sheffield Hallam University) and an MBE for her work as an international writer. Her poetry collections include *I Was that Woman*, *Albino Gecko*, *Animal Antics*, *Jade Horse Torso*, *Words Spit* and *Splinter*, and *Namaskar: New & Selected Poems*. Her edited anthologies include *The Redbeck Anthology of British South Asian Poetry*, *Rainbow World: Poems from Many Cultures*, *Generations of Ghazals* and bilingual books like *The Snake Prince* and *Who Cares: Reminiscences of Yemeni Carers*. Twisting Yarn Theatre toured her multilingual play for children *The Honoured Guest* in 2000 and 2001. Anthology appearances (among others) include *Wasafiri India South Asia & the Diaspora* (London: QMW University) edited by Sudeep Sen. She has chaired the Arts Council of England's Translations Advisory Group and the National Association of Writers in Education. As a patron of Survivor's Poetry and a Royal Literary Fund Fellow, she has mentored many writers. She lives in Sheffield, England, and visits India from time to time.

MY CUP OF TEA

Both hands cup my mug
as I sip my future dreams,
swirling its contents.

My cup runneth over with
rich liquid satisfaction.

SHEFFIELD TANKA

Passage to England
for a writer's life – and more.
Green dreams at eighteen.

The hallmark 'Made in Sheffield'
fiercely shines at fifty-six.

ASYLUM?

Behold this asylum we call the Earth,
where pain and sorrow are objects of mirth.
You are our Keeper and our Healer too.
Help us change before you measure our worth.

A LOWLY TRADE

Like headless chickens running round and round,
we follow those we know to be unsound.
Politics has become a lowly trade.
Elections leave us in apathy drowned.

AN ASIAN CHILD ENTERS A BRITISH CLASSROOM

Before she stepped into the classroom:
she removed coat, mittens and *chunni*;*
mentally undid her shoes for entry
to a temple of secular mystery.

She also shed her:
language, name, identity;
donned the mask of neat conformity,
prepared for lessons in cultural anonymity.

* *A long scarf worn with some South Asian clothes.*

DEEPANKAR KHIWANI

DEEPANKAR KHIWANI'S (b. 1971) first book of poems, *Entr'acte,* a selection of poems exploring interrelated themes of detachment, masquerade and ambivalence was published in 2006. He been anthologized in *Both Sides of the Sky* (National Book Trust / edited by Eunice De Souza); *50 Poets, 50 Poems* (Open Spaces / edited by Priya Sarukkai Chabria), *Wasafiri India South Asia & the Diaspora* (London: QMW University/ edited by Sudeep Sen), and others. His poems have also appeared in *Atlas, Wasafiri, London Magazine* and *Fulcrum*. Currently, he is working on his second book, which collects islands of themes, including sequences about a photography exhibition in the South of France, about travelling around the world, and about reflections on what it means to live in Bombay.

THIS IS THE WAY

My phone's wallpaper frames our holiday,
The sands so carefully separate from the sea.
This is the way that it was meant to be.

And I wait for your next message, your reply,
I've met your deadline, answered you at last.
The sands so carefully separate from the sea.

Would life reject a frank appeal for grief?
My throat's been hurting since the afternoon.
And I wait for your next message, your reply.

I slept post-lunch, and got up at sundown,
Send me an SMS by eight you said.
I've met your deadline, answered you at last.

1 message received now on this unreal beach:
'Kill me before you go, I will not live'.
My throat's been hurting since the afternoon.

The resolution on the phone's quite good.
Strengthen yourself, delete it from the screen.
My phone's wallpaper frames our holiday.

My daughter plays by me, taking apart
The clockwork of her doll, insistently.
I've met your deadline, answered you at last.
This is the way that it was meant to be.

from LIFE ON AN ISLAND

I

They say this city is an island city,
Much of it reclaimed, connecting
marshy landmasses;

and connecting
these narratives of islands, muddy water,
red concrete mixers, unfamiliar connections,
sweet tea with a fly in it, creeks,
confections of silt and yelping dogs,
riots and unexpected rain, the straits of
grunting tarred ropes, dead pigeons,
lost wedding bands with barnacles on them, and

the waiting, waiting, endless isthmus of
waiting,

for this collage to dry
of concrete quicksand
that men bridged, pieced, reclaimed
from an ambition ascribed to them.

And so we may spend ourselves
reclaiming what never was from what will always be,
this sullen silt, this city we animate, nostalgic, for
the tenements of Lalbaug or the Watson Hotel,
connecting season, landscape, decay to this spot

you first discovered I was married, and narratives of
its gimcrack beautiful people, the sweet glittering
adolescent now-no-more Bombay, its vodka bars
and its intolerance, judgements seeking a tentative
kinship, fighting the island, fighting the sea,
the inevitable decay, the yelping dogs, the muddy water;
and now

my child at Bandstand, looking out
at nothing and the unexpected rain.

IV

I grew up in this city,

now thirty seven I sometimes still sit at Mocambo
and write on my napkins the usual questions;
what growing up meant, what the city is,
What *I* means.

As usual, the questions are neither answerable
Nor, after many drinks, interesting.

Then I walk past my old school
and hear them practising the anthem
School first, House Next, Self Last.
And comfort myself with that order of things
Beyond the high stone wall.

V

Outsiders need to leave, they're saying
With calm and specious reasonableness in press rooms
On the streets they've been roughing up taxi drivers

At night I watch all this on TV, and my wife clucks
And talks of divisive politics. I think the man looks earnest,
And has a point, and nice glasses; and, well, has heated things up

And given us something to talk about, so that for some time
We forget the email that didn't come, and the coldness of bed later.
A man shows off his wound to the reporter. An outsider's wounds.

VI

Today they pulled people off the trains, and beat them
Partly because a fading actor made his uninteresting films
In other languages. I'm getting around

To understand that I'm an outsider too, like that actor
And his films that belong nowhere. But where do I go to,
With a father from Pakistan, and a mother from Bangladesh,

Growing up in Bombay, married to a Jat woman who grew up in Jabalpur,
And with a Tamil lover? (Whose Konkani husband, raised in Mazagaon,
Is my only faithful claim to kinship with this place).

VIII

At Bandra Station the hustlers stand
Smelling of sweat and deodorant, and all
The arrogance of those who are bought and sold

The passengers mill past1, as composite, as only those
Who have nothing in common, the Philosophy professor,
Back from Grant Road, the girl with a torn bra and new shoes;

We are all configuring this place, this day,
Upon each others retinas, with all the rich collaborative detail
Of perfect tumult, that this is life, the 23rd of August, in Bombay city

framed by a girl with grey eyes, a child who will be raped,
the laughter of the eunuch, and the koli fisherwomen
with their baskets of glittering fish, that have their eyes wide open,
staring as only the dead can look at you.

IX

From my permanent seat at the Sea Lounge I look out
What's Bombay, I ask the sea, do I stay in Bombay?
Do I stay in Powai? Do I stay in 606 Wing G
Of a building called Lake Homes that looks out on another building?
What is my Bombay? Is it that space
of daily driving past a peepul tree and a shuttered post office
Over four speedbreakers, is that my city, my home,
Or do I stay in the headache, in the dislike of rain,
Stay in the offer of Elephanta I've never seen but send guests too
Stay in the thoughts of those who pull up their covers or fling an arm
Over their heads each night, on pavement, bungalow, hotel, or in my bed,
Within Wing G, in the Air France lounge near Gate 12, in the humidity,
In ambiguity, inebriety,
The island; the corrosive boundaries
of shifting salty tides.

RENCONTRES D'ARLES

Father, photographer, my one-time friend.
Am I now, seven years on, to construct you
Like this, from these luminous hallucinogenic slides,

That announce themselves in the dark cuboid?
What do you think of them, you ask
with a shy faltering pride, as we stand together

At the boy with the Hanuman mace
and a Yankees tshirt, lost in TV
the girl faking fear as her brother displays a snake.

I don't know your children, I want to say,
I am stuck, the boy who drank with you. You've grown up,
I see your life, the wife in the lace bra, the colleague shot in black:

All I see is what is missing, The sword motif,
I say, is repeated – it doesn't work, I'm fumbling in the swamp,
And the red in the garden photograph needs relief...

You nod at something, at the corner of my eye,
And the images move, and move again.

DESMOND L KHARMAWPHLANG

DESMOND L KHARMAWPHLANG (b. 1964) is a poet and folklorist and a native of Shillong, Meghalaya. He has published several books of poetry and essays, including *Mawshamok/Touchstone; Here; Ki Matti Byrshem; Narratives of North-East India I &II; Folklore in the Changing Times; Conference, Confluence; Attributes of Khasi Folklore;* and *Khasi Folksongs and Tales.* A Folk Fellow of the Finnish Academy of Science and Letters in Helsinki, he is on the executive board of the International Society of Folk Narrative Research, and serves as national editorial board member of the *Journal of Indian Folklore Research* in Mysore. He is currently the Head of Department of Cultural and Creative Studies of the North-Eastern Hill University in Shillong.

THERE WILL BE TIME

Is my tongue capable of birthing
those hundreds of signs,
you make on paper like
the flowers our women
make on looms?

When your fingers fly across paper
do you read signs and portents
like I do on leaf and lime?
Do you alter meanings in the
scribing of words?

Perhaps there will be a time
when your reading and writing
will make sense to mine
and our words will be joined
by the same benign shadow.

In that conjoined realm,
I say, let the words of mouth
and words of pen latch together
like the starry belt of the eastern sky
bearing the infinite weight of the universe.

THEY

They came for him one evening,
Packed his bag and even
Carried it to the jeep parked
On the roadside, near the dry public water tap
Where oil containers line up,
Marking space in a spaceless locality.

They offered him cigarettes
Calling him uncle as the jeep
Sped away from the city in
Throes of a dusk he was
Not to see, as he told me,
For sometime.

The moon was already stripping
Off his gossamer robe ready
For his bath.

They plunged into the orchestra
Of night insects and followed
The moon as he swam the length
Of his misty pool.

They rested at dawn,
Waiting for the fifty-four-year-old frame
Of their captive to revive.

It was not easy with gout
Beginning to torch flames
In my friend's joints.

They called him teacher and
Urged him to lecture on the magic
Of myths to make blood
Sing about unity.

We are one, they said, and
Our common history is inscribed
In memory of stone.

My friend did his share of
Tutorials in the jungles but he
Confessed that the practicals
Were too exciting for his old bones.

When the month was over, they
Half carried him through the
Bamboo jungles.

He woke up by the side of
His gate. The water tap was
Still dry, and the oil containers
Still jostled for space on ground
Where no space can be seen.

LAAMI — 18 JULY 2002

By the light of the bonfire
I sit quietly listening to
the murmur of branches.

Leaves fall like stars from
the sky and pile up on
the mossy floor. You say we
are condemned to witness
this theatre of guilt and I
yield my defence to your
knife-edged clarity. The hours
we have abandoned tumble
like a spiralling doom to bury us
in the chill of sculptured night.

Whatever happened to the pact of
the summer sun? Though
embracing, we shiver in the garden
of syllables and groan
in the emptiness of
midnights' luminescence.

IT IS TODAY

It is today
that the bank of
clouds are broken up
into tiny spoors of
the ploughing cat.

It is today
that streets
fill up with people,
invading shops like
swarms of flies.

It is today
that fools
and poets alike salute,
raised glasses bridging
day and night, levelling worlds.

It is today
that I am frenzied
thinking of your honeyed
lips and the pain it
would do me to nibble them.

It is today
my own and another's espoused
that I am alone,
walking with winter mind
and a
sliver of a dream
for company.

LAST NIGHT I DREAMED

Last night I dreamed that I
was a sperm swimming in
the womb of folklore.

I was born an idea and
delivered into a naked nation.

Mating with the elements,
I was raised on speeding clouds
skywards, to be forged in fire.

Rains bore me to earth
and I crawled on all four
scribbling ragged mythology
on the subsoil of time.

I entered the food chain and
became one with the *sohtung* leaf
to be consumed by the eri-worm.

I wintered in its silken cocoon
and a season later, was spun into thread
on whistling looms.

Deft fingers plucked me
and I exited the tale,
grafted my flesh on tongue
of experience:

I became a proverb.

I went from place to place
but always came back to you,
searching the coast of your lips
for clever words to trade:

I became a riddle.

In another lifetime, I would
dream of becoming a sperm in
the womb of poetry.

DIANE MEHTA

DIANE MEHTA (b. 1966) is a poet whose book, *How to Write Poetry*, was published in 2006 by Barnes & Noble Books. Her poems and criticism have appeared in *Agni, Slate, Poetry, The Literary Review, The Gettysburg Review, The Harvard Review*, and *The Southern Review*. Anthology appearances (among others) include *Contours of the Heart* (USA), *Twelve Modern Young Indian Poets* (Edinburgh: Lines Review), and *The Literary Review Indian Poetry* (New Jersey: Fairleigh Dickinson University), the last two edited by Sudeep Sen. Her journalism appears regularly in the mainstream American press. She lives in Brooklyn with her son, and is working on a novel set in 1946.

SOPRANO EXPLOSIONS

Silver jets provide backup for sparrows
like Shostakovich in thirty words, ridiculous
but true to the blur of feeling.

The silky outer radials of a spider's orb
on the porch's limestone edge
quiver in the engine's aftermath.

Soft shade darkens the sparrow's belly
in a blue-tinted tilt. The rhythms of sky
fill my son's almond-black eyes.

The moment collapses into soprano
explosions over bugs and birds,
the flush of genetics and spontaneous feelings.

Illuminated shapes: fence-iron pikes
skewering the slant of Sunday light,
the atomic spaces inbetween.

The effusions of childhood
sashay like a concerto over the page.
Let's sync our life completely into it.

OPTICAL DRAWINGS: WILLIAM KENTRIDGE'S *ERASURES*

I

Charcoal on paper, erased and redrawn, pulled off the page and twisted like a flip book into the colours of South Africa: the jowls of an industrial shape turning into a man who flowers into oil rigs, whose coffee press becomes the gallows where a rhinoceros leaps out or settles into mud.

II

The wife becomes the trick, her lover the dissolved, the lack of shape. Oil trickles back into the carnage that is quickly forgiven. In search of truth, and reconciliation, the government pretends it too reshapes. Giraffes strut with their necks in the trees.

III

He feels the world mowing down around him, his desk becomes the outlines of his room. It has no opening to comets raining over the backs of antelope. Sometimes the sadness reappears as blue instead of charcoal and he thinks he is free.

IV

She meets him momentarily, then folds into a spoon and then a shovel, and then a pumpjack – he waits for her to take the body of a woman. The sun blazes over her in yellow fields but she is simply irrigation. That too turns into tears.

A SOCIAL HISTORY OF IMMIGRATION IN THE FIVE BOROUGHS

Buildings shake to the refrains of worship. Language scatters in the dust of sun-shafts pressing the pews, overcome by the saturated sounds of organs.

The Bronx: Blazed, that family from Mali, entering the burnt ghosts of 87 people at the Happy Land Social Club. Fire, like impassioned knives, digs the life out.

1911, before trees were ravaged throughout Europe and fire blossomed in the hearts and ovens of the countryside. Triangle Shirtwaist, 146 women chalked in asphalt like dress patterns.

The booming 80s. Turks, Willie. Avenue X, Gravesend, Brooklyn. Report reads: Between the salt-saturated breezes and Coney Island's freak show, transit worker stops for beer and a New York bagel. Italian gang in transit. Race rage #2: White mob in Howard Beach; Griffith, Michael, chased onto the Belt Parkway. #3: Hawkins, Yusef, black youth gunned down in Bensonhurst. Rage unchecked, like the swarm of the morning commute.

Greenwich Village, branded with happy hour murders: bullets in a bartender who said too much and execution of two auxiliary cops whose mothers bear the crush of time.

By blood we live through it. It fades, headlines warn, to a glimmer. The next day's news creates new funerals. Buildings shake to the refrains of worship.

THE ENERGY OF SHAPES

Supposedly the brain rewires itself at two, time of taking shape, of shapes, of time-free days marked by meals or who he sees before or after sleeping, not the universal feelings or an outward-edging science of expanding universes. His memory expands, shoulders widen, verbs insert themselves. The moon shimmers; he wants one, calls it *silver circle*. He thinks all shape is outside, where evening hides during daylight, an illuminated *on*. Shards of snow diminish at the harbor, which shivers below the harp of a bridge; beyond it energy courses, a week's journey, through clutches of waves to warm Gulf waters. His mind curving underwater: Intricacies of language, a continuum that vibrates through the minutes whose internal beat is more cacophonous than emergency, last-breath sirens. Physics is the shape of a feeling, eyesight racing, a restructuring of the savage, unfiltered life of physical properties, and, incidentally, the mind's way of seeing.

LOCAL APPLES

The Baspa boils past the bridge strung with epic prayers. Fluttering in the monsoon's north-pounding fist, Tibetan flags honor the walk of old women bent under baskets bulging with local apples. Serene leaves, Buddhist earth. Jagged slopes, striped with ancient patterns the sun clutches. Teak homes on stilts populate the foothills. Below the holy Kinner-Kailash range, trekkers stamp out bonfires and monks in quiet formation ascend to Shiva's rock lingam, at 5,000 meters. Across the valley, days are work and baskets are the commerce of winter after the road closes. We climb through the orchards, past the breezes. The afternoon slants and the trail opens. Yellow meadows curve around a lake, stone fences and a lean-to illuminated with dusk is stocked with metal pans, wood, and wool for winter. Two children race easily in the altitude. They chase me across sunlight into saffron fields. Laughter echoes in the valley where the river is a drumbeat and old men sharpen the hour with black cumin in their tea. The air drops icily; I can hardly breathe. Their mother has no teeth, she has everything she needs.

GLASS OF TEXT

We figured the Talmud talked about the question of the window, each Jew's window, like Chagall, refracting the essential lights. The soul of a bug, seasons, and so on.

Then, our mother at rest. It was in Hebrew, that scent. Know your opinions, she said. Questions full of dusk, answers that have no end.

Still, there's a sense of holy scripture left, especially the ceremony and the rhythms of text. We like reading out loud. Prayers angle through synagogues like the dead in cemeteries and quote their book of text.

Germans crouch on bookshelves, Jews play their pianos to death. Old dachas don't house anything; she lived in her opinions, thinking svelte.

INSIDE THE FERN

Photosynthesis-green interior of ferns,
jade shade, each ruggedly skeletal vein

bursting through leaves, humidly breathing.
Effervescent turns of science.

Heat of minor and magnificent years, of moments in eras,
including grief, which passes. And slow raptures summer

unleashes: monsoons or the farmer's irrigated fields,
that water necessary, and so baptismal.

The fern growing in a spray like a jittery peacock
guarding its place on the perpetual, cliff-side

incline under a fog-infused canopy of green,
tree-line so distant you can hardly see it break for the road.

GAYATRI MAJUMDAR

GAYATRI MAJUMDAR's (b. 1963) poems, short stories, and articles have been published in numerous newspapers and magazines in India and abroad. Her first book of poems, *Shout,* included her poems written since she was nineteen. Born in Kolkata, she lived in Mumbai and worked as a journalist at the Press Trust of India, *The Independent, Debonair* (where she also edited the 'Poetry Page'), and at All India Radio, where she was a DJ. A number of her poems have been translated into Italian. She was also associated with the Indian Chapter of PEN. Currently, Gayatri edits the critically acclaimed literary magazine, *Brown Critique* (recently re-launched as an online edition) and manages a team of copyeditors at a publishing house in Noida. She is also working on her first novel, which she hopes will be out soon. Her other interests include music, movies and travelling.

VERSOVA BEACH

Last night was something else.

The sea licks the face of a sky,
trawlers in the cold shadow of clouds
and two black birds.
A woman in green and gold
searches for crabs and perfect shells.
Another morning leaves
her watermarks on my nape and eyelashes
and lines my womb
with her unformed delta.

Such is the beauty in struggle
and hunger. Small boats flutter blue flags
of peace, economy, and I sniff
for distant thunders, spices, and men –
from Africa, Oman, Afganisthan,
and some unnamed islands
hidden in the large intestine of water.

ANTENNA

We enter into the sweetest
of the brown cookies,
dig a hole
and make provisions for the rains
during the rains.
In this stickthing lovedough
we lock antennas,
sting poison into each other.
Then we about-face: antidote.
We listen to rain
as we eat through the light
on our ceiling;
fatten our sex,
make time in here.
Meanwhile, the bridge
to a neighbourhood constellation
is crumbling.

MY AUNT'S HOME

Her backyard is a ruin in green
On which topaz black giant snails feed.
They have grown lumpish with age,
Prosperity, and charity to reign here
Where we used to whistle around bonfires
Made of crackly walnut-brown leaves
Every Christmas night. The room upstairs
Is a skeleton of its florid cushioned self
With ragged furniture and lights
That strain the eye. It would seem
That an unendurable hurricane has left
Here a disaster zone on the terrace
Where books lay mutilated in the rain.
It takes more than money
To be loved, I said. But does it?
My old aunt knows.
There were once rooms for trespassers here.
Now my aunt complains; demanding
Her share in the ancestral property.
I know she wants to defeat time
And be at that place,
Which is more than a shelter.
She now searches for words that offend.
A little muddled herself, she cannot
Disentangle hope from the weeds
That are scaling her mildewed walls.

H MASUD TAJ

H MASUD TAJ (b. 1956) is an oral poet. His first book of poems *Alphabestiary* (exegesis by Bruce Meyer) had him present at the 2011 International Festival of Authors, Toronto. His audiences range from officers of the Indian Navy to a lone Bosnian refugee in Vienna; in venues such as Kingdom Café in the red-light area of Amsterdam; Hall of Philosophy, Chautauqua, NY; Poetry Place, London UK; a 400-year-old Sufi Lodge, Istanbul; Roman Abbey, St. Albans. Anthology appearances include *Reasons for Belonging* (Penguin India); *60 Indian Poets* (Bloodaxe UK); *The White Collar Book* (Canada); *Wespennest*, *Atlas 'New Canadian Writing'*, *The Literary Review Indian Poetry* (New Jersey: Fairleigh Dickinson University), *The Yellow Nib Modern English Poetry by Indians* (Belfast: Queens University), and *World Literature Today: Writing from Modern India* (Norman: University of Oklahoma), the last four edited by Sudeep Sen. His calligraphy is archived in the Special Collection of Carleton University where he is Adjunct Professor of Architecture. He lives with his family in Ottawa and spends each monsoon as an architect in India.

ANT

I do, therefore
Unmindfully, I am

A passing thought embodied.

A neuron on six neurotic feet
Crossing synapses in frenzy

Saying, 'Read me! Read me!'

For I cannot read.
The sum total of all that I do

Is the thought that escapes me.

While I relentlessly fabricate
Mind, mindlessly.

FLAMINGO

The City of God
Is a pink city in the sky.
It alights into fragments.
Folded wings
Embrace a montage:
Ribs of a Stork
Eggs of a Heron
Webbed feet of Geese
When the City of God
Comes to rest in wet mud
Intertidal zones turn pink.
Constellation of yellow eyes.
Pairs of long legs
With opposing orientations:
One displaced ankle
Folding the sky.
The other extended
Webbing the earth
Swaying back and forth
Mapping wind tides
Laying foundations
Of a new City of Mud
Moulded into mounds
With volcanic depressions
Receiving blue eggs
That turn into a white
Constellation of moons
That crack into a crackle
Of red bills and red legs
Turning black with grey bodies
The eyes of the new City
Of God are grey
Seeking red milk from
Mother City of God
That seeks geysers
Sans salt in the sea
Boiling water
To quench thirst
Before taking flight
At night when pink

Turns grey and the City
Of God recedes
Into vanishing points
Erasing perspectives.

HORSE

My body is all gravity,
My ankles all grace.
My skin is a seismograph:
Shock-waves
Ripple beneath the sheen;
Earth tremors that connect
Shiva's shoulders with Parvati's shanks
The rest of me cope with my androgyny.

My movement is meditation.
Canter is mere foreplay,
When I break into a gallop
The circle of horizon
Begins to slip away,
As I touchdown to beat
The world with my feet
So that it may spin.

My eyes are twin holes;
My eyelashes: scorched rays
Of light that could not flee.
At the twitch of my nostrils
Stars flicker away.
Each time I turn my head
Swirling my mane, spiralling off galaxies,
I watch the universe change.

JELLYFISH

You dream of form:
I appear in water.
You dream of time:
I begin to pulsate.

You dream of life:
I, made in water,
Made of water,
Move in water.

(Somewhere, on land
There is a missing umbrella.
Somewhere, on land
You are drenched to your skin.

Somewhere, on land
You have given up searching
You have taken to dreaming.
Somewhere, on land,

Your missing umbrella
Is waiting for someone
Somewhere, on land,
To open its wings).

Somewhere in the ocean
A portion of water
Is refracting light
In unseen ways.

IMTIAZ DHARKER

IMTIAZ DHARKER (b. 1954) is a poet, artist, and documentary film-maker. Her five poetry collections are *Purdah* (OUP), *Postcards from God, I speak for the devil, The Terrorist at my table*, and *Leaving Fingerprints* (all Penguin India & Bloodaxe UK). Her poems have appeared in many journals and magazines. Anthology appearances (among others) include *Midnight's Grandchildren: Post Independence Poetry from India* (Macedonia: Struga Poetry Evenings), *The Literary Review Indian Poetry* (New Jersey: Fairleigh Dickinson University), *The Yellow Nib Contemporary English Poetry by Indians* (Belfast: Queens University), all edited by Sudeep Sen. Her poems have also been broadcast on BBC Radio 4, BBC Radio 3, BBC World Service, and BBC Television. She has had ten solo exhibitions of drawings, pen and ink on handmade paper, often on a large scale. She scripts and directs documentary films, many of them for non-government organizations in India, working in the area of shelter, education and health for women and children. She grew up in Glasgow, worked for many years in India and now lives between Mumbai, London, and Wales. She can be contacted at www.imtiazdharker.com.

OUT

Get me out, you said. *Now.*
Get me out. The unfamiliar bed
a prison, your body behind bars,
your bright spirit locked away.

I say I am better now, I was lucky
to have you for that precious time
even if the years escaped like
a single day. But as I pay

at a till for milk or bread,
as I board a train, as I turn and turn
on the pillow where your head should be
Now, you say

and it slams shut around me, that last day
when I chose not to understand you,
when I tried to keep you, keep you
in my custody, walled in by my will,

when I tried to make you stay.

AFTER

We have done all the things you
would have liked us to do.

Your brother has been across the country and back
to fetch your comfortable shoes.

We have dressed you in your black wedding suit
and the ironed shirt. Someone has combed your hair.

This is exactly as I wanted it, you will say,
after the tributes have been paid,

when the organ has been played
and the hymns have been sung

when all the well-wishers have gone
and we settle down to talk.

Exactly, you will say
when it is all over, when you come back.

VIGIL

Your eyes open, blaze silver
for one second, close.
Your hand stops, falls still.
You send me no more messages.

The machine by your bed
is saying prayers for you.
It keeps watch, tenderly interpreting
your body's needs.
It listens and records your every breath,
the turning of your blood, your heartbeat.

All night, all night, it pays close attention
to you. At dawn it stops.

I try to read its face.
The machine is blinking back
its tears.

SIGNS OF LIFE

If I were to write a pineapple like a poem
I would look at its eyes to see
what it wanted to be, and then I would
make it what it did not expect to be.
I would slice off its crown
and its thorny skin, slash it and cut it
down, turn it inside out and around.
I would examine it for signs of life,
hold up a mirror to see if it still
had bite, check for pulse or rhythm.
If its heart was still beating
I would eat it alive.

If I were to dig up a poem like a potato
I would root it out of cold soil
and bang it hard against a rock
to shake off the dirt. I would wash it,
gouge out its eyes and look at its skin
to decide if this poem was worth
baking or boiling or mashing or roasting
or cutting in cubes and frying with cumin.

Then I would give it to you to read
and you would say, 'That was a good potato.'

SAYING NOTHING

Our clothes are amusing, tangled
on the floor, thrown into improbable
positions. Outside
people are asking where we are,
passing notes through letter-boxes,
ringing, sending text messages
and your lips are at my ear
saying nothing
but I can feel you smiling.

JEET THAYIL

JEET THAYIL (b. 1959) was born in Kerala, India. He was educated in Jesuit schools in Hong Kong, New York and Bombay. A poet, novelist and musician, he is one half of the contemporary music project Sridhar/Thayil. His four poetry collections include *English* and *These Errors Are Correct*. He is the editor of *The Bloodaxe Book of Contemporary Indian Poets* and *Divided Time: India and the End of Diaspora*. His writing has appeared in *London Magazine, Verse, Stand, Agenda, Wasafiri, Lines Review, Poets & Writers, The Cortland Review, Drunken Boat, The Independent* and *Poetry Review*, among many other journals. He is a contributing editor to *Fulcrum*, the Boston-based poetry annual, and an editor of the multi-media arts journal *Rattapallax*. He is a recipient of grants and awards from the New York Foundation for the Arts, the Rockefeller Foundation, the British Council and the Swiss Arts Council. His debut novel, *Narcopolis*, was published in 2011. He lives in New Delhi.

FOOL AND FLEA

Dearly beloved,
we are gathered here
to join together
this fool and this flea
in holy matrimony.

Fool will sing,
flea will suck.
Fool will work,
flea will pluck.
Both will learn

the virtue of obedience.
Fool will give up his freedom.
Flea will give up
whatever chance
she may have had

at happiness.
Both will die.
Fool first.
Flea so full
she'll burst.

THE HEROIN SESTINA

What was the point of it? The stoned
life, the chased, snorted, shot life. Some low
comedy with a cast of strangers. Time
squashed flat. The 1001 names of heroin
chewed like language. Nothing now to know
or remember but the dirty taste

of it, and the names: snuff, Death, a little taste,
H — pronounce it etch —, sugar, brownstone,
scag, the SHIT, ghoda gaadi, #4 china, You-Know,
garad, god, the gear, junk, monkey blow,
the law, the habit, material, cheez, heroin.
The point? It was the wasted time,

which comes back lovely sometimes,
a ghost sense say, say that hard ache taste
back in your throat, the warm heroin
drip, the hit, the rush, the whack, the stone.
You want it now, the way it lays you low,
flattens everything you know

to a thin white line. I'm saying, I know
the pull of it: the skull rings time
so beautiful, so low
you barely hear it. Itch this blind toad taste.
When you said, "I mean it, we live like stones,"
you broke something in me only heroin

could fix. The thick sweet amaze of heroin,
helpless its love, its know-
ledge of the infinite. Why push the stone
back up the hill? Why not leave it with the time-
keep, asleep at the bar? Try a little taste
of something sweet that a sweet child will adore, low

in the hips where the aches all go. Allow
me in this one time and I'll give you heroin,
just a taste
to replace the useless stuff you know.

Some say it comes back, the time,
to punish you with the time you killed, leave you stone

sober, unknowing, the happiness chemical blown
from your system, unable to taste the word *heroin*
without wanting its stone one last time.

THE SONNETEER

I was famous, I won the Hawthornden prize.
Girls flashed me. One said, 'You're the poet, right?
What a godawful waste it would be, otherwise.'
I told her my talents would not last the night,
and it *was* a waste, you bet, any which way.
She said, 'Poetry boy, I don't give a damn.
I've got time to kill, make a sonnet for moi.'
'She hawks her beauty in the night,' I began,
and stopped, unable to motor my mouth.
One morning I stepped out for cigarettes
and hopped a subway to the south —
I thought I'd vanish myself and my debts.
For months she heard my step on the stair.
It wasn't me, brothers, I was taking the air.

LETTER FROM A MUGHAL EMPEROR, 2006

Nothing here's worth a tick.

I hid everything except the heads. They respect slaughter.

They respect only slaughter. They forget the other things we brought them, the ghazals, the gardens, the ice and symmetry.

It's an affliction to grow up motherless, with your lady mother living beside you.

They have many images, but they have no God. They're fit only for war.

Even the dogs are second rate.

In Tashkent I had no money, no country or hope of one, only humiliation. But among the people I found much beauty. No pears are better.

There are no accidents. There's only God.

Tending to his doves on the eve of battle, my father flew into a ravine at the fortress of Akhsi.

He became a falcon. I became emperor.

Sometimes, when I eat a Kabul melon, I remember my father and you.

I've forgotten more than I've seen, but I haven't forgotten enough.

There's only one way to live in a place like this, with your disgust close at hand.

One night I took majoun because the moon was shining. The next day I took some more, at sunrise.

I enjoyed wonderful fields of flowers, flowers on all sides. I saw an apple sapling with five or six leaves placed regularly on each branch.

No painter could have done this.

I made a schedule. Saturday, Sunday, Tuesday and Wednesday for wine, the other days for majoun.

Your letter puzzled me:

The people are caught between constant spiritual anguish and a faith that will give meaning to the question that consumes them: the dual substance of Krishna, the yearning of man to know God. Between the spirit and the flesh, a great unwinnable war.

Dear friend, write clearly, with plain words. Writing badly will make you ill.

Once, in an orchard, I was sick with fever and vision. I was young, but I prepared myself.

A hundred years or a day, in the end you'll leave this place.

Long ago, my grandfather's face looked into mine, I think with love.

Now when we speak it's of ghazals, of metrics and rhyme or of our most famous massacres.

When he conquered Lahore he planted a banana tree. It thrived, even in that climate.

His memory is so good it gives him a second life. Mine gives only a partial one.

It's no more than I need.

2007

Locked in your head with English,
you number a beat that feeds the day,
but a system exists to deny English
to you who know no tongue but English.
The word with which you order time
is a kindness, a gift made in English
from your years in a house with English.
At dawn, someone's voice calls your name
for pleasure in the sound of your name,
its meaning plain, but only in English,
in a page that passes from hand to hand
and lifts like a bird, white, from a hand.

You hold to the world an empty hand
that fills with the shapes of English.
In your city, someone's prayerful hand
ignites a street, a square with light. A hand
that waved to you — was it yesterday? —
returns as a chalk outline of a hand.
What will you read in the lines of a hand
outstretched, with nothing, not even time,
inscribed in it? It says too much is time-
bound, love, luck, the seasons, the hand
you deal, are dealt — fixed as your name
on a stone, and the dates below the name.

Cruelty without reason, in whose old name
some reject the lovely arm, the hand-
some face, the unfamiliar name,
and learn to husband evil in god's name,
holds nothing dear for me or you. *English
spoken here* was the promise near your name.
You could've been The Man With No Name
for the way you drifted through your day-
dream which transformed each holiday
into mythic disaster, something name-
less that struck a town in the pages of *Time*,
and would do so again, time after time.

Misfortune works in cycles beyond time.
These meanings are contingent, the name
attached to an object, divisions of time,
the fragrance in a room of dead time.
Unchangeable and correct, the minute-hand,
its formal drop — Greenwich Mean Time —
that tells you nothing will turn back time
or tragedy. You, solo chewer of English,
spit your lines of broken English
to God who's busy and keeps no time.
You'll remember stray details of the day,
'I'm my own ghost, I too died today.'

In a damaged city, you take each day
express to the top, where a custodian, Time,
places no bulwarks against the day
his work fails to separate night from day,
forgetting from love, silence from a name.
What sets the week in motion each Monday
sets you off in your own *Groundhog Day,*
stuck on repeat, unable to lift a hand
to change or delay the blood-black hand-
made conclusion. The outlines of day
blur, and the actors have no English.
There's no help for us but in English.

So I speak to you now only in English.
I'm walking with you, hand in hand,
hoping you remember, this is my name,
here's where we met, this is the time
we had together, an hour and a day.

JERRY PINTO

JERRY PINTO (b. 1966) has been a journalist for more than twenty years. He is the editor of *Reflected in Water: Writings about Goa;* and the co-editor of *Bombay Meri Jaan: Writings about Mumbai,* and *Confronting Love*, an anthology of love poems by Indian poets writing in English. He is also the author of *Asylum*, a collection of poems; and of *Helen: The Life and Times of an H-Bomb* for which he won a national award in 2006. He has written a book for children *A Bear for Felicia,* and celebrated Bollywood's poster art in *Bollywood Posters*. Anthology appearances (among others) include *The Literary Review Indian Poetry* (New Jersey: Fairleigh Dickinson University) edited by Sudeep Sen. He teaches journalism at the Sophia Polytechnic, is a consultant editor with Penguin India, and a contributing editor with *Man's World.* Jerry Pinto just published his debut novel, *Em and the Big Hoom*, and lives in Mumbai

SEVEN TYPES OF ANGER

The first: rehearsal rage.
Pacing the streets, an internal tirade
Aimed at bosses, lovers, family, friends,
All turned dumb and guilty,
Stricken by the knowledge that
Behind my impenetrable façade
Of logic-as-I-construe-it
I am in tears.

The second: the quick acid spurt at the self
Always such a tempting object,
Such a sitting duck.
The alkaline self redux
Turns all into the salt and water
Of self-pity.

The third: shimmering
quivering
shaking
sweating
incoherence.

It breaks down here: who's counting?
Saboteur, saviour, sucker,
Naming you does not help.
You're not dead yet.

NIGHTMARE

Left unsung
the world
became a better place.

'WILL YOU MISS ME?'

Yes, I will.
That's no answer, of course, not for you.
Nor for me.

I shall miss you as a broken needle misses its thread.
I shall miss you as the bones of Nureyev miss his jetés.
I shall miss you as Beckham missed his penalty in 2004.
I shall miss you as ISRO misses Chandrayaan.

And I shall miss you as I would a stone in my shoe.
And I shall miss you as New York misses its twins.
I shall miss you as I would miss a splint in my shins.
Oh yes, in those ways too.

But I shall miss me too
Shall miss how you made me.
I shall miss what we made of each other.
The stain of your voice in mine.
The phrase I fed you one evening.
The outpost I still man in your mind.
The anicut you built in mine.

I wish I could say I would not miss you so much because of this.
This coming and going, this uncanny symbiosis, this more than friendship,
This more bizarre than love, this sense of a connection forged before we met.
I wish I could say: you're in me, I'm in you, what's to miss, who to miss?

But I'm not that way.
I will miss you.
Some days it will be bad.
Some days will open into darkness and only music or chocolate or yoga or language will lighten them.
Some days will close into darkness in which I will store up things to tell you and lose sleep, panicking that I might forget.
And there will be other days when it will only be a moment
When something opens up a you-shaped whole in my life.

Hold on.
I will miss you.
But you're going away.
I'm here.
If you don't want to be missed, stay.

I know the answer to that.
You're off.
You're a truck without brakes running down a hill road.
You're a comet being whipped around an orbit by some
dark sun.
You're what you want to be.
You're off.
I'm staying.
And you're asking, 'Will you miss me?'

You have some cheek.
I will miss that cheek.
I will miss you.
I don't have much choice.

THE SAYONARA ALPHABET

I would bid you farewell, friends
And would say:
You served me well.

Omega and alpha, sayonara
Aleph and bey, ciao.

But I know that a few furlong further
I will find inksmears on my soul
And you will feel
The four humours I left with you.

I would say adeus, word and vowel
Consonant and diphtong.
Farewell, plosive and labial
Adios.

We smeared each other you and I
through constant use.
Detachment will not be easy.

JOHN SIDDIQUE

JOHN SIDDIQUE (b. 1964) is the author of *Full Blood*, *Recital – An Almanac*, *Poems From A Northern Soul*, *The Prize* and the co-author of the story/memoir *Four Fathers*. His work has featured in many publications, including *Granta*, The *Guardian*, and *Poetry Review*. The Spectator refers to him as 'A stellar British poet'. The *Times of India* calls him 'Rebellious by nature, pure at heart'. He is the Honorary Creative Writing Fellow at Leicester University.

NAME

Put your hands on me to remind me who
I am, put your hands on my face and heart
and say my name to stop me still, make me
human, teach me to wait until I can open
with self blessing, as a rose buds to the sun,
as a seal on a rock sings the sea.

All it would take is a word, and day
and night would separate, the oceans would
move back to reveal the land, until one day
a figure would emerge from the tall grasses,
he would look out from his own two eyes
– the seed heads ripening, the wind causing
them to hush, the hills in the distance,
he would stand in the newly made
and know his own name again.

VIA NEGATIVA

I could have loved each of you so much better
than I did. You remained sitting at my table
and sharing my bed for so long.

For so long I heard my own voice instead
of each of yours. I had not learned
to make anything, to put a brick
on top of another brick, to plant seeds
in a field, to put one word up against another.
To know a day and to name it summer.

Each of us choosing and chasing
the reflections that suited the feeling.
We could not be other than we were.

Dark trees before bud.
Hands reaching for hands.
Blood seeking blood,
voice for voice, and bodies
looking to quench themselves
without learning seawater
from freshwater.

We could have loved so much better
than we did. For so long we sat at the table
waiting, while not one of us served the other.
For so long our voices were filled with only
the words we knew. Without knowing what lay
between those words. Brick by brick, seed by seed,
body next to body, summer day by day.
Without knowing who lies behind each feeling.

The bud before blossom.
An open hand.
Knowledge of the sanguine.
Waiting for the other to speak.
We could not be other than we were.

Four Wishes:
A leaf with knowledge of the root.
Hands working with love then taking your hand
at the end of day. A moment rather than
more words. A jug of clean water on the table.

WE WILL WAKE AT DAWN

Waiting beyond suffering,
our lives are entangled.

There are snakes.
There are hours filled
with dreams of march hares
with black tipped ears.

I wait for you to come,
heart-bruised and naked,
carrying a price that I will
take on my own head.

In dreams we are new.
The wild moon lighting
the blown-away sky
with a halo.

The wild moon lighting
dark high fields above the town.

Between your breasts – a kiss
to penetrate, to love, the torn places
you made in your leaving for home.

I give you water, eggs, oranges, toast.
I give you my arms and chest, my root.

You are dying to be born anew,
to become a bride with her dress
blowing around her, as we stand
together on the hilltops entangled
like tree branches grown close.
How wild the moon.

We will wake at dawn,
married, beside each other,
as if we have always been.

ADULTERY

Finally I reached across the table
to touch your face, the pads of my fingers
on your forehead first, drawing down near
the inner edge of your ear and under
to hold your chin, lifting your head slightly
as if I'm about to kiss you.

We are burning as if we are adulterers.
The table is between us to keep us apart.
I think if we are going to have to pay for this,
I want to have at least touched your skin.
We do not kiss, don't go home, or make love,
we drink tea – green for you, regular black tea
for me. I eat, you say you can't.

We are adulterers of talk and desire,
pretending that by not coming together
we are somehow still standing on the good side
of the line.

We sit amongst other lovers, no one knows
we are not supposed to be, *say my name,* you say,
and I say it. *I want to show you so many things,*
you say to me, it goes right into the place
I have covered up, armoured, and pretended
didn't exist any more.

AFGHANISTAN 1970, STOPPED

We're somewhere
in Afghanistan. The five-year-old in me
can't remember the town's name.
Our minibus up high
on a police transporter, for our own protection.

The hill bandits
are raiding, kidnapping at random.
We don't know the roads.
We're stopped for the night. Father climbs down
the lorry, finds seekh kebabs
from somewhere. They are hot and flecked
with green chilli.
An illicit midnight picnic in a country
that's closed for take-away.

The shutters are down.
There is no news on the news.
Night, dust and heat still in my mouth.

JUDITH LAL

JUDITH LAL (b. 1975) was born in the Cotswolds. She moved to Norwich to attend the Norwich School of Art and Design where she completed a BA in Cultural Studies before going on to do a MA in Creative Writing at the University of East Anglia. She received an Eric Gregory Award in 2001. Her poems have been published in various magazines including *Poetry London, The Rialto, Ambit, Magma, Mslexia, The North* and *Aesthetica*. Her collection *Flageolets at the Bazaar* was a winner in the Poetry Business Book and Pamphlet Competition 2007 published by Smith/Doorstop Books and was chosen as a Poetry Book Society recommendation.

TIGER HILL EXPECTORATE

A thousand men
bringing up the toddy mucus of night,

beating in dawn
on a tabla of aniseed gobbets,

the catarrh heavy
clearing of string dogs with a peg of breath.

The less and more of women
calling *cough cough coffeecigarettes*,

tea is for those below
the penlights of shock absorbed jeeps,

Tata groups
figuring their ascent,

who are not witnessed or witnessing
the earth's curve to Everest's acrimony,

a sunrise of compacts
competing for flash,

but know the dawn sob
in its gourds and clavicles.

AMARYLLIS

Gone is Diwali
when the lovers
find a way out of darkness,
a forest coming back on itself as an echo,

and not yet
the birthing of an end
to hold a candle to.

Days dark as
last honey
from the pollen of ivy.

The kitchen gifted with oranges
and in between
the green sword of memory
before the head rush of petals.
The bulb itself heavy as a head,

oesophagus coloured
through with
a song to winter,
ripples of noted oxygen.

Close bleeding,
short waves
arranged against
watermarked glazing.

Once I walked to a place
that such flowers made famous
under a sheeting of cloud
from the improbability of a bathroom door
left open in the valley

fluid with inkcake and inkstone,
the liquid jottings of trees.
Rain intoning on pavilions,

falling on timbers and voice,
a way cleared with blunderbusses.

Blouses equidistant
around the raw materials of a home,
on sun-made bricks
they ran around like a line

escaped from a nursery rhyme,
or bagged and broken out of a nursery
in their own daylight robbery.

Each celebrated a placement,
and to live there
was to feel the charm
of standing inside a circle.

LIBATION

Seven bowls of water,
each one a step that was taken
and where they fell lotuses grew.

No lotuses here,
air stretched tight
as the skin of women

mending a road
so a journey can be completed.

MONKEYS OF MAHAKAL

The old plays have monkeys in
and here are the monkeys seriously playing.
The prayer flags carry long murmured wishes

on the wind, they catch on the
wide comb of teeth, punctuated on
points of Frey, Simvo, Pandim.

The prayer flags carry monkeys
and the monkeys carry babies
with minute heads filled up to the brim with eyes,

until the string bridge shakes like a oud
plucked with long fingernails
reaching the footsteps of each quaver.

The dextrous monkeys sew themselves
through this world
then give it the slip up a lode gold stupa.

Food is offered to the Gods
and the monkeys eat it with
soft clicks believing themselves to be Gods.

Sunlight hits the entrance bell,
the Gods are pleased to recognize
themselves in monkeys

and you who leave to collect
your highly polished shoes with stepped-up shine
that have been kept safe from monkeys.

OOLONG

In a dance with two fingers
they pluck the first two tips of camellia
when the season is a sterling flush.

A sometime heat finds out green
humming a recipe to itself.

No time for the Krishna butterfly
to smoke into the concentration of perspiration.

With their crèche of babies
rocked high further on
they must fill the quota and over.

Delicate, where foothill rings
step close together
under layers of a wide skirt,

ghats where the sun is still young
before the pukka guesswork of rain,

where an umbrella is a basketed idea
in service to monsoonal silver.

A few rupees flow down. Needs must.
They laugh with us who drink dust.

CHIT

In Calcutta hospital there are forms
asking if you are single or married,
outside a black box you write *cohabiting*,

the girl with long fingers hands back A4,
asks you to leap to a v squared,
to plant a leaked tick in one of the two,

gives you a receipt for 600 rupees.
You think of a gaggle
answering *yes* on a winter sky.

The skin specialist is busy and out of range,
you watch a programme on tiger corridors
and get up to leave. Someone demands
you get that lolly Ghandiji cash back,
you say it's alright really.

Someone next to the girl explains
you are a registered patient now,
for the next twenty years you get treatment.
Someone next to you explains
that you are from England,

that you'll not be coming
back to Ruby General soon.
The girl takes out your file,
gives you a long fingered chit for a refund.

A rib waved man sweeps ankle puddles from the entrance.
Outside it is festive with children
deep in traffic, the taxi driver wakes
as if from a dream where he is still falling,
lights are strung with ending rains,
lights drive with you all the way past middens.

At the hotel reception there is a sign,
An apple a day keeps the doctor away.
They hand you one, cricket ball red,

a caught smooth drop from Kashmir
and ring for a practitioner
He looks at the hives mounted low on your stomach
and asks if you have been in a wooden house
in the north founded with bamboo.

He says *these houses scare the vowels out of me,*
they have insects in and under them,
moving atomic proof cases into our homes,
moving us to stillness in our homes,

all gold greeting and toxic resin,
covering their backs with black,
what surfaces on your skin is just superficial
it is what is happening here that it is my wish to know.
He takes his finger out, points to your throat.

I knew a man, he was just sitting down
to eat, inside he swelled up, no flying lying
he fell on the ground. Take these and
don't have shellfish tonight.

Ring me if
you cannot swallow or if it spreads
quick as this Oberoi's sister sheet.
You hand each other over to money.

At the airport they don't know
if you can board with an inhaler,
compressed gas is a danger.

Paper chains, paper planes
handing over your flight number
in carbon neutral refrain.

Close your eyes, breathe over Afghanistan,
concentrate on each exhale
dai raita cool over the ocean,
to the last flushed pan and touchdown,
think of the thanks you will
pack into a line from a London lounge.

KARTHIKA NAÏR

KARTHIKA NAÏR (b. 1972) is the author of a poetry collection, *Bearings* (HarperCollins India, 2009). She lives in Paris, and works as a producer in performing arts. This proximity to performing arts and to dance, in particular, is refracted in much of her poetry, which has been published in several anthologies and journals including *Indian Literature*, *Caravan India*, *The Asia Mag*, *Live Mint*, *Terre à Ciel*, Penguin's *60 Indian Poets* and *The Bloodaxe Book of Contemporary Indian Poets* (both edited by Jeet Thayil), *The Literary Review*, *The Poetry Review* and *Atlas* (all three edited by Sudeep Sen). Her poems have been translated into French and Italian. Naïr wrote the script of British-Bangladeshi choreographer Akram Khan's new full-length piece, *Desh* (which won the Laurence Olivier Award for Best New Dance Production of 2012), along with performance poet Polar Bear and Khan himself. Young Zubaan will soon be bringing out *The Boy, the Bees and Bonbibi*, one of the stories she wrote for *Desh*, as an illustrated children's book. Naïr is currently working on her next collection for HarperCollins.

SOLEÁ: FROM LYON TO ANGERS

ghazal

Phoenix in front, dragon on your back; both soared in that dance of solitude.
A wingtip shattered the moon that night: shards illumed your dance of solitude.

Onyx, obsidia'n glacier for muscle, bone and blood: in which chasm
was he forged? Whose the arms that raised him, this necromancer of solitude?

Delhi, Detroit, Forbach, Sydney? No, by a sleeted airstrip in Annecy,
on an aquamarine noon was first blood drawn by the lance of solitude.

Look carefully and you can spy them everywhere: in bedrooms, on beaches
and battlefields. The time has come to globalize the brands of solitude!

There were so many roads from Lyon to Angers – highways, bylanes, and some
seasonal tracks through dreams – but none detoured the greygreen strands of solitude.

Chiselled with the heartbeat of her dancers are Sevilla's streets, her heavens
arched by a spine; days spiralling back to flamenco's trance of solitude.

Another age, another sphere. In Gent, Tomorrow flared in high-octane
whirls: half-faun, half-unicorn, tethered by a ruthless glance of solitude.

Across latitudes and almanacs they have prospered – poets, peddlers, priests,
palmists, songsters, also publishers – on the high finance of solitude.

We might have met under Dhaka skies, beside a marché in Nantes, Marseille?
But the E.U. in Brussels had blueprinted our romance of solitude.

Shrek it was, at the Cigale, that spilt amber from laughing eyes on the path
of raven seekers: their alloyed gaze dashed the happenstance of solitude.

Once more morning, once more Montreal: the words were calligraphed, then branded
on memory's skin, "There will be no stemming the advance of solitude."

Daughter of the Pleiades, born nomad, whom fate leads far from hearth and kin:
stellar forces play sentinel as you embrace a France of solitude.

FAR FROM CHAGALL

four triolets

1. MONTREAL: FALL

Tell me it must be the weather
that dyes my mind white, congeals thought —
not meltdown of that myth: *Together*.
Tell me it must be the weather
not your ire, nor eyes that ether
memory, blaze the words we wrought —
tell me! It must be the weather
that dies: minds in flight can seel thought.

2. ROME: WINTER

We drove to Rome to unreel pride
and pain, staunch the blame, drain dissent,
graft content. The last galactic tide:
we drove to Rome to anneal pride
with 'art and rain. When the Tiber died —
riven blue-black by rage misspent —
we drove from Rome to unreel, ride
the pain, staunch the blame… feign consent.

3. NEW DELHI: SPRING

As you move into yesterday,
the sky runs copper; trees stain blue
on sleeping earth. But seasons stray
as you move. Into yesterday
spills blood from my breath: I must pay
for the ground sunshine, for these hues.
Then you'll move into yesterday.
The sky runs copper, stains trees blue.

4. ROME, THE RETURN: SUMMER

I'll come alone this time, serene
if songless. I'll have lambent night
to bathe the pines, restore life's sheen.
I come alone. This time — serene,
knowing you gone — breathes, slight, between
relief and grief. No wraiths alight.
This time, I come alone: serene,
for the songless have lambent night.

SONG SHAN IN 36 SHUFFLED SLIDES

haiku sequence

I.
Traversed two sunsets,
six time zones, tongues — to carve you
in blithe silhouette.

II.
Mount Song, the first sight:
his tonsured peaks crowned claret
by a dying light.

III.
They unlace the skies,
stride indigo earth by night —
deep freeze at sunrise.

IV.
Paris, Amsterdam
Beijing, Zhengzhou… we vetoed
the Three Gorges Dam.

V.
Dark and day arrive —
without pageants, or war cries —
fully clad, alive.

VI.
Shaolin's phalanx:
monk-mountains in mute vigil,
but uneven ranks.

VII.
English, Polish, French,
Belgian, one Indian: cloudburst
of brogues, a guide's drenched.

VIII.
Here, light the crescent,
seek the God of Verse — chthonic
spirit or volitant?

IX.
It isn't just hearsay:
we meet the Six Perfections
on temple pathways.

X.
Dusk, hour of still thought.
You become the Eightfold path:
transient, but unfraught.

XI.
Remember 'Lulu'?
Almond milk: chemical, canned.
Cravings caught from you.

XII.
Tongues tumble forth, vexed
(nine-selves-ten-square-feet-three-hours);
vote hot showers next.

XIII.
Forest of Steles sieves
from cedar trees the essence
of Light for cursives.

XIV.
More chapels, eastwards.
Steles in Pali beckon me —
my roots glint in words.

XV.
You will never know:
I owe you this day, belief
touched in granite flow.

XVI.
Dying feels easy
in Song Shan: the breath, like breeze,
chooses when to be.

xvii.
Back at the hotel,
Winter lingers; the State bid
him to melt pell-mell.

xviii.
That's you, Szy, Ali:
mindless as sunbeams hopscotch
over dreams in glee.

xix.
You walk scents of pine,
cypress, oak to Wuru Peak —
Boddhidharma's shrine.

xx.
"No fish in eggplant,
please, for vegans. No, meat's worse!"
Meals get a fresh slant.

xxi.
Yes, I doused this one.
Three years on, the day your words
scorched my world, homespun.

xxii.
Time takes off his shoes
outside the Hall of Abbots —
Sutra does mean ruse.

xxiii.
I smelt myths, moonbeams,
mist for ink; write on oak leaves.
Poems float upstream.

xxiv.
The stone lions of Qing,
warrior monks, your dancers:
March, with Spring's blessing.

XXV.
Invite from Zhengzhou
to judge Thai Kickboxing Crowns.
The Buddha laughs now.

XXVI.
His left arm Huike
slashed for Damo. Blood won't help —
here, drink my today.

XXVII.
Dragon and phoenix,
dancing beasts, boxing Buddha….
the Divine frolics.

XXVIII.
Midnight, scale model
of sets; three a.m., light design.
Prayers at dawn? *Swell.*

XXIX.
Devaraja Hall,
built, burnt, restored: Heavenly
Kings, Four, never fall.

XXX.
Generals Hum-Haw —
brick, blue — guard the Truth and you.
I detour to bow.

XXXI.
Pain pervades as mist,
evening dew I strive to hide:
you snag a choked fist.

XXXII.
Chicken claws, pigs' balls?
(packaged, coloured) preen on shelves.
By night, they may *crawl.*

xxxiii.
Noon at Pagoda
Forest hums — sleep-filled relics
greet the young stupa.

xxxiv.
Sixteen monks and you
scythe the air, stoke stars with spines;
Earth's heart beats anew.

xxxv.
Dark mares run riot
beneath eyes: will they unseat
this reign of Quiet?

xxxvi.
The end of *Sutra*,
"nothing's lost, things just change form,"
becomes my mantra.

KAVITA JINDAL

KAVITA JINDAL (b. 1964) was born in Delhi, and grew up in three cities by the sea. She now lives by the river in London, following a nomadic life lived between Hong Kong, England and India. Her work is inspired by her observations of different cultures, landscapes and people. Apart from performing regularly in London, she has been invited to read at universities and literary festivals in Asia and Europe. Her poetry collection, *Raincheck Renewed*, was published by Chameleon Press in 2004. Since then her poems, short stories, reviews and essays on the Arts have been published in literary journals, anthologies and newspapers including *The Independent, The South China Morning Post, The Mechanics' Institute Review, Cha, In Our Own Words, Asia Literary Review* and *Not A Muse*. [www.kavitajindal.com]

SUCH A THING AS A CLOUD WOULD SULLY YOUR TONGUE

Such a thing as a cloud would sully your tongue
the particles in it unpurified

Such a thing as a kiss would break no ice
the floes having melted fast

Such a thing as freshwater would cool your temper
that's if you can find it

Such a thing as life - if you come to it -
will expel you or exhaust you

Such a thing as our world will drown you
burn you, bury you

Such a thing as ingenuity may see you through
the gloom of predictions

But when you bow your head the earth
won't grant you forgiveness

All this has been before; and it is yet to come.
The nomads of the deserts remember

and they kiss the ground in homage
before stamping hard on it to dance.

IT WAS IN MAY. THE SKY POURED.

The day the gutters overflowed
I left Kotapuram Port.

Abandoned on the platform were black trunks and tan suitcases
forsaken to their drenching while the porters huddled
under the whipped red awning.
The long brown train awaited the flutter of the guard's green flag
as with slick-wet hair, from the window I stared
at a shadow I thought was there.

Friends wrote after long silences to say they'd told you
I'd shed tears on a platform awash with water
Scraped on to the train and cried again.
It was too good not to repeat.
You were puzzled when you heard this
or that's the version I received.

It wouldn't have changed anything, you said
if you'd been there, if you'd spoken
It wouldn't have erased the train timetable
or the date of leaving Kotapuram
If you'd said 'best of luck in life, my friend'
or another farewell equally inane
I'd have lived exactly the life I have
it would all have panned out the same.
I would've left on the day the sky poured
the day the gutters overflowed
Even if you'd stood there
to say 'Hello. Goodbye. I care.'

'Tears?' you'd asked, with perplexed brow when the story was repeated
of rampant lightning and umbrellas twisted by the storm.
Of the face squelched to the streaky window.
'Tears, for what purpose?'

There were pillars on the platform
Posters on the pillars, imploring us to
Stick No Bills
The yellow of the posters was shiny-succulent, water-lashed.
The pillars were white and round, the sodden green flag was down,

the train slipped out, pulled away my stare,
away from the shadow I thought was there.

It was in May. The sky poured. The gutters overflowed.
I left Kotapuram behind. The trains ran on time.

ALJEZ AT MIDNIGHT

I try to speak to her but she ducks backwards into the moon-drenched cave
Called under the duvet
It is where loops loop, corkscrews take the first turn, lyrics hunt for melody
Or become babies' rattles

I was thrown, she says, thrown into the arum lily marshes
Like a discarded baby's rattle
Complete with first bite marks, indentations on red plastic
Hidden jangly bells

Arum lilies absorbed me as I sank
Lifted their proud heads to the sky
Their fluted petals tight and mysterious gave nothing away
To light or dark
To silence or sound

I try to speak to her, crawling forwards into the moon-drenched cave
Called under the duvet
It is where loops loop, corkscrews take the first turn, babies' rattles are sown
In arum lily marshes.

KAZIM ALI

KAZIM ALI (b. 1971) has worked as a political organizer, lobbyist, and yoga instructor. His books include two volumes of poetry, *The Far Mosque* and *The Fortieth Day*; the novels *Quinn's Passage* and *The Disappearance of Seth;* and a book of lyric prose *Bright Felon: Autobiography and Cities*. He has taught writing and literature at various colleges including The Culinary Institute of America, Monroe Community College, Shippensburg University, and New York University; and currently teaches at Oberlin College and in the University of Southern Maine's Stonecoast MFA Program. His poetry and essays appear widely in such journals as *American Poetry Review, Boston Review, jubilat,* and in the *Best American Poetry 2007*. Anthology appearances (among others) include *The Literary Review Indian Poetry* (New Jersey: Fairleigh Dickinson University), and *World Literature Today Writing from Modern India* (Norman: University of Oklahoma), both edited by Sudeep Sen. Ali is the co-founder of the small press Nightboat Books.

MORNING NEWS

I left myself
dizzy in the sky

flint-thinking a foray
kith and kin

humans are silent now
rude and unshaped

do you really have to sin
to be saved

what I was sick for
a glass we are filling

tool that binds me
between zenith and obscene

another season cut to pieces
soiled and squandered

what everyone knows
no one will say

FREEZE TAG

Why agree to this awful treaty

To share the fate of fire and flesh

Released from stillness by a single touch

For barely one moment being able to think "I"

Through stone or muck running as if on fire

Fingers reaching to save all the others

No return home but an eternity of transformation

Everyone cries out *not-it*   *not-it*

THE PRICE OF FIRE

Daily I wish stitched here to live

Facing west watching the last light

Tattooed on my left wrist, "let-go"

Tattooed on my right wrist, "not-it"

Daily you make me dizzy with messages

Nightly torn open by brute sky and eagle claw

The strongest man in the world is on his way to release me

Although touched by fire I am fire

Upon release I may disappear

PRAYER REQUEST CARDS

I would like the church to pray for

a clear reckoning
the core unearthed
what's best born skyward
searched

who's most easily followed
seared

who's most faithful
beckoned to
queer

I would like the church to pray

my psalm to unsettle the case
my askance umbilical lust to review
and refute the evidence

to enter my gilt-edged tongue
as final proof
of innocence

I would like the church

on the inside of my sin
to spell out my breath
to draw a wing

SINKING

you became real to me father
when I saw you fly over me from beneath the waves

a bone-white door against the cloud-white ceiling
looking for me, flapping and furious

I watched you in the dark as you slept
knowing the edge of you only by the deeper darkness

below you now in the blue-black, a star
winking out, I am thinking I may wake up in the labyrinth

and not ever do this
not seek for the sun

oh father my storm-dark coast
nothing fills

LABYRINTH

Unmake yourself year by year
your urge

surges in your ear
no purpose at all but dispersal

lost in the labyrinth
desperate to wring yourself

dry of lust
wanting exhalation

to mean disappearance
in the space between lightning and

thunder
fling yourself skyward, son-storm

a hagiography of feathers
glued to your sin-singed skin

arrowing sunward
singing the whole way

I'm leaving you behind ghosts of a prayer
leaving you behind shining thread—

KYNPHAM SING NONGKYNRIH

KYNPHAM SING NONGKYNRIH (b. 1964) is a poet, short story writer and translator belonging to the Khasi tribe in Meghalaya. His poetry books include *Moments, The Sieve* and *The Yearning of Seeds* (HarperCollins). He has co-edited two poetry anthologies: *Anthology of Contemporary Poetry from the Northeast* (NEHU), and *Dancing Earth: An Anthology of Poetry from the Northeast* (Penguin). Anthology appearances (among others) include *The New Welsh Review*; *Planet: The Welsh Internationalist*; *PEN International*; *Poetry International Web;* and *The Literary Review Indian Poetry* (New Jersey: Fairleigh Dickinson University) edited by Sudeep Sen. He has also published books of translations and short stories. He received the first Veer Shankar Shah-Raghunath Shah National Award for literature from the Government of Madhya Pradesh; the first North-East Poetry Award; and a Fellowship for Outstanding Artists from the Government of India. He is an Associate Professor in the Department of English at the North-Eastern Hill University in Shillong.

WINTER WEEDS

He watches the weeds in his kitchen garden,
thinking of the girl down the road
with whom he has been having a fling
for some time.
He determines: today I must take them out.
And so he does, picking each weed by the root
until a thought strikes him: but when shall I root out
the weeds from my heart?

BELOVED IS THY NAME

Unexpectedly, today he remembers Akhmatova,
composing short poems and committing them
to memory and the memory of friends, till after
Stalin when they became the famous "Requiem."
He too has been receiving love messages
too dangerous for pen and paper.
Therefore, he devours them with relish,
consigns them to memory till they become
harmless as thoughts for his poetry,
which his wife neither reads nor understands.
He too plans a long poem
comprising a cycle of short poems.
He already has a title—
he may have to suffer and mourn because of it—
but come what may,
he will call it by the name of his Beloved.

THE COLOURS OF TRUTH

A siesta phone call
oozes friendly warnings.

Insurgents have grown
incredibly urbane, these days.
The question is, must we subterfuge
to shield a pedagogic stooge?

I close my eyes
turn towards the sun.
The colour I see is
disgorging blood.

I close my eyes
shade them with my palms.

the colour I see is
life-erasing black.

These are the colours of destiny
of immutable truth
and the colours also
with which warring pawns[1]
are daily decorating our towns.

[1] The north-eastern region of India, including the state of Meghalaya where the Khasis live, is a place troubled by insurgent groups whose agenda range from greater autonomy to outright independence.

HAIKU

1
autumn sky spreading
heaps of cotton wool — all set
to make winter rugs

2
first spring rain
the bus-shelter
only half-finished

3
trees planted —
a blue-winged butterfly
perches on my arm

4
rain for days —
only soldiers' clothes flapping
on a sagging line

5
last haiku of Bashõ
alone
facing blank page

6
city's cluttered drains
even unwanted infants
are thrown in

7
never knew bulbuls
feeding at dawn, noisy as
Khasi funerals

8
fiery pomegranate
bursting with ripe seeds — earth
bursting with humans

LEELA GANDHI

LEELA GANDHI (b. 1966) was born in Mumbai. She received her BA in English from Hindu College, University of Delhi. As an Inlaks Scholar, she went to do her postgraduate work at Oxford University. Her poems have appeared in *Creations, Indraprastha,* and other magazines. Anthology appearances (among others) include *Wasafiri India South Asia & the Diaspora* (London: QMW University) and *The Yellow Nib Modern English Poetry by Indians* (Belfast: Queens University), both edited by Sudeep Sen. Her debut collection of poems, *Measures from Home,* appeared in 2000. She is also the author of a book of literary criticism, *Postcolonial Theory,* and the joint editor of the journal *Postcolonial Studies.* Gandhi taught in the School of English at La Trobe University, Melbourne, Australia, before moving to Chicago where she now teaches.

SHEILA CHAWLA

Now you've gone too my little comma on the lean settee
unused TV-turned-table between you and him.
'Funky furniture', I'd say. You'd chortle to the brim,
taking all allegations of impropriety on the chin. Some habit of concluded time
made you release the present to others as their confine
too readily; the constant drama of our youth in your eyes, before they went
with all the rest: muscle, fibre, tissue, all spent.
In those last blind years, haunted by children,
you struck at them along the edges of your bed:
an unruly crowd, demanding, jealous, ill-bred.
Was it us, stripped of your courteous vision,
or shadows from some former brutal playground in Lyallpur,
the day you first stepped out of line?

SEASONAL | ANTI-PASTORAL

My keeper scatters even as she binds.
Every leaf knows this figment of design
as the grammar of seasonal iteration,
making light its tenuous habitation
in the abstract sequence of leaf-events.
Most generalities are given for the order of most things:
for each leaf, on every tree, in some continents,
there'll be green, copper, russet, sere, passing;
occurrence, transience, recurrence,
on, off, hot, cold, birth, death, the shifting tense
locutions of it all. Were this were all.
No errata in nature's covenant,
no random perpetuity in wet cement,
no broken bird's adamantine fall.

ON REPRODUCTION, AFTER DARWIN

In the theology of descent a catechism
of improvement consumes most little things.
The listless pigeon, distracted barnacle, poet-mammal,
each pausing in uncooperative contemplation
of inessentials, miss the amendment
of tooth and claw, beak and tail.
Neither rising, nor falling, they gather,
ephemerally, against other contingencies:
the storm in winter, the PhD colloquium,
the end of man.

SWAYAMVAR: SITA

The way you bent that bow
made me love the place
your spine begins its declensions
(base/apex, high/low),
yet dread the symmetry
of man and weapon;
the deadly circle
of your combined inversions:
you rigid
with complex curvature of bone,
the other turning all that is liquid
into stone.

NOCTURNAL (I)

This time the move is egregious,
the dreams juridical.
I must leave for a foreign place
before dawn intercepts my deportation
to a small, featureless town.
My preparations are immaculate,
even banal. All belonging has been shorn
of possession. Yet my effects refuse annulment
of their own compact with the world:
a fridge, chaotic with animal remains
and soy proteins will sustain guests
to come once I have gone away.
And so on, and on, perennially,
more ends for more beginnings.

NOCTURNAL (II)

1.
In a psychic turn toward the popular,
my most mundane anxieties
now feature assassins and a car chase,
or two, most nights.
Bad news if you can't drive
and are comatose in pajamas:
floral, frayed, beyond repute.

2.
Sleep, my father said, is the courage
of fidelity to a benign universe,
faith in the absence of *constitutively* hostile others;
so we subside in war zones, traffic, terminus, intersection,
punctuating the vigil of wakeful reason with bravado:
'I'm alright, you can go now'.

3.
Alone in this sensorium, who watches as we sleep
our nervous rest exact a toll for credulity?
We recompose matter, we become the hostile world.

MAHENDRA SOLANKI

MAHENDRA SOLANKI (b. 1956) was born in Nairobi of Indian parents. He has lived in England since 1965. After graduating in English and philosophy he has worked in publishing, bookselling, adult and community education and the theatre. He now teaches at Nottingham Trent University, having previously directed the MA in Writing. He has worked as a writer in schools, colleges, libraries, universities and has had a year-long residency at the East Midlands Forensic Mental Health Centre, a secure unit for prisoners with mental health issues as well as taking up residencies for the Arts Council, the Poetry Society, and the Arvon Foundation, amongst others. He has been a Visiting Writing Fellow at the University of Massachusetts. He co-edited *Other Poetry* (with Anne Stevenson et al) and has edited individual poetry collections for Blackwater Press. His collections include *Shadows of My Making, Exercises in Trust* (Aark Arts), and *What You Leave Behind.* Solanki's poetry has appeared in magazines and journals in Britain and abroad, including *The Observer* and *Poetry Review* and been broadcast on BBC Radio 3 & 4. Anthology appearances (among others) include *Twelve Modern Young Indian Poets* (Edinburgh: Lines Review), *Wasafiri India South Asia & the Diaspora* (London: QMW University), and *The Yellow Nib Modern English Poetry by Indians* (Belfast: Queens University), all edited by Sudeep Sen. He has also undertaken public commissions, collaborating with artists such as Kay van Bellen (for the Riverside Commission) and film-maker Jaharlal Sen (for the Royal Festival Hall).

SLAUGHTER

We offer as sacrifice, a goat
Stunned into two by a sword.

A ritual made real by blood;
An act to make us whole.

DAYS

Your days are laid out
in a row for me
a pull of dates
torn from a calendar:
an abacus of hope

EGGS

I make it the way you did:
cracked eggs spiced with
nuggets of red chilli,
catching my breath.

Each plate, stained
like my fingers with
turmeric, forever marked.

THIRST

And what good will come
to tell now, of how for years
your mother took you to see
the priest, who once alone
with you, talked you out of
your shorts, and with you emptied,
would plead for you to piss into
his mouth; his thirst not quenched?

WISHES

What do you think about
When you think about me?

I think about your wishes

About my tongue inside you
About the wind outside
About your scent around me

About the give of figs just opened
About the feel of warm asparagus
About your mouth as my container

About how wishes come in threes

from THE RIVERSIDE COMMISSION

I

the A frame stretched tight
against a familiar sky

take a step, a start

II

a canal, a river
through a lost green corridor
a well-kept secret

III

a man runs on this path
between grass and water
like a feverish race horse
blinkered against distractions

IV

a to and fro

a giant see-saw rocking

a give and take:
the hiss and spill of the past

V

we who left behind our lands
we who crossed the black ocean
we who miss open fields and running water

we seek comfort in this pull of green
we seek rest in this flowing bed

MAKARAND PARANJAPE

MAKARAND PARANJAPE (b. 1960) has published five volumes of poems: *The Serene Flame, Playing the Dark God, Used Book, Partial Disclosure,* and *Confluence*; a collection of short stories, *This Time I Promise It'll Be Different*; one novel, *The Narrator*; and more than thirty academic books. He has also translated *Boats* from the Marathi original *Hodya* by Hemant Govind Joglekar. His own poems have been translated into Hindi, Marathi, Bengali, Greek, Spanish, Portuguese, Korean, and Chinese. Anthology appearances (among others) include *Midnight's Grandchildren: Post Independence Poetry from India* (Macedonia: Struga Poetry Evenings), and *The Literary Review Indian Poetry* (New Jersey: Fairleigh Dickinson University), both edited by Sudeep Sen. Some books edited by him include *Indian Poetry in English* (Macmillan); *An Anthology of New Indian English Poetry* (Rupa); *Sarojini Naidu: Selected Poetry and Prose* (HarperCollins India); *The Penguin Sri Aurobindo Reader*, and *The Penguin Swami Vivekananda Reader*. His latest monographs include *Another Canon: Indian Texts and Traditions in English, Altered Destinations: Self, Society and Nation in India,* and *Making India: Colonialism, National Culture, and the Afterlife of Indian English Authority* (forthcoming). He is professor of English at the Jawaharlal Nehru University in New Delhi.

Day
ST. ANTHONY'S ART

1

At the heart of every looking glass
is an image. A solitary mirror also
dwells inside each heart, hiding in it
the likeness of an unnamed beloved.

2

The kiss she blew from the half-open
window of the taxicab, entered his
thoughts, became this poem, which
even as she departs, wafts back to her.

3

It is the ring on his finger that deceives
onlookers: a married couple, they wonder,
smile at his speaking a foreign tongue—
how will this *translated* husband work?

4

Someone has stolen the baby from the arms
of the patron saint of impossible causes; our
guide married for seventeen years is childless:
will his wife's prayer ever be answered?

5

After lunch, he buys chewing instead of
bubble gum; mouth full, asks, do you like
to blow? Giggling, she says she loves bubbles
bursting with a pop, face sticky afterwards.

6

They're in a church gilded with half a ton
of gold, every nave and cornice sports
an ornate angel or god, and beneath the
wooden floor boards, bodies of the pious--

7

but walking over sacred bones, all he can
think of is sex; to touch, hold, caress, kiss,
stroke, penetrate—the madness of skin,
saliva, semen, smell of concupiscence.

8

The necklace around her bust, rosary
going all the way down below to the
very gash, to stroke it, bead by bead,
to ecstasy would also be a prayer.

9

Underneath, dead saints or sinners,
decaying flesh or mere skeletons, but
the brush of her hair or accidental touch
of skin on skin—ah! such oblivion!

10

Remember that you have forgotten,
she says; no, remember to remember
and once remembering, forget forgetful-
ness—that is the way of the non-dual.

11

I want it now; no postponement; no
promises of future fullness or past
perfected; to see in the midst of all
this pain, the same, serene continuous

12

always complete, never mitigated;
that's relating to reality. What we
call flux is itself firmness, to see no
difference in them is to transcend.

Night
REALMS OF (IM)POSSIBILITY

1

Tonight, I feel shaky on my feet.
If I falter, hold me lest I fall. You who
drank all evening are steady; I who
only looked into your eyes, totter.

2

Like Ulysses, tie me up, but let me
hear the sirens' song; you laughed:
am I a siren then? Quite; that's why
we must sleep separately tonight.

3

You thought I was adventurous
but actually I am risk-averse; I can't
do until I must; it's the opposite of
doing until I know I mustn't.

4

I had so many things I wanted
to try with you, but how could I
put my mouth where my mind was
or give tongue to my thoughts?

5

The truth, I told you, was simple:
men were romantic, women practical;
but I was not anxious because the
realm of possibilities is unlimited

6

while actuality is more restricted:
to have a hot shower together after
a tiring day and discover the mis-
demeanour of incarnation—or

7

just lie in bed, wake up scared
to flee from oneself and everything

else, the anguish of heartache,
the agony of incompleteness?

8

How could I tell you that I
had only one day to offer you,
not even twenty-four hours,
but only sunrise to sunset.

9

In the empty playhouse it became
clear. What else was it, but an opera
fit for king or commoner, this wretched
thing called romance, nothing but
a flight from reality, an obsession?

10

How dualistic! Virtuality vs reality?
They are no different. Myths are
also real as reality is mythical. How
to be free, to love without fear?

11

In the end, we see hearts everywhere,
balloon shaped hearts, lollipop hearts,
hearts on shop signs, in flowerbeds,
even a trash can shaped like a heart.

12

So this madrigal to you in the morning
dew; a raga of mist & snow, sun & soil,
the music of spirit mingled with soul,
And the gasping joy of convergence….

EPILOGUE

Breasts, buttocks, and lips,
Fruit of the body,
Make a nice offering.
But they don't have to be eaten entirely,
Just touched or tasted
To be sanctified like *prasadam*,
And returned to the votary.

MANI RAO

MANI RAO (b. 1965) is author of eight books of poetry and a translation of the Bhagavad Gita. She published essays and poems in journals including *Atlas, Indian Literature, Kavya Bharati, Chandrabhaga, Wasafiri, Meanjin, Washington Square,* and *West Coast Line.* Anthology appearances (among others) include *The Literary Review Indian Poetry* (New Jersey: Fairleigh Dickinson University), and *The Yellow Nib Modern English Poetry by Indians* (Belfast: Queens University), both edited by Sudeep Sen; and others published by Zoland Poetry and W.W. Norton. She has performed at literary festivals in Las Vegas, Melbourne, Vancouver, Hong Kong, Singapore, Chicago and New York PEN World Voices. Translations of her poems have been published in Latin, Italian, Korean, Chinese, Arabic, French and German. She was Visiting Fellow at the 2005 Iowa International Writing Program, and won the 2006 University of Iowa International Program's writer-in-residence fellowship. [www.manirao.com]

BRAHMA'S MOMENT

Brahma unfolded
Four petals on a shoulder

TimeSpace emanated
Twinned at the hip

Quarreling who's older

FOR POOTANA'S SAKE

The beast
now in the guise
of a babe

Exuding
Sweetness

Draining the
Poisonous wetnurses

SHIVA'S DIGS

Fragrant floured
Nude blue bloat
Last seen by the boy who
Wanted to be a ghost

The scavenger hooks
Fingers in the rim
Bone pots conk
Dangling swing

Finger a ring ran away with
Knobs and bits
Found in ash spills

It's his job but gravely notes
Soil bored with air
Fluids laying cesspits

PANCHALI

Five limp fingers
A useless hand

Who draped Draupadi

Yudhistira sorry
For himself

So sure he was
The eldest son

LOOKING FOR LETHE

Lingering waters Mnemosyne

Slave to recognition the sommelier sips
History's arias – mountain under ocean – crystal chambers – singing salt
Sudden body – undercurrent – slow release – cleansing nourishing bitter
Sharp – teeth – opening – vanishing citrus
Something buried – buried hint

Along her shores infinite coves
Amuse the helpless odysseys

At the end of each day
Livedness by people

REJECT

The gods took one look and tossed him

Dented
De-fizzed
Rocket to space junk
Fell

Wayward washing
Ragged upon the crags

Penalty: not liver but a part more tender:
A frequent-flowering incorrigible phoenix heart

Now flooded by the moon the startled thief
From the day he is engorged and cannot hide
To the day he is mute and will not show
In the shadow of the eagle he sees keeping watch
A luscious rested tongue
And thirsts for it

MARILYN NORONHA

MARILYN BAYROS NORONHA (b. 1952), studied in Mumbai at the Convent of Jesus and Mary, and read English Literature at St. Xavier's College. She went on to teach, after obtaining a B.Ed. degree, and later worked in a nationalized bank for twenty-three years. A long-standing member of the 'Poetry Circle' of Mumbai, Marilyn has read her poetry and spoken at several forums including British Council, Kala Ghoda Festival, and Prithvi Theatre. Apart from poetry and short stories, she also writes plays and musicals for children. These have been performed by various schools on stage, as well as on radio and television. Her short stories have been published in magazines and one story, 'Jyoti Means Light', was read on the BBC World Short Story Programme. Her first collection of poems, *Different Faces*, was published by Allied Publishers in Mumbai (2003). She has a master's degree in education and teaches music and creative writing in Mumbai.

ANOTHER STACK OF HUTS

We are nameless, faceless,
concealed in cartons.
Cradled in rags,
our children
dread bulldozers.

Tsunamis come,
the earth erupts,
fine causes
rise and roar,
rip continents apart.

We cower
in the rubble,
still scavenging
our dignity.
Neglect…disgust…
these maim and blind us.
Eyesore!
Embarrassment!
Attempts are made
to obliterate us!

But we are adroit
too adept at existing
on nothing,
to oblige and let go
of life so easily!

Rummaging in the debris
crouching in the refuse,
clutching our children,
we piece together
another stack of huts…

IT'S TIME

When your mouth is pursed up
and narrowed like a beak;
you must carefully pick
every word you speak.
No sincere opinion
has the slightest chance.
You skirt round issues
like a minuet dance.

It's time, it's time, it's time to go,
to make your curtsey and get off the floor,
to make your curtsey and head for the door.

You must jump up and run
at their slightest cry.
When your world falls apart
they're sure you'll get by.
But they're loaded with burdens,
you must understand
when your hi-five
turns into a flailing hand.

It's time, it's time, it's time to quit,
when you have to ask what you're getting out of it.
when you have to ask why you're taking so much ****.

They seize your exuberance
and wring it out,
ensure that your confidence
is punctured with doubt.
But take it from me,
it's time you went,
when they start to mess
with your inner content.

It's time, it's time, it's time to say "so long!"
Before you yell, over an' out, I'm gone.
You can go to ****, now I'll sing my own song.

URBAN EQUITY

It is wise, the seed,
it has no need to know –
"What colour is the skin
of the hands that sow?"

A beggar, who's starving
for more than a week
won't ask hands that feed him
what language they speak.

When you're catching a train
and you're falling out,
hands grab you and hold tight,
as you start to shout,
do you then claim the right,
as the train gathers speed,
to ask those hands questions,
"What caste?' "What creed?"

MAYA RANI KHOSLA

MAYA RANI KHOSLA (b. 1963) was nominated for a Pushcart Prize in 2011 by World Literature Today. She is the author of *Keel Bone* (Dorothy Brunsman Poetry Prize from Bear Star Press), *Heart of the Tearing* (poetry from Red Dust Press) and a book of non-fiction, *Web of Water* (Golden Gate National Parks Conservancy). Her poems have been featured in *Fog* and *Wood Smoke* (Lost Hills Press), *Water: Culture, Politics, Management* (Pearson Press) and in journals including *The Literary Review*, *Wisconsin Review*, *Seneca Review*, and *New Orleans Review*. She is currently co-directing the Turtle Diaries Project (http://saveourseas.com/projects/turtle_diaries), which is supported by two awards from the Save Our Seas Foundation.

AMLA IS READY

When its flowers shrivel to rust
and time has no color
at the sky's edge, when rivulets
of a richer season have dried
to barely a memory,
like two straight lines of chalk,
converging in the red distance,

when fog's scarf is torn up
by cold branches, many of them
shorn of leaves, then it is a time
of falling fruit. And what falls
falls fully equipped, ready
to begin life, stiff-skinned,
perfect, pungent with proteins.

Each is radially symmetrical,
with seeds at its heart like unlit bulbs
coded to carry the full strength,
the full brilliance,
of an upcoming season. To tap
the wild crimsons of solar fires
and turn them into fruit.

SYNCHRONICITY

for A. Sze

In Bhutan my camera's *click* jerks a yak
from her suckling young. Miles up-mountain

a goatherd struggling to lift her dead goat's feet, stuck
in blue junipers, finds a snow leopard jawing the head.

As I reach for water in darkness, a half-human
half-animal call creates a gold bowl of sound.

Dawn's butterflies alight on pines miles
from their home while the yak herders say *not yeti,*

maybe bagh, leopard. As potential prey, we taste
each word for balance between fear and surrender.

Deep in a village a child is torn off its mother's back
like a postage stamp. Coffee steam from a cup I grip

on a rooftop joins smoke from the sunlit bazaar.
Thunder rolls on the ground. Mountains don't answer

the goatherd shrilling for the rest of her flock.
The guard dogs' hoarse barks at the leopard's howl

are swelling its silence.

REMEMBERING THE POTTER

for Gouri Khosla

I open the envelope and rain begins
to pull free from purple summers
that hung above your tomato vines
over a decade ago. What pours down
washes each soil-grain of memory carefully,
as if for the last time. And so the thin
and minimal salts are carried deeper
where they feed a tangled underworld
linked to the stems and sweet-sour globes

of red. I let the note slip out. Each word
can be tasted without salt or seasoning.
There may be regrets, seeds stuck
between teeth. But nothing can alter
the texture of leaves that brushed your face,
the focus as you plucked tomatoes.
Nothing can erase the sky full of hawks,
whose circling you continued in spun clay

that was glazed, then bathed in flames.
We take nothing with us. I will
burn the note, be true to the journey
that cleansed your body and freed
its nutrients. I will allow the wind
its curtain of ashes. And be nourished
by soup from the cup with your initials
neatly scratched underneath.

A POET'S KEYSTONE

Is easy to lose, yet achingly familiar in most ambits.
Sphere-shaped, it remains elusive as sound-bubbles
surfacing from a winter wren's depth among dogwoods.
The search can continue among the sand-guarded eggs
of a western pond turtle, under the threatening gestures

of fish-hook cacti guarding their hidden globes of water,
in the still-untorn ball and socket joints of an ibex carcass,
descended on by lammergeier vultures. The search
can continue inside the rattling cup of a beggar child.
Don't quit. Persist, even if the skin of wild cucumber
forbids with thorns, even if the night-dark gnarl of tree rot

is visited only once a year by slant of sun. When it's time
to rest, settle into a shelter that once housed ancestors.
The dance of their hands, thrown against walls in candlelight,
will renew a belief in the mud-dark path of mid-river boulders
rolling in flood. The silence of that space, emptied of all but cups
and silvers, that silence will be round as a stone in your palm.

PANTOUM ON A HALF-SENTENCE

for T Basu

You left mid-sentence. I tried everything to stop
rain's echo, a second shower, willow leaves.
Before the pyre I took coma earrings from your cold ears.
O moon's chuckle, you scattered the clouds.

Rain's echo, a second shower, willow leaves:
shimmering like silver saris, like a departing sky.
O moon's chuckle, you scattered the clouds
a dance that continues, after the drumming has ceased,

to shimmer like silver saris, like a departing sky.
Still, you live in bird glitter, in willow's spring brio
a dance that continues, after the drumming has ceased,
in green silk fin of morning, gold silk fin of day.

Stay close to water. Come near, dove-foot girl—
You left mid-sentence.. I tried everything to stop
Bud jasmine, jamun flowers from being placed in your hair
before the pyre I took coma earrings from your cold ears.

MEENA ALEXANDER

MEENA ALEXANDER (b. 1951) was born in Allahabad, India, and raised in India and Sudan. Her work includes six books of poetry *Illiterate Heart* (The PEN Open Book Award winner), *Raw Silk,* and *Quickly Changing River;* the memoir, *Fault Lines*; the book of essays and poems, *Shock of Arrival: Reflections on Postcolonial Experience;* two novels and two academic studies one of which is *Women in Romanticism: Mary Wollstonecraft, Dorothy Wordsworth and Mary Shelley.* Anthology appearances (among others) include *Wasafiri India South Asia & the Diaspora* (London: QMW University), *Midnight's Grandchildren: Post Independence Poetry from India* (Macedonia: Struga Poetry Evenings), *The Literary Review Indian Poetry* (New Jersey: Fairleigh Dickinson University), *The Yellow Nib Contemporary English Poetry by Indians* (Belfast: Queens University), *World Literature Today Writing from Modern India* (Norman: University of Oklahoma), all edited by Sudeep Sen. She is editor of *Indian Love Poems* (Everyman's Library). *Poetics of Dislocation* recently appeared from the Poets on Poetry Series, University of Michigan Press. She has received awards from the John Simon Guggenheim Foundation, Fulbright Foundation, Rockefeller Foundation, and the Arts Council of England. She is Distinguished Professor of English at the Graduate Center and Hunter College at the City University of New York; and currently serves as an Elector, American Poets Corner, Cathedral of St. John the Divine.

BIRTHPLACE (WITH BURIED STONES)

I.

In the absence of reliable ghosts I made aria,
Coughing into emptiness, and it came

A west wind from the plains with its arbitrary arsenal:
Torn sails from the Ganga river,

Bits of spurned silk,
Strips of jute to be fashioned into lines,

What words stake – sentence and make believe,
A lyric summoning.

II.

I came into this world in an Allahabad hospital
Close to a smelly cow pasture.

I was brought to a barracks with white walls
And corrugated tin roof

Beside a Civil Aviation Training Centre
— In World War II officers were docketed there —

I heard the twang of propellers,
Jets pumping hot whorls of air,

Heaven bent,
Blessing my first home.

III.

In an open doorway, in half darkness
I see a young woman standing.

Her breasts are swollen with milk.
She is transfixed, staring at a man,

His hair gleaming with sweat,
Trousers rolled up,

Stepping off his bicycle,
Mustard bloom catches in his shirt.

I do not know what she says to him,
Or he to her, all that is utterly beyond me.

Their infant once a clot of blood
Is spectral still.

Behind this family are vessels of brass
Dotted with saffron,

The trunk of a mango tree chopped into bits,
Ready to be burnt at the household fire.

IV.

Through the portals of that larger chaos,
What we can scarcely conceive of in our minds —

We'd rather think of starry nights with biting flames
Trapped inside tree trunks, a wellspring of desire

Igniting men and gods,
A lava storm where butterflies dance —

Comes bloodletting at the borders,
Severed tongues, riots in the capital,

The unspeakable hurt of history:
So the river Ganga pours into the sea.

V.

In aftermath — the elements of vocal awakening:
Crud, spittle, snot, menstrual blistering,

Also infant steps, a child's hunger, a woman's rage
At the entrance to a kitchen,

Her hands picking up vegetable shavings, chicken bones,
Gold tossed from an ancestral keep.

All this flows into me as mottled memory,
Mixed with syllables of sweat, gashed syntax,

Strands of burst bone in river sand,
Beside the buried stones of Sarasvati Koop,

Well of mystic sky-water where swans
Dip their throats and come out dreaming.

AFTERWARDS, YOUR LONELINESS

in memory of Mirza Ghalib 1796– 1869

1. INDIGO INTERIOR (DELHI 1857)

You were holed up in the cold
No oil to light the lamps, even mice started shivering.
You had to sell your clothes, the camel hair robe,

Woolen kurta knit with finest lambswool,
Turkish cap, all of it,
Down to the cotton coverings she stitched

For your bed, all this to get a few morsels of food,
For yourself and that mad brother
Who tore cotton, silk, off his own flesh

And started scratching —
Unbearable itch, he had,
Poor Yusuf.

At night you waited for a lightning flash
So you could put out your hands,
Touch paper, ink.

The lane where you lived
Was shut with stones,
Huge stones to keep out the Brits, shoved

Against the mouth of the gully.
Roses shriveled,
All their color sucked

Into crevices of rock.
Keekar trees high on the Ridge
Held out crowns of thorn,

They were calling, calling out to you —
Half dressed, you tried to set out, stick in hand,
All the way from Kashmiri Gate.

2. SCARLET EXTERIOR (BOMBAY, 2008)

In Bombay where you've never been
People clamor by India Gate.
So many in starlight and smoke

In the blood spotted alley way,
On the causeway
At dawn, clouds cling to a spittoon of fire

Dragon flies shimmer on burnt metal.
Raving threads of light
Pierce us into other selves we long to be

Ruinous shimmering metamorphosis.
Who are we? Where are we?
Stuck in the mess of Delhi, what can you tell me?

3. SCRATCHED SILVER

You pretend to be hard of hearing.
You say – Why is no one coming to see me?
My mirror flickers.

Can no one come?
The postal system is in utter chaos.
The letter I wrote to the British Queen

Victoria — Diamond of the Sky , Maker of Kings —
Concerning my pension,
Who knows if it was even delivered to her?

4. GASHED GOLD

Be near me, you cry, as dung spills
Down your lane and you try to stumble out.
Were you speaking to the ghosts who live in your head?

'There is one world of mud' you wrote 'another of spirit'.
What did you mean?
Mirza Ghalib show us where the horizon goes,

Where sight must cease.
Your loneliness makes fiery footprints in the sand.
At night, stars throw down their spears.

They beckon,
Making spirit signs
Coming closer and closer.

JUNE AIR

All summer I wanted to hold tight
To what I felt was the truth --

A penurious thing.
All I had our breath, an unsteady pulsing

With holes enough
For a swallow to fly through.

I remember one in our room
Hovering by the portrait of someone else's ancestors

A girl skirts askew, eyes half shut
Seated on a tricycle.

Behind her, hands cradling her shoulders
A boy bruised by paint.

The bird swam by the gilt ceiling
Then startled, dashed itself against the window frame.

After the beating wings were done
Hills clarified in darkness,

Bits of light fell from the sky.
We watched not knowing what it all was,

The air hurting us into happiness
We never really thought was possible.

GRANDMOTHER'S GARDEN

I.

A space without history —
At the rim of the pond

Grandmother loosens her sari
Steps into water

Her skin glistens, utterly naked.
No one remembers this.

Lotus petals flicker
Float to the axle-tree

Tree of Heaven
They call it in the family.

By its roots
Grandfather made a fire

Tossed in her poems
Poor things, penned in black ink

She had folded them
Into finicky squares

Buried them
In her jewel case

With molten rubies
Slow sift of sapphire

Poems of no climate
Words halting, quick with longing

For a man whose name no one knew.
She dreamt him up?

Who can tell?
Two whole months she took to her bed

Her hands bent under her
Broken winged

Refusing what food she could.
One night

Half mad, she stumbled out
Ran her fingers

Over scorched bark
— *Alstonia Scholaris* — what was left of his body

Imagined reliquary
Blushing like koi fed from her own hand.

II.

Syntax surrenders
To an axe biting into wood

And hearing small shocks from my past
I know it's all over — the years of childhood

The Innocence of Before and After
Seasons of rain, fragrance of burnt blossoms

And under the axle tree
Stars musk scented, acutely unreal.

In the shadow of that tree
Mirza Ghalib comes to me

Lambs wool cap askew,
Flecked with blood —

I tried to wash it
In your grandmother's pond.

He took off his cap
I saw it was crowned

With pale freckled eggs
He knelt beside a hole

Where the tree once stood.
I can see through this pit

To the island city
Where you've gone to live, he said.

In the glory of the Beloved
All borders vanish.

I saw her then in moonlight,
A girl, my close familiar

Her wrists were stumps
Her black hair

Blew into resurrection waves,
She could not comb it back

She was grandmother
And she was me.

She strode up the invisible
Stairs into the sky.

III.

In glowing heat
In blessed synchrony

I saw what Ghalib saw —
Houses with their eyes torn out

Books knifed, goblets shattered
Townspeople, some in soiled dhotis

Twirling from the lampposts.
O lilies he wrote on his sleeve

Your mouths
Are filled with syllables —

Love draws us down into history.
Men on horseback bearing myrrh and fine paper

All the way from Mecca to Manhattan
Dream of a garden where

A poet sips wine
From the crook of your elbow —

O girl with moonlit hair
Whose wrists are stumps!

Then whispering
So I had to stoop to hear:

Beloved my body is scarred with age
Fit for burial

While yours gleams,
Rainbow colored.

In the rain washed trees
There is nothing to see but nakedness.

IN THE GARDEN OF FREEMASONS

Gnats flee into thickets
Swans too, in search of periodic water.

I brood on Jibanananda Das, poems tucked
Into a notebook, returning from the Book Fair

Struck dead by a tramcar, aged fifty-four.
On tendrils of dirt, in the spot where he fell

Spirits cluster. Children sing to each other
Tossing balls as children do

A mechanical bird tethered with wire
Circles a stall of neon colored bras, panties too.

Needing a place to wait for you
(Chowringhee undid me)

I sit on a flat stone in the garden of Freemasons.
What did the poet say about swans, nine of them, mystical?

He did not know why there were nine
Vanishing into trees, but that there were nine

He was sure.
It's dark in your city, clouds cover the moon

The House of Freemasons tilts
With the weight of gnats wings.

Under a crystal chandelier,
When he's sure no one is looking

A man with red hair polishes his own shoes.
Don't go away, think of the poem

I hear you say –
It's all you need to do now, or ever really.

MENKA SHIVDASANI

MENKA SHIVDASANI (b. 1961) is a founder member of Poetry Circle, which began in Mumbai in 1986. Her first book of poems, *Nirvana at Ten Rupees* (XAL-Praxis), was published in 1990. Her second poetry collection, *Stet*, first appeared in 2001. She is co-translator of *Freedom and Fissures*, an anthology of Sindhi Partition poetry (Sahitya Akademi), which has been subsequently translated into Marathi and Gujarati. Her poems have been published in numerous journals and anthologies, both in India and elsewhere. Shivdasani is director of The Source, an editorial services company based in Mumbai. She is also Mumbai coordinator for the global movement 100 Thousand Poets for Change.

FOR WOLE SOYINKA

My solitary confinement does not run
deep as yours; my pen is plastic,
not of chicken bone,
and no coffee wakes me up
like your makeshift ink,
with which the poems brewed.

You speak of freedoms I cannot
begin to need; mine
are like cockroaches in the dark.
This cell is noisy;
their scurrying is too loud.

Yet we belong to confined worlds
in different ways,
even if my gun is just the kind that melts
into vivid, useless bits of molten sound.

My plastic world lies
liquid at my feet,
and no battles are being won.

DEPARTURES

The clothes are perfect,
neatly folded,
taking as little space
as they possibly can,
flattened by the heat
of the iron hand.

It's the books that get unwieldy,
falling out of the suitcase,
their edges sharp enough
to rip the bag. They
flap their leaves
and just will not fit in.

Take a deep breath,
sit, press hard.

Now zip it up.

BIRD WOMAN

On one of those days
when the key refused
to fit the padlock,
I turned myself to air
and squeezed through
the keyhole.
It was bright outside,
and I was tired
of all the jostling
women inside the house —
Nomad, with her fraying
suitcase, Devil Woman
with her lacerated
tail, and that sad little lady
with her stained apron,
who seemed so familiar,
disintegrating
in a thousand homes.

All these women,
and a few more,
were crowding in,
and the keyhole
that sat on my shoulder
was at cracking point.

I knew I had somehow
lost my way
in the brightness outside,
after all those years
in a dank and dingy room.
Stretching my legs
was a strain and breathing
was a whole new experience,
but folded up
behind my back
I found some wings —
who knew where they
had been all those years?
They were slightly dirty,

but once I got used
to their rusty screech,
I found,
they worked.

I am making friends
with the birds now,
and discovered
I have talons too
which sink perfectly
into the eagle
with his beady eyes.

Breathing is still
a problem sometimes,
but the blue air
is warm and best of all,
I have left those
jostling women behind.

I couldn't help it.
I know I let them down
and they are wondering
where their hostess
disappeared.
But what could I do?
They simply took up
too much space
in my head.

HOME-MAKER

It's time to break the kitchen,
take your fires elsewhere,
watch time and space curl up,
waft out through windows.
Just one last time,
hear the clanging
of the steel, recognize
the drawers no longer fit;
they scrape and drag
along channels tucked inside.

The workmen said these granite slabs
would never splinter; they did not speak
of tilted angles, wooden cracks
that would widen, swell, stay
stubborn on their hinges,
refusing access to the sharp-edged tools inside.
They did not speak of choked-up pipes,
and roach-infested drains.
You wipe the spills off shining stone,
but what's the use?

Stay quiet now,
and watch the hammers fall.

MINDSPACE

Begin with the familiar. There is
a reason for the warmth of flesh,
the slow parting of lips
and ways, and the gyrating
thighs that slice the moving air.
There is a reason for the thrust
of bone on skin; the nervous
shiver of the veins, the reddening scar,
the slit across the face
where the smile should be.

Start with the familiar;
the rapacious grin you try to beat
out of your mind;
the silence beneath your skin.
It will begin
to feel like an old friend,
leaping out
of hidden corners in the dark.

Then, let go.
Let go of the cracking twig,
get a grip on solid ground,
step away
from that chasm at your feet.
Stay focused on the thought;
it may be heavy on your back,
but in its warm, deep pockets,
there is sustenance, jagged
though its can-opener edge might seem.
Hear the whisper in the bloodstream;
slake your thirst.

The unfamiliar
is on the other side,
and there is time.

MICHELLE CAHILL

MICHELLE CAHILL (b. 1969) is Goan-Anglo-Indian. She wrote *The Accidental Cage*, short-listed in the 2007 Judith Wright Poetry Prize. She was highly commended in the Blake Poetry Prize, the Alec Bolton Prize, and received the Val Vallis Award and the Inverawe Poetry Prize (minor). *Vishvarūpa*, her second poetry collection was highly commended in the Wesley Michel Wright Prize. Her chapbooks are *Night Birds* (Vagabond) and *Ophelia in Harlem* (Kilmog Press). Anthology appearances include *The Yellow Nib Modern English Poetry by Indians* (Belfast: Queens University), *World Literature Today Writing from Modern India* (Norman: University of Oklahoma), both edited by Sudeep Sen, *The Best Australian Poems 2009*, edited by Robert Adamson (Black Inc.), *The Best Australian Poems 2011*, edited by John Tranter (Black Inc.), *30 Australian Poets*, edited by Felicity Plunkett (UQP, 2011), *Not A Muse* edited by Kate Rogers and Viki Holmes (Haven, Hong Kong, 2009) and *Collective Brightness*, edited by Kevin Simmonds (Sibling Rivalry, 2011). Michelle writes fiction and essays. She has been awarded grants from the Australia Council, the Copyright Agency Limited, the Australian Society of Authors, a Fellowship at Hawthornden Castle and a residency at Sanskriti Kendra. She is founding editor of the online magazine, *Mascara Literary Review*.

PARVATI IN DARLINGHURST

So I lay on the body of a pale Shiva. He spoke
not a word, bothered perhaps by my nut-brown
skin; my slow dance calmed his electro shuffle.
A slap of limbs pinned him down to my earth.
I hadn't bathed in sandalwood, flouting legend
with a preference for Estée Lauder. The moon's
crescent tangled my hair, my breasts were bare,
our timing synchronised. Night fizzed, vanishing
into day, the club's hypnotic rhythms subdued.
We scorned the Puranas, our tryst no Himalayan
cave, but a hotel bed I had draped with stockings,
lingerie, and the crystal ice of a Third Eye. I admit
that's why I spoke with the speed of an antelope.
It seems the acharyas were mistaken: I hadn't
dated for marriage or adultery; nor with a wish
to deck his house with flowers or sweep his floors.
I am too busy, I declared, for dalliance or abstract
gossip. I have no interest in honeybees and birds.
All I wanted was a good time. I swear as the river
is my sister, that this guy was not my sun or my sky.
No way did it even enter my mind to have his kids.
His first wife's ashes are scattered all over the city.
Goddamn it, Shiva is a walking disaster; whatever
he touches burns. Restraining him with handcuffs
I said, forget it babe, your lingam and my yoni are
made for one thing only, improper and unchaste.
It's little more than conjecture to think our sweaty
helix could ever be whole. Then I offered to grind
and gyrate him silly, suspend our want indefinitely,
and he fell utterly silent with this new meaning.

THE PIANO LESSON

My hands are stricken. Do they not brush your sleeve?
Are they not stripped by this embrace? Such brevity:
light aslant on the maple, flooding us with its promise,
as if there were things outside our selves, or our words.

There are cities whose landscapes we chart. How dry
the river seems as dusk blanches. I twist in your arms,
where my aches and stings are electric.Your hammers
strike my strings, then rest, until the sound uncouples.

You have spent epistolary days rehearsing a solitary
composition; variations on the same étude, to balance
what you have abandoned for loveliness. No exception
to this, I fasten my bra, as you lie, perfectly naked.

There's no indignity. I think we're saved by the purple
darkness. I return to the street, unable to disguise a flush
in my cheeks. Absorbed by stilettos, subways, the slow
traffic, for a few hours, I feel immortal as any fugitive.

What bitter chords should I wait for? I forget to ask.
You have tried to get behind all the music this world
makes. My hands are stricken by the lustre of ebony
at my keyboard. Now I work. Play the silent harmonics.

KALI FROM ABROAD

Kali, you are the poster-goddess, sticking out your black
tongue, like Gene Simmons from Kiss, a kick in the teeth,
with your punk-blue leggings, your skull and scissor charms.

You swing a trident, a demon's head and dance on the bones
of a pale Shiva. I recall the convincing eyes of a girl cripple
carrying your bottled effigy, as our bus careened to a dusty halt.

Some say you morphed from Parvati, drunk on blood,
others cite your superhero leap from Durga's brow to slay
the self-cloning serpent before a Haka dance on mythic soil.

By a hundred Sanskrit names, India claims you in a single text,
while in *Zen and the Art of Motorcycle Maintenance*, you are
'the grass and the dew', on screen, our contemporary Judge Judy

having a bad hair day. I'd argue for your cosmopolitanism,
a global denizen, you're adroit in drugs and aphrodisiacs, a nude
Dominatrix, a feminist export with a sadomasochistic bent.

A figure of partition you were cover girl for *Time* magazine.
A Neo-pagan diva, your wholeness is darkness fashioned
from light, moon-breasted, with eyes of fire, with Brahma's feet,

Varuna's watery thighs. You rise from the grave, step over
carnage, feeding the world and your severed self with blood.
Stripped bare as Duchamp's Bride, you set Bachelors in motion.

CHILDHOOD

The afternoon cruises,
after badminton, lemonade,
and chutney sandwiches.
Voices are like ribbon made
for unwrapping the past.
Syllables of imaginary laughter
blend with the real, as I recall
the warmth of uncles, aunts, cousins
left behind in foreign cities,
Mumbai, London, Goa.
I think of the bright day when dad
flew our kite on Primrose Hill.
It's hard to say what matters.
Everything fragments,
defers to time's calibrations,
the long shadows are deceptive.

I piggy-back my daughter
in summer's leaf-light.
We swim laps in tandem
riding a pink foam noodle, sinking fast,
her tiny arms a choker for my neck.
I'm weak to her commands, her tears.
In any competition, I must lose.
The dragonfly's flight is a tease
never kissing its reflection,
a cross stitch lacing the pool.
The distant hum of the freeway
sounds like a hole in the heart,
the softest turbulence.
The garden is a green humidicrib.

DYING TO MEET YOU

for Aravind Adiga

Maybe it wasn't deferred by the hardness of rain,
my lack of sincerity, your lover, an unfinished book,
a hangover; the cigarettes I didn't smoke to save
my lungs. I wasn't breathless last night. I dreamt
an email I opened from a publisher wishing me well
was an awful sign. You didn't even enter my dream,
though it would make poetic sense to mention loss
in imagined fragments: how I left my bangles by your
bedside table; how you asked me to slide them off
so they wouldn't chafe or ring the way memory does;
how you covered my pillowed face under a cold sheet.
I woke with a slight headache to morning's amnesia
— some days I know not who I am, or how to begin.
Yet, you're right. No one *is* dying to meet someone
like you. The poor are buried alive in seismic rubble,
their children swallowed by tsunamis are casualties
of global warming, over-population, urban planning.
How then to measure a grief which I sometimes desire
to share? How not to read your remarks as if you came
like an electronic prayer into my head? Is it worth you
knowing I trembled this morning at the very thought
of our real bodies meeting? Would I be grave? I am
so brittle lately, imperfectly divided. I am untouched.
In my yoga, you're not the Brahman from whom I draw
breath. Perhaps, by now, I might know the epic nature
of suffering; the way we can be prisoners and still free,
not by purchase or design. By readiness for what this
day brings do we exist, in the spaces between words.

MICHELLE YASMINE VALLADARES

MICHELLE YASMINE VALLADARES (b. 1963) is a poet and filmmaker. She is the author of *Nortada, The North Wind* (Global City Press). Her second book of poems, *The First Map of the New World*, is forthcoming. Her poems and essays have been published in *The Women's Review of Books*, www.poetsagainstthewar.org, *The North American Review*, and included in the anthologies *Language for a New Century: Contemporary Poetry from the Middle East, Asia & Beyond* (Norton) edited by Chang, Handal & Shankar; and *The Literary Review Indian Poetry* (New Jersey: Fairleigh Dickinson University) edited by Sudeep Sen. She has produced several award-winning films including *Landscapes of Memory/ O Sertao das Memorias*, a Brazilian feature which won Best Latin American Film at Sundance and the Wolfgang Staudte Prize at the Berlin Film Festival in 1998. She was born in Mumbai, grew up in Kuwait and the US and currently lives in New York City. She is a Lecturer in English at the City College of New York, and the poetry editor of *Global City Review*.

ARJUNA'S PENANCE AT MAMALLAPURAM TEMPLE

The archer stands on one leg,
looks through a prism of his own hands,
meditates on Shiva.
Arjuna in a stance of penance
leaves the forest for the Ganges.
He is hoping that Shiva will
part with his favorite weapon,
the *pashupatashastra*,
his magic arrow.
Shiva keeps Arjuna praying
while the *nagas* swim in the river,
and the elephants and mice line the banks.

My mother and I join Arjuna,
praying for good fortune,
my father's health, shade
on a hot south Indian afternoon.
Our minds dance like the goats bleating
between stone cliffs and young boys
trying to sell soapstone elephants.

We pray for an end to the suffering in Gaza,
that change will follow a new American president.
We suffer our penance, each in our own way,
while Shiva dances and the Shore Temple
sinks into the Bay of Bengal.
We'd aim the Golden Arrow
at the melting of glaciers,
choking of rivers, overdependence
on fossil fuels, and wars.

The fading light shines with prospects,
each branch of the trees glow with the favor
of goddesses and gods who are with us
by the ocean, in the rivers, and rice paddies,
and the offerings arranged by street vendors,
flowers, saffron, and malas of *rudraksha* beads
You can hear the arrow's hum
beneath our busy lives.

THE CONSORTS

They are curved to the bodies of the gods,
their heads bent, looking upwards,
milk, honey, flowers, a perfect union
offered in harmony
        Draupadi, Parvati, Saraswati
  even their names are offerings

Thousands of years past, at Mammalapuram,
the carvers knew, as they took chisel to stone
cliff, each breast and nipple, flower
garland, jeweled headdress, hand
in a perfect mudra of compassion, love,
union, they were carving
the Goddess, herself,
not a stone replica.
Those nights with their wives,
the goddess satisfied
their deep hunger.

I'm afraid the priests have gotten it wrong.
We, the men, must serve the goddess,
cook for our wives, daughters,
sisters and nieces, bow
when they enter the room,
touch the edge of their saris,
and feet,
circumambulate
to their beauty and intelligence.
We are alive because of our mothers,
Goddesses of childhood. In our old age,
women surround us.
Our crops flourish with their blessings. Fish dive
into the nets and boats.
The sun rises.

Heresy or truth. Walk among the ancient statues,
listen to the waves
crash at the Shore Temple.
Rewrite history at home. Awaken your consort,
She is singing as veena, flute and drums,

the mantra *Om*.
She is the reflection of moon, the force of the sun
guiding you to the clear light
of your own mind.

INCHMAHOME PRIORY

Those giant boughs that wave around
My aged hoary head,
Were then the tenants of the ground,
— W M STIRLING, 1815

In our ancestral selves, floating above and blue
we ferry over the Loch of Menteith with your father,
where once we fled from the English
to hear the Augustinian canons sing the hours
at Inchmahome Priory. The boatman asks
where we have traveled from?
New York in this life, but in others
I returned from a month's
journey through the Highlands from the Isle of Skye,
where we lived a stone's throw from the sea.
Scotch pines and a large beech circle
the ruins of nave, choir and cloister.
Under the voices of the Glasgow school children
I hear the monk's tenors soar.

TRANSFORMATION

This bit of betel nut
turning over and over on his tongue
is a mantra.
— ARUN KOLATKAR, from *Jejuri*

The goddess arrives in Brooklyn
this morning, as two cardinals
red and vibrant orange sit still on the wire
fence separating us from the duck pond.

The labrador I step over is resting on the path.

I stop walking
hold my breath.
The first cardinal cocks
its head to the left
then right.

The second cardinal
flies above the Russian woman
singing between the magnolia and cherry tree to her grandson.
lands on a bush beside the old arch stone tunnel.

Should I continue working, living, eating in the same way?

This morning, spring, earth and I have changed.

I call my husband and divorce him.

We begin to live as two lovers,
cardinals in the park,
happily ever after in Brooklyn.

JANUARY 1, 2010

*Havering**, Malcolm says,
is Scottish for talking nonsense.

I rescue two owls, plastic
and plaster, from the garbage.

Athena's representatives appear,
as guardians against duty,

antithesis of wisdom.
This year's resolution is

an ode to curiosity.
My brother laughs in a photograph at 20.

The Ajanta and Ellora Caves,
will shut to tourists and a replica

will be built in the parking lot.
The Goddess Tara appears as the woman

with wrinkles giving directions.
and the young girl with a pink backpack

skipping through the first
poem of the new year.

** haver from the German word for oats*

MONICA FERRELL

MONICA FERRELL (b. 1975) is the author of a collection of poems, *Beasts for the Chase* (Sarabande Books), and a novel, *The Answer Is Always Yes* (The Dial Press/Random House). Her work is included in many anthologies, including *Language for a New Century* (Norton), *Legitimate Dangers* (Sarabande Books), and *Asian American Poetry: The Next Generation* (University of Illinois). Her novel was named one of the 'Top Ten Debut Novels of 2008' by *Booklist* and received warm notices in *The New Yorker* and elsewhere. Her poems have appeared in *The New York Review of Books*, *Paris Review*, *Tin House*, *The Nation*, and *Fence*. Anthology appearances (among others) include *The Literary Review Indian Poetry* (New Jersey: Fairleigh Dickinson University) edited by Sudeep Sen and *The Bloodaxe Book of Contemporary Indian Poets* edited by Jeet Thayil. A former 'Discovery'/*The Nation* prizewinner and Wallace Stegner Fellow at Stanford University, she is an assistant professor in the creative writing program at Purchase College, and lives in Brooklyn, New York City. [www.monicaferrell.com]

THE THRALL QUEEN

You've said you were done with love.
You threw it off from you, a poisoned apple.
You poured graffiti over its temple,
Smashed the windows, ran away

And feasted with vandals, with cannibals;
Eyes bright with drink, you glittered in mirrors
When midnight showed you clearly your future
Dissolve into a graveyard settled by weeds

Whose waving's long since washed those stones
Clean of names — ah even the dead, your memories
Taken from you into the ward of insignificance too.
You've said you were done with love,

You stupid bitch, still you wake me now at midnight
Shot through with a dream's light, the sight of his eyes:
Malevolent blue, blue of lasers, of the gas-ring
On a stove that will burn without feeling.

What is he thinking now? Don't bore me.
And perhaps…perhaps we could… I ought to leave you
In a corner alone with such trife like an old woman
Rocking through the hours with her knitting.

You used to be a lot more fun, you know. Remember?
We dreamed up Molotov cocktails, Roman candles.
We made up brilliant speeches holding a dagger.
Next thing I know, you'll say you want a baby,

Wedding cake, the red sari, a summer invitation.
Malevolent blue, blue cornflower glowing through dark,
A stove that hurts you and it isn't even personal,
Blue kiss on the matchstick that burns our house down.

CONSOLATIONS OF SOLITUDE

Imagine your craft has crashed on a foreign planet.
You're alive. You stumble from the hull
Testing your radio, which gives a promising fuzz:
But the mother-ship does not return your call.

So you are forced to find food and water,
But the food is green, and the water purple.
Furtively you try them, one night, cursing,
Ravenous, in the open, under pale, circling moons —
Sweetness of daffodils, water clear as dimes.

Still you're searching some key thing, you suppose.
Parts? Gasoline? At the time you like to call midnight,
Long spokes of smoke rise from mountain pools
And when the violet sun gashes you awake
You see how everyone on Earth is retreating from you
Starfish beneath soft, repeated waves.

The way starfish slide off beneath soft, repeated waves.

Scrambling over the crags of this new planet,
Strange but not unpleasant, with angular black rocks,
Periodically you may gasp, checking over a shoulder
But then you'll recall *there is no one else here*,

RIME ROYALE

You need me like ice needs the mountain
On which it breeds. Like print needs the page.
You move in me like the tongue in a mouth,
Like wind in the leaves of summer trees,
Gust-fists, hollow except of movement and desire
Which is movement. You taste me like the claws
Of a pigeon taste that window-ledge on which it sits,
Like water tastes rust in the pipes it shuttles through
Beneath a city, unfolding and luminous with industry.
Before you were born, the table of elements
Was lacking, and I as a noble gas floated
Free of attachment. Before you were born,
The sun and the moon were paper-thin plates
Some machinist at his desk merely clicked into place.

VETIVER

All right, put your hands on my breasts one more time.

For a last time, take down the evening's hair
and introduce me to the dark.

It's true what the others say: your place
does smell of old man,

so much fear of everything
that you can't destroy.

When I close my eyes, I am thinking of what is inexhaustible.

Outside this window
you have trapped in heavy velvet,

fields of vetiver and clover
where love is.

SNOWFALL

Bridges that cross in space but go nowhere,
Transistors that fall from here to there:
For a long time the soldiers waited, guns in their hands,
But that white did not relinquish the sky

I welcomed you into my house
Your hands were two coals
Laid on my back

Snowflakes are inhuman as balloons.
They are finned with complicated shapes like the legs of insects
Falling through a black that is atmosphere

This snowflake music is of a xylophone:
Pastel, the high soft tones

I welcomed you into my house
Piece by piece you cut me open
Like a drowned girl dragged in from the ocean
Just to see if her heart still beats

Perpetual is the spheres' music,
It is eternal as Genghiz Khan's caravan across Asia
Or Napoleon forever gathering his troops in a hollow of bone

Snowflakes are perfect, sublime as anatomy
Your body begins with the mouthwell
I shall never complain of the richness of your skin
Where my fingers sank searching buckets

We begin again with *A.*
We begin with the grooves of letters.
Like a motel sign, twittering neon,
The semaphore mind, barbarous, flashes *Yes All right*
No Stay home

We begin again with narrative.
I loved you once. Could that have been so long ago?

Snowflakes falling on the beaten copper of nightwater,
Filling up the mouths of drowned soldiers,
Snowflakes filling the sidewalk cracks,
Edging the trees with a blue light

O silver flashes of mercury, of manna,
Falling on the house of the girl who waits by the window,
Falling on the branches that will snap,
Dazzling hypnotism — o seraglio of deficient stars!

MONICA MODY

MONICA MODY (b. 1981) is the author of two chapbooks and her first book, *Kala Pani*, is forthcoming from 1913 Press in the fall of 2012. Her work can also be found in journals such as *The Boston Review*, *Wasafiri*, *Upstairs at Duroc*, *Apocryphaltext*, *Horse Less Review*, *Nether*, and *Pyrta*, among others. She received her MFA in poetry from the University of Notre Dame.

NOT IN MY NAME

PREFATORY ADVICE:
The Delhi Government plans to make the city beggar-free by the 2010 Commonwealth Games

vaulting over
civilized noise

view from fenestella
others scurrying

city has
abyssal pockets

spotless mirrors
grafted in irises

project chimeras
conditioned aloft

breathing habits
exclusively clean

colonies of
disinfected franchise

sell the view
sustainable fable

printed on blue
beauty crease

schedule
cosmetic procedures

plant landscape
worldclass green

garden of
curtailed subscription

dispel defects
centrifugal

RESCUE

PREFATORY ADVICE:
The Delhi Government is developing a state-of-the-art sports village on the Yamuna riverbed, a high-risk seismic zone

hundreds of warriors
jumped in cracks
opened
by the quake

landed on their
fluffy bottoms

dumpty dumpty
woke up on the wrong
side of dawn

I sniffed remainders –
nothing much

this handsome city

people patiently
queued up for their turn
noiselessly plopped

sky
opened
into suppurating wounds

trickled into cracks

trail of time led me
back today

dumpty dumpty
blenched at the
lack of self control

I pitied workhorses
but was busy watering
polythene

I ran my tongue
along fissures

love my shining eyes

in 2033, I am a dog

SHADE A RIVER BLUE

PREFATORY ADVICE:
Garbage, untreated sewage, and industrial runoff continue to flow into the Yamuna even though the Delhi Government has spent millions on its clean-up

shake it out
that magic hat

    worn
    shopped

nothing wasted
nothing gained

    get momentum
    matted locks

sprinkle with dust
fine gold

    talking doll's head
    swollen

girth
strange offshore

    tie in rope
    unregulated smoke

taupe that
self replenishes

    grit
    timeless

running out
rising

I, OR
I

i
Still a great city
I shame private
parts into steel

run
counter to
national crisis

How much does the crisis weigh?
How does it spell?

There is nothing more to be said

ii
Monkeys shake fist
give rides

to stuck people
with stick stories

How many times can you circle the earth?
Any other time, what would be

possible

?

Whoever left the door open forgot about the draft

iii
My veins spill
warnings
down roads

lights on full display
beaming
underground moles

Who knew this story being told?

It is not about me
I have not understood the charges

iv
Not small
but flat aground
ready to take on the world

I stuff
the feeling into my mouth
become a crow

device to scratch throats
trash bins

Do you wish I hadn't?

Everything I do for you, for me

v
I power my way
to the center of the world

slam my throat with foggy
cloth and yelp

joker

beware, we are letting
loose crazed bipeds among you

How can I write myself off?

It needed to be said

vi
I leap
land amidst landfills

swarm dead cows and cabbages
rummaging for a good story

a trickster bulb
bulging

into the swill I add
more tears, stir

Nothing smells here, see?

NEELANJANA BANERJEE

NEELANJANA BANERJEE (b. 1978) is a writer and editor whose poetry and fiction have appeared in the *Asian Pacific American Journal, Nimrod, A Room of One's Own,* and *Desilit.* Anthology appearances (among others) include *Desilicious, The Literary Review Indian Poetry* (New Jersey: Fairleigh Dickinson University) and *World Literature Today Writing from Modern India* (Norman: University of Oklahoma), the last two edited by Sudeep Sen. She received an MFA in Creative Writing from San Francisco State University in 2007, and was a Hedgebrook Fellow in 2008. She has worked in mainstream, ethnic and independent media for the past ten years. Since 2003, she has helped young people tell their own stories at *YO! Youth Outlook Multimedia* and the *San Francisco Writerscorps.* She is also an editor and blogger with the Asian American magazine *Hyphen.* She is a co-editor of *Indivisible* (University of Arkansas Press, 2010), the first anthology of South Asian American poetry. She currently lives in Kolkata.

TELEGRAM FROM MOUNTAIN VIEW

for RN

natives are friendly stop am learning the names
of trees stop there are caverns of soapstone stop
I detect a glow stop

underneath he is rainbow trout stop

I have seen a pink tadpole stop the discovery
of my jellyfish stop

my wrists regenerate stop ears have
dissolved stop learning to tune
with tendon stop

in retrospect stop I stop have stop
surrendered stop
there is no such skin stop

have cut out my eyes stop will send
back melanin

THE LEGEND OF JAREK

you ride horses across the Gobi

a nomad wrapped tightly
by distance   only your scarred
knuckles chapped red

at night just a shifting of sand
a growing of mountain

you think: this is the civilization
that I will build, this transience

mirages outnumber the red trees

there are ancient bear tracks
at the spring, turquoise
blooms in the sky

black-haired girls appear
leaping like gazelles

through your broken heart

PROGENY

we envision the color
posterity will assume.
you are sad
because blue is de-
feated, darkened by the weight
of my subaltern

eyes. understand this:
our child will shimmer, the sun
drowning among gold

petals, hyacinths
in a village pond. her cheeks glowing,
the orchard blossoms

of your grandfather's
unmapped land. wrists, veins frail as
these loose visions but

knobs of spine sturdy,
rugged as the snarl of my
mouth against your lips.

GOURI

Between us: a wide, scarred
ocean, the swollen-tongued
struggle of language, the shelter
of my undarkened skin.

Still, you lead
me through wheel-
rutted lanes, catching
my foreign stumbles with
a quiet word
shabdan. Careful
I repeat, watching the dust
layer our feet gray.

Later, we listen
to village dusk in the
tone of cow-bells
and frantic mosquitoes.
You stop to light
a lantern, turning the flame high
and then low.

FIRST MELT

How sweet the past is, no matter how wrong, or how sad.
— CHARLES WRIGHT

I watch the icicles
                    unravel from the rooftops of this winter town,
everything   everyone   turned lazy toward the sun's
yellow-gold tease.

Clutch of mud at my feet and I'm reduced.

Once on that field near the flat blue horizon, we sat
on raincoats, poured gin into cans of orange juice –
our mouths metallic, surrendered.

I remember the wide canopy of sky,
that incessant suck of mud, the tender shoot
of my heart.

On days like this, everyone fades transparent.

Even that boy
sitting on the steps, flesh and stone and cloth,
just a smear of mud against the collar bone.

I walk past green courtyards of trespass,
filled with the smell of musk and breath,
the planetary motion
                                        of rolling under and under.
                                                            The bodies left
buried in the soft earth, imprint of elbows and shins.

It's the words that have dissolved, a slow-molasses disappearance
of everything I thought was finite.
          At dusk, a red wash against the buildings, nothing but
the shape of a bone in my mind.

PRAGEETA SHARMA

PRAGEETA SHARMA (b. 1972) is the author of three books of poetry: *Bliss to Fill* (Subpress Collective), *The Opening Question* (Fence Books & winner of the '2004 Fence Modern Poets Prize'), and *Infamous Landscapes* (Fence Books). Sharma's poems and writing have appeared in *Art Asia Pacific, Bomb, Boston Review, Fence, Indiana Review, Vanitas, Women's Review of Books* and other journals. Anthology appearances (among others) include *The Literary Review Indian Poetry* (New Jersey: Fairleigh Dickinson University) edited by Sudeep Sen. She received an MFA in Poetry from Brown University, and an MA in Media Studies from the New School in New York (2002). She is an Associate Professor of English and the Director of Creative Writing at the University of Montana in Missoula.

WILL YOU LET GO FOR RANSOM?

NO.

And so deep was the fall, what a drop; I had nicks on my knuckles.

There is a passage of time, for all of it to hold you,
then you hold it,
you wring it by its neck,
it's murderous and invisible—a darkling spot that grips.

And on some days, we would head to the bar—in the middle of the river,
the wail or the cries there found us.

Some colleagues had tears down each eye.
Some other colleagues made them cry.

We tried handing them words, but it all became inaccurate fast.
I held my purse in my fist.

Not sure if this was a place I could get mugged,
I was reminded that it wasn't. I was still unsure.

I told you—
we are all like fish, happenstance, troubled, out to the river and to the undergloom.

And glad I am, I took you in, and pushed all of the urchins out and off the deck.

I didn't have to tie you—
you tied me with several words, several serious words.

It's been something I've been wanting to suggest for a long time:
this intentional community can withstand the social pressures of the corporation.

It won't matter that its patent will expire; we can and will reissue it.

Though it may take a kind of erudite plea—
to push the corporation
into that certain sphere of word-fuss
that they continually resist or make do without.

The willful dropping of real time for imaginary foes;
foes that rattle the head and heat the heart.

But patents aside, it's the way the poem always usurps instrumentality,
rhetoric or pleasure: a thief too benevolent, a wish to entertain.

So give the poet a martini glass, an abstract painting,
a patent to keep existing, to be an exuberant foe

since the corporation with its misgivings
may want to preserve all of the things that merely *make* the table decorated,
not what invites *spilling*.

The overused idea of "voices" provides me no useful markers,

no atmospheric noun or adjective for how to describe

the moment of powerlessness that dug deep into me.

Of how the mind speaks in cries.

I am a sentence but not much more.

I am full of cunning and able functions, but not much more.

I am quantifying this smallness
that I admonish; but, somehow,

I then embrace
it in the abstract,
as the theory of humility,

and hope it's concrete
enough to be much more,

and not the tyranny
of arrogance nor the trouble of tiny.

DEAR POET

Are you the dark
orange tree of night?
A persimmon ebullient
                    in a cave of little thoughts?
                    I'm following your thoughts
and not another trend in poetry.

But I can't be like you,
because you are wrapped up in you,
and your purity is the color of orange.
          Believe me, I grew up with that color.
It's everywhere. It debuts as saffron.
          I know what it might mean when
sifted through a sieve, or a thread.
Perhaps all colors find us neutral--
          the scent of *mock orange*.
We can be stuck in poetry, in the things

needing attributes when
we can't color them away.

A riotous mob blanched heedful poets with fever.
Accordingly, the poets found a clone heart forming someone's human shape;
but it deceived, sucking souls out to Rome, Harvard, and Hell: cleave in cleaver,
montane in Montana, and yet finally an obdurate effect occurred: fate

had all the poets for dinner, no feelings were left. It was then that something sunk,
a pediatric antic. And sojourning students played Orpheus
with the underworld; henceforth, no established rescue to the dunk
of morale, no point of refute, and no megaton in the nefarious

phylum. It was a physic of how the pincers prick with pinch;
how poetry, too, can be pistol-whipped by the haters
who had originally enunciated each syllable of the chant, inch
by inch, pressing noses down to the large lacuna: healers

looking for headfuls, in order to find the right verbal phrase to heed.
Why were they all feasting on the heavy head of one stinking weed?

PRISCILA UPPAL

PRISCILA UPPAL (b. 1974) is a Toronto poet, fiction and non-fiction writer, and academic born in Ottawa. Among her publications are eight collections of poetry: *How to Draw Blood From a Stone* (1998), *Confessions of a Fertility Expert* (1999), *Pretending to Die* (2001), *Live Coverage* (2003), *Ontological Necessities* (2006), *Traumatology* (2010), *Successful Tragedies: Selected Poems 1998–2010* (Bloodaxe Books, U.K.) and *Winter Sport: Poems* (poems written in her capacity as Canadian Athletes Now poet-in-residence at the 2010 Vancouver Olympic and Paralympic Games); the critically-acclaimed novels *The Divine Economy of Salvation* (2002) and *To Whom It May Concern* (2009); both with Doubleday Canada; and the academic study, *We Are What We Mourn: The Contemporary English-Canadian Elegy* (2009) with McGill-Queen's University Press. Her work has been published internationally and has been translated into Croatian, Dutch, Greek, Korean, Latvian, and Italian. *Ontological Necessities* was short-listed for the prestigious Griffin Prize for Excellence in Poetry. Anthology appearances (among others) include *The Yellow Nib Modern English Poetry by Indians* (Belfast: Queens University) edited by Sudeep Sen. She is a professor of English at York University in Toronto. As editor, she has also published several books, most recently *The Exile Book of Poetry in Translation: Twenty Canadian Poets Take On the World*, and *The Exile Book of Sports Stories.* She is an active participant in several arts committees and organizations, and is on the Board of Directors at the Toronto Arts Council. [www.priscilauppal.ca]

BOOKS DO HOLD ME AT NIGHT

As I open my eyes in the morning, so do books.
Eat breakfast, lunch, dinner and dessert at my side.
Amuse on subways, trains, and planes.
Hold my tongue in meetings and during the news.
Take my temperature when I'm feverish.
Mourn when I'm sad.

I've had orgasms with books, alone and in unison.
Travelled to the ends of the earth.
Teetered on the edge of pools and baths.
Waited patiently in cafés for my safe return.
Stayed tight to the chest in the dark.

Books dressed me during puberty.
Held their own at university.
Knew before I did that *he* and *he* and *she* were not the one.
Stood quietly aside while my babies were born.
Sometimes beat me senseless.

Books sweat with me on the elliptical.
Idle on summer porches.
Recognize my neighbours, and crawl
into my children's hands.
Sing on birthdays, and treasure old memories more
fondly than I do.

Change hats: father to uncle, daughter to professor.
Books are survivors.
Harness the crowd. Rewire the individual.
Know when to hit the brakes, when to risk it off the cliff.
I even believe, though you insist otherwise, that you know
how to die.

And now that we're on the subject.
My most loyal companions, I leave you
all my worldly and unworldly possessions.
Don't let me down. Beware of fire.
Please, do something grand.

A DIORAMA OF YOUR ANGER DRIFTS DOWNSTREAM

It's not in a rush; heavy, plump,
enjoys the splash of water on skin, mud
on frame; speed builds
in time.

Your anger has built a raft, a life jacket,
even scuba diving equipment. This anger
goes deep & turns exotic colours. Parts
of its species are yet to be
named.

To onlookers: the ordinary calculated
occurrence of aberration, deviation
from an outside temperature gauge. A coke
can or an olive branch, a tear off a teenager's
sweater, a plastic lunch bag.

Sometimes fishermen bait you,
then throw you back.

Not famous enough. Can't compete
with no feet for the mob to kiss,
then trample.

Patience. Rumours study
maps of the falls.

Ancient men sing songs of grief.
You drag their notes along.

THERE ARE NO TIME-OUTS IN HISTORY

At best there are pauses between rounds
to stitch skin, wipe blood, spit into the bin,
& except for a few predictable platitudes,
wave to what's left of the crowd.

IDENTITY CRISIS

My cat thinks it's a dog.
My dog thinks it's a horse.
My horse thinks it's a car.
My car thinks it's a train.
My train thinks it's a submarine.
My submarine thinks it's a skyscraper.
My skyscraper thinks it's a museum.
My museum thinks it's a carnival.
My carnival thinks it's a funeral.
My funeral thinks it's a birth.
My birth thinks it's an episode.
My episode thinks it's eternal.
My eternal thinks it's hope.
My hope thinks it's cynicism.
My cynicism thinks it's time.
My time thinks it's anachronism.
My anachronism thinks it's pride.
My pride thinks it's a cat.

THE WOMEN IN MY FAMILY ARE BOXERS

Hard quads & black eyes
to prove it. Father gave us

each a belt on our twelfth birthdays.
And a gold ring.
We toughed it out.
Then ate our cake.

Did I mention the women in my family
are all boxers?

And the years punch back.
While we search for a title
worth defending.

PRIYA SARUKKAI CHABRIA

PRIYA SARUKKAI CHABRIA (b. 1955) is a poet, novelist, essayist and translator. Her publications include the speculative fiction *Generation 14*, *Dialogues and Other Poems*, *Not Springtime Yet: Poems* and *The Other Garden*. She edits the website Talking Poetry. Anthology appearances (among others) include *The Literary Review Indian Poetry* (New Jersey: Fairleigh Dickinson University), *The Yellow Nib Modern English Poetry by Indians* (Belfast: Queens University), both edited by Sudeep Sen and *Language for a New Century: Contemporary Poetry from The Middle East, Asia and Beyond* (New York, London: W.W. Norton & Company). She is translating, with poet Ravi Shankar, the Tamil mystic poet Aandaal's hymns excerpted in *Post Road* (Boston College Department of English). Twice recipient of the Senior Fellowship for Outstanding Artists from the Indian government, she has experimented with the Rasa Theory of Aesthetics in her writing; learnt Pali to read Buddhist Jataka Tales; co-founded Friends of the Archive that screened silent films; and co-scripted the Oberhausan Critic's Choice film, *Daara*. She has collaborated with classical dancer, Malavika Sarukkai on several productions. Her publications in 2013 will include the poetic journal *Immersions: Bombay/Mumbai* with photographer Christopher Mark Taylor and a book on Indian cinema. She lives in Pune with her husband. [www.priyawriting.com]

1.

I'll meet you here.[1] In the meantime I check the mail, call the booksellers, iron clothes dowsed in yesterday's breeze and consume cups of jasmine tea. Sunlight slides down the far wall and eddies across the floor to lap around the walnut wood desk near the windows; the wine red Persian carpet with its central shamsa sunburst medallion and borders of neat diamonds grows dimmer underfoot. I will await you; I will wait long past the rush hour, even though the sun has crossed over to the other side of the house and readies to slide into tomorrow between a tangle of trees and far buildings and then curve beneath them.[2] I shall wait till lights come on in the buildings, and until they are turned off. If you do not come, I shall say it does not matter. You could believe this.[3]

---

1. field at the edge of the Milky Way: brilliance behind, black vastness ahead, at the rim, wheeling galaxies
2. "*What if I say I am you?*" ibid pg.154
3. … though the adult heart is usually about five inches in length, three and a half inches in breadth at its broadest and two and a half inches in thickness. However, the organ is extremely sturdy, beating without a break from its formation in the womb until death. The glistening appearance of its inner surface is due to the transparent endocardium membrane. Wounds of the heart are often immediately fatal, but not necessarily so. They may be non–penetrating, when death may occur from hemorrhages, or subsequently from pericarditis, or on the other hand, the patient may recover.

2.

Sometimes light wants to clutch whatever it can:[4]
space, as it falls through, igniting it like a cloud from within
as if in an act of visual echolalia while in
the softening dusk that grows from earth upwards
beyond trees-buildings-clouds-sky
something, not a leaf, falls like a leaf.[5]
and something unheard gargles like an inky fountain[6]
and someone living prays to give up the dead[7]
and fails.

---

4. George Szirtes
5. Derek Walcott
6. Bao Jing
7. " *... veils of such transparency blew across her face that she no longer knew what she was seeing...*" ibid, pg. 260

3.

Ap	ple,	pear,	man	go:
He	cuts	fruits	for	me.
I	make	him	daal	rice.
To	get	her,	read	books.
How	man	y	more	days
Are	we	thus	gift	ed?

4.

A vase of flowers squats in sunlight.[8] On the sideboard, a bowl of fruit. Above it, branches reflect in the mirror's bright rectangle. On the polished wood[9] of the dining table I lay mats, plates, cutlery, napkins. Pour a thick stream of water into a crystal decanter cut with diamond designs; it is an object of great beauty that cannot be replaced. Each time I touch it, my heart beats a little faster. Curiously, the water looks heavier with sunlight streaming through.

---

8. whales beached on the white continent as far as the eye can see: stormclouds swept up from the ocean, lumpy, dark, lying on their sides, not gasping. Like elephants that seek out secret cavernous graveyards to die in, their ivory yellowing like dusty tallow, ribcages like broken teeth, the whales swim here, on to this melting shore of ice led by their song; they beguile themselves, become their own sirens, become liquefying moonstone
9. Voyager has proved beyond doubt that storms the size of Earth rage on the surface of Jupiter. Winds reach speeds of 15, 000 miles per hour. The sun is too far away to cause these effects; therefore Jupiter's storms are caused by something else.

5.

As I wait, I scan a questionnaire sent by a literary journal. Their last issue was a special on terror to which I contributed; now this. Does terror affect my daily life? What do I deem as terror? Did… I close the page and browse. The bell rings. A couriered package smudged with a scrawl and foreign stamps.[10] Inside, a book of poems of the rarest elegance, rigour and luminosity.[11] D has kept his word.

I return to the room. A pair of pigeons, startled, flies towards the window, their smooth shapes becomes oval flurries as they thrash wings, pppada-ppaada-ddaa-daaa against partially closed panes before escaping. On the slim marble of the windowsill, curls of down, grey on veined white, which I blow out. Should I leave the room, the pair will return to roost amid bookshelves. They never learn.

---

10. … under skies of cracked crystal, plum wine trapped in its veins, darkening the fractured dome, spins a mirror that captures those who look into it and reflects to each an identity they as yet do know, but which exists in their future or their past; what is more, this is an identity they will meet. [LR]
11. for it is well known that people can transform from hatred to forgiveness for no apparent reason as is frequently witnessed in survivors from war zones: having lost everyone and everything such people become apostles of peace and love. Ref: Amazon, Gaza, Kashmir, etc.

"*… the sparkle in a drop of dew is sieved through dawn so all that remains is sparkle*"

6.

Salammbo leans at an angle on the topmost shelf, a 1908 edition. Repeatedly read and passed over, today, in the space of waiting, I reach for its musty red hardcover. [12] Blow on it. Open it with the care brought on by neglect and its tainted delicateness. Page corners crumple on touch.[13] Dark moons, wormdrawn, burrow through, chapter after chapter. I pluck fresh neem[14] leaves and place their acrid scent between pages to drive away silverfish.

---

12. However, certain possessions refuse to be tattooed into a particular time, or a specific space, such things do not abide by the rules. Rapture is foremost amongst these: it rises unbidden at all times. Moreover, it continues to rise.
13. Drenched rapture, as in lotuses filled with rain, swollen pollen and drowned bees.
14. … especially the skid of moonlight underfoot as it rolls on dew

7.

Pastry flakes on white plates. Forks gleam, sun–warmed. The wine bottle's lengthening shadow pauses[15] as I drowsily blink. Distant laughter opens its eyes, then snoozes.[16] I reach for your hand and place it against my face; it fits exactly, curving like mango flesh around its seed. Knowing you are nearby, I drift into sleep. I return to the dream that I constantly dream these days, that dream whose meaning I know but cannot share because my words are also only of this world[17]

15. ... for, between the dissolution (pralaya) of the universe and the beginning (sargam)of the next one is a pause of complete equipoise, one of "pure duration" as time has not yet come into existence.
16.
17. The translated significance of this stanza does not seem clear but is possibly worth investigating

PURVI SHAH

PURVI SHAH's (b. 1972) *Terrain Tracks* (New Rivers Press, 2006), which explores migration as potential and loss, won the Many Voices Project prize and was nominated for the Asian American Writers' Workshop Members' Choice Award in 2007. She is the winner of the inaugural SONY South Asian Social Services Award in 2008 for her work fighting violence against women. In 2011, she served as Artistic Director for Together We Are New York, a community-based poetry project to highlight the voices of Asian Americans during the tenth anniversary of 9/11. She believes in the miracle of poetry and the beauty of change. You can find more of her work at http://purvipoets.net or @PurviPoets.

YOUR FACE STILL BEARS THE DEW OF TOMORROW

If you evoke in me song, ravish the day.

If you evoke in me complaint, ravish the night.

If you forget to stroke the air, witness of dew, I'll bring supple

body instead. Tired of the ifs, make certainty
certain – bring a scarlet fabric the stretch of the universe

& lay it across my kitchen table. Together we can eat

stars as if they were figs, spin
a circle of parallel lighted paths, aligning

not to road for escape but the spectrum
of rainbow, you & me the elements
of colors primary & secondary – no longer

jumbled nor separate, no longer
distinct nor unified, simply arcing

heaven, arcing home.

WAITING TO DEPART

The boat is prepared to ferry, the airplane shrunk
its line of boarding, the train just one whistle

from exiting platform – all docks unroped, air
crisp with departure, even the molecules drunk

with buzzing. Yet the air

hovers on your face, revealing
this one heel spun towards
new journey and one arch

affixed in your gaze – we break
clasp and remember: even Achilles

faltered, before a final storm.

Somewhere a child is longing to have a birthday. A mother longing to bring forth a child. A midwife circling the bed, expectant, organizing crisp towels, boiling water. A web of friends suspended to phones. This life: consumed with searching for pulse.

The young man has his back to this buzz. He steadies the door frame before the vinyl sheen of a cookie-cutter development. He is examining the inner lids of his eyes, painting the Ara, the Auriga, the Orion, in the shape of names, in the arc of features – a plump toe here, his mother's bent nose there. It has been years since his mind drift to dreams. His father's sound. He involuntarily snaps. His father's sound – one who couldn't but make too much noise through the shrinking house, one who pulled out leather straps this day, the next day, any day. The competing pulse of his mother's whispers: *He'd do so well with a sister, a brother*- And before the words attract, his father has commanded speech: *This one's already too much. Your family gonna work to afford the next one?*

Cringing in the one-pillow bed and star-covered pajamas, shivering under the ceiling's glow, tracing the hunter, the dogs, the belt – until the voices buzz. Before the tears well, he catches the wail. He indulges cry. As he turns, illumination lifting gaze, one by one, the stars go out. One by one the stars go out: he turns to illumination.

HIS HEART COLLAPSES, WHEN TIME STILLS

Boughs still
bend, hungering
for unsheened fruit.

Breath still
lungs, aching
to undestined travels.

Clouds still curl, *quivering*
unspent drizzle.

Still the hair stretches
for gray, this unavoidable
unbecoming –

And you, nestled
between silence and song, palm
Nature's pacemaker, regulate

its march back
to untuned rhythm.

AFTER·LIFE

With night, the oxalis curls in, a baby nesting.
We know the morning will raise the plume, spreading.
But these fading fuchsia tropicals, the kind that green

year-round in Costa Rica, droop yellow
with decay, gaunt like an old man over
a cane. I pluck from the pot, stem slippery

through my fingers. The remaining appear earthworms
shriveled or a series of cut wires littered
across a dusty floor. With surprise, weeks
later, next to the sole blushing leaf, I watch green

shoots emerge from the split stems, like shiny
lipstick swiveling out from the tube or hesitant
well-wishers with gifts peeking round the hospital door.

Despite the jagged quick
of the cut, life presses out, irrepressible –
dealing death a blow, the fragile
guarantee of resurgence.

R RAJ RAO

R RAJ RAO's (b. 1955) two poetry publications are *Slide Show* (Peepal Tree), and a chapbook, *BomGay* (Aark Arts). He has also published a book of short stories, *One Day I Locked My Flat in Soul City* (Rupa); *Wisest Fool and Other Plays* (Brown Critique); and a novel, *Boyfriend* (Penguin India). His poems have appeared in magazines and journals: *Atlas, Poetry Wales, Kavya Bharati, Gentleman, Debonair, Femina, The Little Magazine,* and *100 Words;* and have been featured in the film 'BomGay' (directed by Riyad Vinci Wadia, 1996). Anthology appearances (among others) include *Yaraana: Gay Writing from India* (Penguin India), *Midnight's Grandchildren: Post Independence Poetry from India* (Macedonia: Struga Poetry Evenings) and *The Literary Review Indian Poetry* (New Jersey: Fairleigh Dickinson University), the last two edited by Sudeep Sen. He has also edited a book of interviews with queer Indian men titled *Whistling in the Dark: Twenty-one Queer Interviews* (Sage 2009). His second novel *Hostel Room 131* was published by Penguin India in 2010. He teaches at the University of Pune in India.

LIFE IN THE FLAT

LIFE IN THE FLAT 1

Old Aubrey Menen,
Smart young *New Yorker* fiction,
And I'm not brain-dead.

LIFE IN THE FLAT 2

Pacing the long room,
I use my footsteps to mark
The passage of time.

LIFE IN THE FLAT 3

Oprah, Dr. Phil.
Hot showers and nightly shags.
Green tea and red wine.

FEMALE EUNUCH

FEMALE EUNUCH 1

The female eunuch
Claps so hard the neighbours think
It's firecrackers.

FEMALE EUNUCH 2

The female eunuch
Exports her castrated part
To America.

FEMALE EUNUCH 3

The female eunuch
Gets the barber to dye her
Pubic hair golden.

THE BOYS I LOVE

The boys I love
Are scarecrows without Salman Khan's biceps.

The boys I love
Do not have e-mail ids or internet passwords.

The boys I love
Scrub their teeth with neem twigs, not Prudent tooth-brushes.

The boys I love
Have hard-ons only when they're hard-up

The boys I love
Apply no deodorant to mildewed armpits

The boys I love
Are dunces who don't know their ABC.

The boys I love
Turn dead rats on taking off their socks.

The boys I love
Can't talk Foucault before or after fucking.

The boys I love
Never touch my tongue with theirs.

The boys I love
Say AIDUS, as if it were anus.

The boys I love are animals
But isn't sex a thing between animals?

FOR HIRE

To flee the ill-fame of Bombay
you go to the hill-station.
Take a cab from base-camp
Where the train dumps you.
Your package begins then and there.
The driver packs his van to capacity,
seats you next to him.
He turns on the ignition, climbs, stops.
To make you sit
astride the car's phallus
so he can squeeze in
one more guy.
He drives.
Each time he changes gears
he hits you in the solar plexus.
South of, actually.
Is he a taxi himself?
For hire?
When you reach the summit
You've been molested forty-two times.
In public!
You ask the driver
how many trips up and down
he makes daily.
Sixty nine!
How promiscuous, you shrilly exclaim,
scandalized to the bone.
And rush back to the city
to get a bank loan
and become a taxi-driver yourself.

RABINDRA K SWAIN

RABINDRA K SWAIN (b. 1960) did his MA and PhD in English Literature from Utkal University in Orissa. His four published books of poetry are *Once Back Home, A Tapestry of Steps, Severed Cord,* and *Susurrus in the Skull*. His translations from Oriya to English include *Bahubreehi* by Rajendra Kishore Panda; *Dear Jester and Other Stories* by J P Das; and *The Cemetery Flower and Other Stories* by Sachidananda Raut-Roy. His critical books include *The Poetry of Jayanta Mahapatra: A Critical Study;* and *Silent Tongues: Writings in Contemporary Indian Poetry*. His individual English poems have appeared in journals such as *Atlas, The Kenyon Review, Shenandoah, Verse, New Letters, Times Literary Supplement,* and *Ariel*. Anthology appearances (among others) include *Midnight's Grandchildren: Post Independence Poetry from India* (Macedonia: Struga Poetry Evenings), *The Literary Review Indian Poetry* (New Jersey: Fairleigh Dickinson University), *The Yellow Nib Contemporary English Poetry by Indians* (Belfast: Queens University), and *World Literature Today Writing from Modern India* (Norman: University of Oklahoma), all edited by Sudeep Sen. He lives in Bhubaneswar where he is the managing editor of the poetry journal, *Chandrabhaga*.

WHAT YOU MISS

All along it has been there.
You feel its presence
but cannot be sure of the space
into which it empties itself.

It played with its shadow
till sundown. With the dark
it crept up to your doorstep.
You felt its rustle but couldn't

touch it, sense its breath.
The walls you stared at
drew only a blank.
It sensed your despair

and dropped its quills.
Failing to get its hint
you sulk and then wilt.
Dawn is petals; dawn is quills.

BALES OF TANGLED FABRIC

But always they leave, by the doors
Unseen, you've not seen.
They leave behind them not turd
As birds do nor the mess they have been in
But gold, the one they found to be leaden.
The gold you need, in comfort
Of words, bold in being battered,
Made pulp, gulping insults, indiscriminate
In being stingy, effacing the mark
Each time a stone pelts at your back.
A spiritless heir, bequeathed with a fire
In love with its ash, ashen by the hour
When deities are made to sleep with lullabies,
When they are to return by the doors, unseen,
Sore, and sour of the world, homesick, their hearts
Bales of tangled fabric.

A CAGE OF RIBS

It occurs when you expect it least.
For fear of nightmares you do not sleep.

It taps on the banana leaves in the yard;
it taps on your shoulders and knuckles hard.

It sits by your side, cajoling you to take this or that
the things you have desired but dared not have had.

It seems to say: it happens, don't worry.
And when you do not yield it swears:

you deserve the fruits of your karmic guilt.
Before you can sulk it is already there

inside you like the kernel in the coconut:
soft, temptingly close, almost in grip yet beyond reach,

playing with your sentimental heart (taunting you?):
reach out to me, take me out, show me the cage

that has for its bars the ribs of those birds
ever suspended in their still flights.

KNOWING ME

Knowing me has made no one lose his sleep.
I keep awake, thinking of those who do not sleep.

Not to sleep is to be caught in the crossfire
between those who suppose you are a police informer
and those who suspect if you have any ideology at all.

Walls
impenetrably insomniac.
Living on the other side of the wall
is to lie on a prickly bed of conscience.
On this side
          are hurt certainties.

The ones beyond them
are not necessarily like the leaves of those trees
which begin to drowse once it is evening.

Not knowing the ones who do not sleep
is to paint nights black and white.
Do not ask the elderly couples about it.
Their kids, grown up, laden with dreams,
have slipped into the jungles
          of the Khondmal district.

They have
no walls to sit.

Knowing them makes no one lose their sleep.

WHAT IF

What if India was to sink
dragging down with her the neighbouring countries

to the earth's mantle,
to her gleeful abyss

What if Orissa is re-spelt Odisha
What if the wheels of the chariots

of her mighty poets sink
in the quagmire of bureaucracy

What if the Parswadevattas
were to seize the sanctum sanctorum in a coup

What if the representatives of the European Union
were to picnic in the riot-torn Khondmal district

What if the European countries
were to declare themselves theocratic

What if beliefs were magical hats
out of which one could produce

an old religious zealot like a rabbit, hacked and shot,
and scores of them wielding knives, cans of kerosene and boxes of matches

What if the forest dwellers were left to worship trees
not wood, stone, medicine, money

What if to dream had not been political
What if to mourn had not been political

What if the artists had not shown
us the faces of gods

What if the poets had not been
in defense of poetry

Would our sorrows have been
anything more or anything less

RAMAN MUNDAIR

RAMAN MUNDAIR (b. 1981) is a writer and artist. She was born in India, raised in Manchester and Leicester and lives and works in Scotland. Mundair is the author of *A Choreographer's Cartography*, *Lovers, Liars, Conjurers and Thieves* and *The Algebra of Freedom.* She is a Rolex Mentor and Protégé Award nominee, a Robert Louis Stevenson Award winner and was identified recently by the BBC/Royal Court Theatre as one of the 'next generation of promising new writers in Britain' (24 Degrees Project). In 2009 Raman was chosen as one of two British writers to participate in the Word Express, Literature Across Frontiers project. Word Express took twenty young writers from twelve European countries by train through South-East Europe to Turkey, where they took part in readings and literary events in every country they passed through. Her artworks have been exhibited at the Gallery of Modern Art, Glasgow, City Art Gallery, Leicester and Kevin Kavanagh Gallery, Dublin.

fingers of rain
stroke
the windowpane

pumpkins piled high
outside on porches
multiple bright suns

the fog clears
three Buddha deer
a holy trinity

bloated olive rivers
play hide and seek
with passing train

lush forest
hugs steep mountain
hints of Autumn

train hurtles East
single track mountain
roads race river

passing through Zidani Most
the rain commits
to becoming serious.

CHATTRI YATRA

'Chattri' is the name given to the memorial erected on the South Downs in Sussex, England, to the memory of the one and a half million Indian army soldiers who saw active service during the First World War. In the course of the war 47,746 Indian soldiers were killed and 65,126 wounded. The Chattri Memorial is in an obscure location deep in the heart of the English countryside. It is not particularly well known and difficult to get to. Having visited the memorial one summer to pay my respects I wanted to know more about these men and their hidden history and visited the archives at the British Library, London.

I

We have a date - I journey
miles to meet
you. Change trains
twice. Crumpled and hungry
I arrive. I am led
to a desk. I sign
my name in bold.
Accompanied, I am led
up the stairs. At
a leather desk you wait.
My name nestling
in ink above you.

II

The man on my left has an impossible,
ancient, volume; he wrestles with both hands,
holds the pages back with soft rope.
I can smell the musk of the pages -
the ink like *mehndi* across the page.
On my right, the woman next
to me bristles as I come
to sit and have my moment with you.
I have waited
days to hold you
in my hands
and wonder at you.

Who are you?
I undo
your file, brown. Legal.
Bound with string.
It's a pleasure
to unwrap.
Marked, in thick, soft pencil,
Mss Eur F143/82;

III

Inside
a smooth sepia image:
'A' Block, Kitchener Hospital
I find two of you
leaning out from the second window -
both of you wear bright, white turbans
that halo you in the winter light.
The trees naked,
struggle to stretch,
to reach you, aid your escape.
I look closer and find more of you,
faint shadows, behind the pane.
Halos at different heights - some of you perhaps
sitting, gazing out at the sky,
the same sky that covered you in France
and home, safe,
in India.

IV

Some of you have gathered
outside under Brighton sun;
bright, young bodies play
card games. Your hand
open, for all to see.
I notice your skin:
smooth, soft, young
- surely not
even of an age
to shave. You are boys,
tender with youth

wounds
healing
under the sun

V

In another picture
there are many of you.
Sitting smartly beside rows
of beds. A rudimentary stove
in the middle of the ward. You
lack lustre. Your eyes meet
the camera reluctantly.
Some of you can't be bothered -
gaze off
somewhere into the middle
distance.

VI

Later, the skies
through the café
window - a tree
offers itself,
to me - each leaf
a tender sacrifice,
layers of skin fall.
Lights from the café
dance
across its slender,
brown, strong frame.

"WHY DON'T YOU GO BACK WHERE YOU CAME FROM?"

Life in a White British Town in the Nineteen Seventies

I never lived Bollywood days
filled with extended family,
with closed *desi* ways

or spoke in bright, quick
tongues that turned pale
heads in public places.

I never prayed
to many headed gods
or kneeled, veiled and ready

to submit, with light
palms together.
I never ate meat - not for faith

but by choice - I never married;
wore the *mungal sutra*, stained
centre parting red or stood bent-backed

cooking *roti* over hot *tuva*;
or had boy children to carry
my husband's name.

I never touched
my elder's feet
or felt my mouth full

with *pindu* Punjabi.
I never learnt the sing-song story -
I sent it back to where it came from.

RAMAN MUNDAIR

RANJIT HOSKOTE

RANJIT HOSKOTE (b. 1969) was born in Bombay. He is a poet, cultural theorist and curator. He is the author of more than twenty books, including the poetry collections *Vanishing Acts: New & Selected Poems 1985–2005* (Penguin, 2006) and *Die Ankunft der Vögel* (Carl Hanser Verlag, 2006), the translation *I, Lalla: The Poems of Lal Ded* (Penguin Classics, 2011), and nine artist monographs; most recently, *Zinny & Maidagan: Compartment / Das Abteil* (Museum für Moderne Kunst, Frankfurt / Verlag der Buchhandlung Walther König, 2010). He is also the editor of *Dom Moraes: Selected Poems* (Penguin Modern Classics, 2012). With Nancy Adajania, Hoskote is co-author of *The Dialogues Series*, an ongoing cycle of conversations with artists (Popular / Foundation B&G, 2011). He has been writer-in-residence at the International Writing Program, University of Iowa (1995), Villa Waldberta, Munich (2003), Theater der Welt, Essen / Mülheim (2010), 'The Promised City' project / Polnisches Institut, Berlin (2010), and BAK / Basis voor actuele kunst, Utrecht (2010). Hoskote and Hyunjin Kim co-curated, with Artistic Director Okwui Enwezor, the 7th Gwangju Biennial (Korea, 2008). Hoskote was curator for India's first-ever national pavilion at the Venice Biennale (2011). He lives and works in Mumbai.

THE INVENTION OF THE SENSES

for Masaki Fujihata

Touch crosses the small distances of this room,
caressing a pebble, smoothing a ruffled curtain.
When you rest your hand on this ebony table,
a book floats to the surface, opens to page one.
Run your fingers along the paper, the edge, the spine,
and a lamp begins to glow faintly in a corner.

Touch unlocks the closed and private cells:
unlike the voice, its ends are not gregarious.
Searching alone, it brings home what you've lost:
open your hands in a shallow fan
of ten fingers, and a door clicks open,
a child looks through.

FREEHOLD

for Mehlli Gobhai

A gash of sunlight on a lemon door.
A cat hacked by the slatted shadow
of a screen, flicking its tail
to show it's alive
to the dripping of unseen faucets.
What can hold them together,
these partitioned moments,
straggling hours and makeshift days?
As you watch, the house falls

into place: walls standing up,
windows forming in pools,
fanlights capping tonsured doors,
a roof dripping eaves on the lawn.

Your feet sink in cloud.
The powdery shadow of a key
blesses your doorstep.

The house finds its breath again. Its past
is an abandoned line of defence.

FERN

This feathered leaf must have fallen from the hand
of the woman who turned around to see
if her child had strayed too close to the slope
of the fuming mountain or the hunting birds,
and left her footprint in ash that hardened
to rock. A spray of seeds released that noon
remains in the thick air, and this gift:

a leaf trapped between layers of mud
that volcanic fire baked into stone.
Drained of light and green, long spasm,
breath dusted with pollen:
a net of veins splayed on an altar
where the river turns in its sleep
and an old woman lights a lamp.

BOTANY

Prickly garden where voices flower and run to seed:
this conversation could go up in a sheet of flame
any time, any leaf could be a bait, any tendril
a booby trap. Watch your words, and hers, theirs,
and all your stranded thoughts. Clove and mandrake
open the mouths of your mind, all dialogue here
is rolling transcript for a police state:
check the names for shadows, the verbs for stains,
turn connoisseur of signs, yogi, give nothing away
except your deep-shelved archive of silences.

BEARINGS

for Michael Krüger

I would go back in time to trawl
these lucid particulars from the tarred drift-tide:
the yellow butterfly poised like a pair
of palms in prayer;
the star climbing to sainthood
at the silver oak's zenith;
the wasp boring its sawdust martyr heart
into the painted window frame;
the full moon, delicious as a flower
pricked by the needle of lyric.

Shuttling between was and is, will I find them there,
unchanged, arranged as bearings, which first came
as chance beats in a music of surprise?
And will I get there before it's too late
to guess at whole systems of weather
that ride the oceans inside our heads
while circling the planet in silent waves?
Keys to epics, I hold these partisan details
that burn the writing hand
and pierce the eye's complacencies.

THE SOLOIST PERFORMS WITH AN ORCHESTRA OF EVENTS

for Ranbir Kaleka

The greenest things happen when you're not looking:
creepers braid themselves around a bridge,
clouds surround a tower, nudge it towards a dead end
and neon measures the length of the cobbled street.
There's no one to hear you read, clearly it's time
to jump off the mind's cold waterfront

and follow the dolphins, whose dance lasts as long
as a notched breath, the naked spasm of a thought,
the yanking away of a hand. You could miss it
so easily and freeze. Is that you or a cut-out
parked in your chair? How wise to plant a proxy:
the greenest things happen when you're not there.

BIHZAD CLOSES HIS EYES

for Peter Weibel

He sits in the centre of the carpet of silence, the last of all the carpets he will sit on, and calls out to the trees by their special names.

Cedar was always good to him, wrapping its fragrance around his books. Cypress offered him the shelter of love. Pine shielded him from angry princes and jealous slaves. Poplar kisses his windows. Willow sweeps his river clean. Every autumn, *chenar* has covered his garden with leaves like hands of flame. These he has trusted. But today they are quiet, respectful, distant.

And his colours? He has fought them through the long dream of his life, powdered them in the mortar of his heart, glued them with anger. They have stung his sleeves and bitten his goldleaf borders. He has dragged them across marbled pages with his brush, forcing them into images.

God made man from clots of blood. A painter makes saints from broken coral, grinds emperors from lapis. While other men sleep, he barters queens for turquoise. Spies bring him crushed cinnabar to finish his tented cities. Traders find him leopards and peacocks to draw. No cabinet is safe from his fingers: he will claw through the flasks and retorts of friends, looking for the lost elixir. Who called him an idle collector of travellers' tales? He listens. He knows every shade will open in its own time, tell its story in the fall of stained syllables.

But Bihzad has not listened to his colours for many years. He has forgotten the boy who beat off the swans and read the deepest pages of water. He has forgotten the young man who slashed through afternoon's sawdust shrubs and the green silk pavilions of evening, the wolves howling in his blood. Too soon, he came down from the mountains and chained himself to the forced march: an album for the king's uncle, a portrait for a merchant, love spells for a princess, the chamberlain's prayer book. To the beat of the sun's hooves, he herded his colours through the gates of floating palaces and honeycombed bazaars. Splashed them on stairways left unfinished when the barbarians attacked, steps locked between earth and heaven. Hurrying north after the retreat, he dripped his colours on sketches that soldiers threw into winter fires, watching them shrivel into veils of ash.

On this last carpet, he does not whip them with strokes of ink or trap them in porcelain cages. He knows the black angel is coming for him in a rain of sand, gardens and houses crumbling in its eyes. Nothing stands between Bihzad and the angel except his colours. He draws his shawl around his shoulders. Once again the song of an open wound, he chants their names: *laleh*, *kermes*, *sikarlat*, *khun-e siyavush*.

Dragon's blood blesses his page.

THE EMPIRE OF LIGHTS

after Magritte

This house has not moved a brick since midnight.
Outside the front door, the streetlamp has brushed
the cobblestones with a moss of delay: the night
glows in a yawn between darkness and day.

The street flows on, soaking the canal
with brittle afterimages of rain.
The bats that have chased butterflies of meaning
up the crescendos of trees all night

are drowsing in their green and icy silhouettes.
It is night here still, it will always be night:
this street is wound up tight to strike
at 3 a.m. and hiss a breath of doubt

into waxy clouds that are talking softly
about the ninja maestro who bled the clock dry.
They remember the day he parted the curtains
and broke the windows with his flame-coloured hands.

They are whispering about the jacarandas
that he drowned in the sky beneath the house
that has not moved a brick since midnight,
and how well cotton burns at noon.

RAVI SHANKAR

RAVI SHANKAR (b. 1975) is Associate Professor and Poet-in-Residence at Central Connecticut State University and the founding editor of the international online journal of the arts, *Drunken Boat* [http://www.drunkenboat.com]. He has published two full-length collections of poems, *Deepening Groove* (TNPR), winner of the 2010 National Poetry Review Prize, and *Instrumentality* (Cherry Grove), named a finalist for the 2005 Connecticut Book Awards; with Reb Livingston, a collaborative chapbook, *Wanton Textiles* (No Tell Books); and two chapbooks published in 2010, *Seamless Matter* (Ohm Editions) with a cover by the late American artist Sol LeWitt and *Voluptuous Bristle* (Finishing Line Press). His creative and critical work has appeared in publications such as *Atlas*, *Scribner's The Best American Erotic Poems: From 1800 to the Present*, *The Paris Review*, *Poets & Writers*, *Time Out New York*, *The Massachusetts Review*, *McSweeney's*, and *AWP's The Writer's Chronicle*. Other anthology appearances include *The Literary Review Indian Poetry* (New Jersey: Fairleigh Dickinson University), *The Yellow Nib Modern English Poetry by Indians* (Belfast: Queens University), and *World Literature Today Writing from Modern India* (Norman: University of Oklahoma), all edited by Sudeep Sen. He has taught at Queens College, University of New Haven, and Columbia University, where he received his MFA in Poetry. He has appeared on the BBC and NPR, been featured in *The New York Times* and *The Financial Times*, won a Pushcart Prize and a Connecticut Commission on the Arts grant, and is Chairman of the Connecticut Young Writers Trust. Along with Tina Chang and Nathalie Handal, he co-edited *Language for a New Century: Contemporary Poetry from Asia, the Middle East & Beyond* (W.W. Norton & Co.). He is currently on the faculty of the first international MFA program at City University of Hong Kong.

AN UNVERIFIABLE THEOREM

The gun once introduced must be forgotten
because its snub-nose gives a pocket the weight
of syllogism: no posthumous event can affect us.

Or, say, after it occurs, death cannot affect us:
it's impossible to imagine what we have forgotten
when who we were no longer has any real weight.

Stripped of consciousness a body has the weight
of water evaporating from a lake: breath leaving us.
Once introduced the gun cannot be forgotten.

The weight of the forgotten: not what leaves us.

GRAVEYARD

With child trammeled jouncing to chest,
I mount thirty overgrown wooden slats
up a frost-weathered knoll that looks

down on the backs of craft boutiques
lining Main Street. Up into a clearing
where carved granite slabs concatenate

in neat rows. Some gravestones specked
with algae are nearly indecipherable.
Others scrubbed with soft bristle brushes

or surrounded by plastic hydrangea sprays
too bright for winter. Walking on bones,
we stop at an incised ringed cross: *Mother.*

THE MANY USES OF MINT

Fresh mint leaves muddled with cane sugar
at the bottom of a rocks glass full of crushed

ice and an exquisite spiced rum don't taste
as good as you, not even close, though sprigs,

intoxicant green and flavorful, spring to mind
when I think of you, consider your nape, flute-

shaped, and your almond eyes that see so far
into me that what I'm yet capable of surfaces

like wet earth gravid with the start of shoots
after a protracted frost has finally thawed.

Or say, I'm new minted in your gaze, unused,
unmarred, coined especially to fit your purse,

to be pawed, turned over, spent as legal tender
in a country whose borders no map could draw

because it extends past this life into the next,
into the past, where we were more verdant

than jade polished to a sheen, were the envy
of every hoarder's greed but could only belong

to each other because in each other we reach
the apotheosis of—dare I say it?—human love.

Then down to Scottish use it comes, *to attempt,*
to intend, to suggest, to dare, to make a mint

at it, no matter the impediments which run
beyond winter, past numismatists, clear of mites

that might gnaw a stem to a well-withered nub,
into infamy of the Capulet variety—*what indeed*

is in a name?—into a gale of forces that coalesce
to enforce such abstractions as "sanctity"

and "family values" even while the rafters quake.
Petrifying yes but fuck it—let's make a mint at it.

UNTITLED, OIL PAINT ON CANVAS, 1958

"Shapes have no direct association
with any particular visible experience,
but in them one recognizes the principle
and passion of organisms."
—MARK ROTHKO

The proposal: luminous drama.
Ensconced pallor meets an edge
of burnished orange for a shotgun
romance. Share a moment
of horizontal bliss. Then watch
as doubts arise. Ardor turns nasty
Recriminations grow ever nastier,
spiraling into black, burning coals
of depression, continually brooding

on death. Timelessness passes.
The whole spectrum gets absorbed.
Somehow the couple emerges aglow,
slightly altered, happily lanced
in yellow, each a part of the other
expecting, miraculously to give birth
When harangued by hue and cry,
they admit to eloping. Step away
from domestic light's embrace

to tally the gradations that hint
at perspective abstracted:
romance, pain, renewal, failure,
the ecstasy of later years, happening
all at once. Step to the surface.
Look there, dead center: the secret
wedding. An exchange of vows
in an effulgent chapel where color
gathers to praise us in our plight.

Appalled and thrilled is what I wrote for its alliteration
but that was pure showmanship, shimmy shuffle
and shoulder roll, not true to the rapt attention I had
trying to pin the technical terms - jab and cross,
hook and uppercut - onto the bodies of two men
who glided across the roped off ring trying to land
blows. Watching the fight, I watched myself watch
the fight, noticing how in spite of myself raw sounds
gurgled up from my throat. Was it to help exhort
Bad Chad Dawson, New Haven's finest, rip into his older
opponent? Or in appreciation of the way he would
slip punches like a speedboat navigating a cove?
Perhaps it was a muscle memory of the only time
I stepped into the ring, with a buddy, to playfully
grapple, until I got hit with a roundhouse in the ear,
which clicked some primal button I could not unblink,
and charged with animal aggression I never suspected
I possessed, I dropped my good friend to his knees?
Or maybe finally it was being colonized by the crowd,
in synchronicity with the growls and curses that made
me yell out in spite of myself. I could have been in
Baghdad 7,000 years ago, where an archaeologist
discovered a Mesopotamian stone tablet engraved with
two boxers preparing to fight, else in 18th century London
eating meat pies and drinking ales while watching
a bare knuckle prize fight. Somehow each feint and parry,
each exchange of fists, encapsulated an essential
idea about brotherhood and brutality that I could not
put into the right words. All I know is that when the final
bell sounded, cauliflower ear and nerve-cell damage
in the periphery, the ring overrun with promoters, corner
men, men in tuxedos and blue latex gloves, cameras
on cranes, the ring girl in her low-cut dress, I was fixated
on the two fighters with their gloved hands raised in the air.
I was galvanized yet not quite satisfied. I wanted more.

Tinsel seldom dominates a domicile's décor the way lofts under the Williamsburg Bridge are strung up in silver, now that trustafarians have arrived to drive up rents, to play alt-country singer-songwriters too often too loud too deep into the night, to bring back the mullet and Member's Only. Decades before them, a few blocks north flowed brick and strips of corrugated steel, busted up factories designated "interim multiple dwellings" to meet code, Puerto Ricans and Hasids fighting for overcrowded flats along a waterfront rife with distilleries, muggings, sugar refineries and rusted turbines that spewed silt into the East River. Now the bodega sells Brooklyn lager, stiff avocados, toupee tape, trucker hats, novelty fobs in the shapes of states, superthin lambskin condoms, Mucha Lucha Wrestling magazines, loose batteries and prepackaged kielbasas that a bearded man hunched in a subway hub furtively devours, poring over pages of Rabbinic Law. He's a Mohel who later tonight while performing a bris will taste blood from a child's penis. Three steps: cut the foreskin with a knife, rip the membrane open with a fingernail and stopper the blood flow with pursed lips. Then it's wine and matzah for everyone! Imagine. Not rubber or *Chinoiserie* or even leopard print. Tinsel.

REETIKA VAZIRANI

REETIKA VAZIRANI (1962–2003) was born in India and emigrated to the United States with her family as a child. She received her BA from Wellesley College and her MFA from the University of Virginia. Her first collection of poetry, *White Elephants* (Beacon Press, 1996), won the Barnard New Women Poets Prize. Her second collection, *World Hotel* (Copper Canyon Press, 2002), won the 2003 Anisfield-Wolf Book Award. Vazirani received a Pushcart Prize, a Poets & Writers exchange program award, the Glenna Luchei award from Prairie Schooner, and a 'Discovery' / The Nation award. Her poems have appeared in many publications: *Best American Poetry 2000, The Nation, The Paris Review, Six Seasons Review, TriQuarterly*, and *Wasafiri India South Asia & the Diaspora* (London: QMW University) edited by Sudeep Sen. She was writer-in-residence at Sweet Briar College and later at the College of William and Mary in 2002. Vazirani took her own life and that of her son, Jehan Vazirani Komunyakaa, on 16 July 2003. Her posthumous collection, *Radha Says*, was edited by Leslie McGrath and Ravi Shankar (Drunken Boat, 2010).

LUXOR

nothing matters but the door   Egyptian
shirtsleeves cotton   my mouth
and nothing   your scent
is breeze and nothing goes
Merle Oberon with Dorothy Dandridge
exiled Sitas?   no we go on our own
out of marriages into ideas
nothing matters now that I ask for
nothing   when you closed the subject
crossed the street
when I want so much the goat
sister of my wish to torch me prone
batter me ring-fingered
nothing matters   I think the horizon
looks so Anglican   stiff and long
with trees and the junk
of yesterday   eyes in the river
I keep on   bedpost
walls don't hold
I tell myself please
make this do   don't ask for anything
among *bulbuls rat-ki-rani* blossoms
arc of a steamer heading east
to begin again a migration
can you hear?
ship's leaving foghorn
is no greeting   I ply
the wrong questions

GRIEVANCE

those days I hung my sleeves on the railing
got them wet if I stayed out till dawn
when clouds fell I could hardly see the gate
I had fashioned you in
absentia   vegetable seedling black clay   last July
my verdandah vigil for the sound of a hoof
untangling braids   Ayah scolds
my mirrorwork   starched *kemize* by the door
why ever change from the night before   forget them
ordinary day clothes I'll never wear
when I imagined we'd undo
the buoyant earth   blue horse

then when I heard you were not arriving
but had turned on the road to Jaisalmer
I was to keep from spitting you out
one day you would title that city
now a son in my arms   I look
far from the gate   I am not
to reproach you but I am full of reproach
your men crossed the desert to my city
you shed your blood on this ground
what did you care for the wind in my veil?

calm me *Ayah*
now as I turn from Jaisalmer why should I chart
the constellations   a figurine who leans
into a telescope   learns to press organ keys
smiles   wears makeup all the time   disposable
like a man's battle plans   these nights
musicians entertain us late   the prodigy Lalita arrives
her beauty a laser on marble
forget your pasha   derelict star   farewell

WHAT A FISHER GIRL SAID IN DEFENSE OF HER ABSENCE

at least he kept his promise
he said I'll make you rich
even though he left
when I close my eyes
I'm hitched to his strides
he's shown me
my house is as broad
as a look over a beak
and there are fifty rainy
seasons becoming paradigms
big future   sometimes
I'm without hope
for light years but he didn't promise
me words   like an athlete
in his element with me he had
no use for talk
and day by day I am stunned to want
him on me unpeeled even
when he leaves
I've let him own me   how
did I contain your
desire for the myth of me?

RESHMA AQUIL

RESHMA AQUIL (b. 1955) is Professor of English at the University of Allahabad in India. She is the author of *Sleeping Wind* (Singapore: Ethos Books), *Shadows of Fire* (Kolkata: Writers Workshop), and *The Unblending* (Kolkata: Writers Workshop). Her poems have appeared in *Poetry India: Voices of Many Worlds* (New Delhi: British Council), *Chandrabhaga, Kavya Bharti, A Hudson Review, Tonight: An Anthology of World Love Poetry* (South Africa: The Poets Printery), on 'www.softblow.com'; and also in *Midnight's Grandchildren: Post Independence Poetry from India* (Macedonia: Struga Poetry Evenings), and *The Literary Review Indian Poetry* (New Jersey: Fairleigh Dickinson University), both edited by Sudeep Sen. She lives and works in Allahabad.

INNER VERANDAH

In its cool inner verandah
I surprise the swallows

Heads swivel, a black eye alerts
Except for one soft belly heavy with eggs
Bulging a nest of feathers stuck to a corner

Others burst forth
Like arrows from a quiver

And shrieking sail, dotted scythe
Over the river

THE BACKYARD

Nothing prepared me
For their low large crop of leaves
Fanning yellow/white flowers

Tight green bell berries
A few reddening, tangy, more seed than pulp
The black ones easy on the tongue

(We called them our nightshade)
Soon the bush will stalk for birds

Yes, nothing prepared me
For this welling up of moistness in my backyard
For this soft hop of winter

BATHING DAY

Festive pilgrims like waterfowls
Meandering upslope
Shrilled our sunset

Birds we mistook
For fishermen's pegs
Flew like pins to a magnet

TIDE

The river left an arch
of our mud-walled-doughnut shrine

A jasmine sky
Hoods its single candle.

We had climbed
Swaying the lantern through cacti, stones

Smiting the soft weeds
Holding up the light for that last climber

Rushed past rows of nozzled pots
Palms full of incense ash.

Again it is the month of mourning
Our rain-oiled streets deserted

A few tea-shops opening for mourners
Boys with rose-bud garlands waiting

A black tide breaking

RISHMA DUNLOP

RISHMA DUNLOP (b.1956) was born in Poona, India, and grew up in Beaconsfield, Quebec. She is an award-winning poet, essayist, and translator. She is the author of five books of poetry: *Lover Through Departure: New and Selected Poems*, *White Album*, *Metropolis*, *Reading Like a Girl*, and *The Body of My Garden*. Publications as editor include *White Ink: Poems on Mothers and Motherhood,* and *Red Silk: An Anthology of South Asian Canadian Women Poets*. She has published in international anthologies and journals including *Blackbird*, *Louisiana Review*, *Literary Review of Canada*, *Canadian Literature*, *The Comstock Review*, *Descant*, *Event,* and *Grain*. Anthology appearances (among others) include *The Literary Review Indian Poetry* (New Jersey: Fairleigh Dickinson University) edited by Sudeep Sen. She won the Emily Dickinson Prize for Poetry and has been a finalist for the Chapters- Robertson Davies Prize for Fiction and the CBC Literary Prizes in Poetry and Non-Fiction. Dunlop was awarded the Canada-U.S. Fulbright Chair in Creative Writing at Arizona State University (2009–2010), and has also received grants from the Social Sciences and Humanities Council, Ontario Arts Council and Toronto Arts Council. Currently, she is a professor of English and Creative Writing at York University, Toronto.

TESTAMENT

In a city ruled by pigeons and doves, I see citizens moving mysteriously in the streets as if in a silent movie. I want to speak out to them but the world is deafened by the cries of birds, by the flap of wings. I imagine voices that taste of colors and flavors. I imagine describing these sounds to the deaf, a voice like vanilla, or orange, or a voice that smells like brandy. I count the birds in the square at City Hall as if some numerical sequence would be a code to explain the digits I have memorized: the phone numbers of the dead. Sometimes I dial those numbers, profess my love to anyone who picks up the receiver. Catalogue of memories in my hands, thickening in spiral notebooks. The city offers me a biography of rain, every vowel beating against its granite heart.

AUBADE

This morning I woke to blackbirds singing
a multitude waiting for me to bless.

This morning I wonder if St. Francis was right—
if Perfect Joy can only be found nailed to the Cross.

This morning I know the love we cling to—
and the constant fear we'll lose our grip

This morning, if I could preach to birds
I'd tell them— fly and kiss, lives depend on this.

SAUDADE

Waiting for you in the square in Lisbon—
the singer beckoned to me.
I followed her shadow along the stone walls
of the deserted abbey near the Tejo River.
As she sang *fado* I took my religion from the city
on a night when I was poured out like water.
Darling, how I loved you then— unflinching.
We slept holding each others' hands in the night
in Stevens' paradise of imperfections, hot with
flawed and stubborn sounds, replete with dreams
of miracles, cinematic—like the scene
in *The Godfather*—
the pulled seam of my feathered dress
releasing a flock of doves.

RADIO NEW MEXICO

Music from somewhere—
air violet over the mesa,
music leaking from the rental car,
drone of tires on the freeway,
some pain drenched country song
in the time lapse day/night/day…
hypnotic, hilarious—
we hover in the ticking car,
minds clear-sighted—for the little
there is to say—hum of the car,
the engine pull a dare—for the room
at the desert motel where
we ache to be taken all ways at once.

Now in our daughters' empty rooms,
the neural storms of their mother.
Our girls lie down with lovers
of their own.
each girl's face
my own.
I hear a trace
of their grandfather's lullabies
Soja, Raj Kumari, soja—
Sleep, Princess, sleep.

On the stereo the Stones' "Paint it Black,"
U2's *Rattle and Hum*,
The Band's last waltz, "Helpless Helpless."

But I listen for strains
of father singing
along to Punjabi and Hindi ghazals

or Roger Whittaker—
Moi j'ai quitté mon pays bleu—

as he slices oranges for me in the morning
as I fold the starched turban
he wears for work in laboratories.
And I see him walking away
down the front lawn's
path like a part
in hair,
humming
with Harry Belafonte:

I'm sad to say, I'm on my way
Won't be back for many a day
My heart is down, my head is turning around
I had to leave a little girl in Kingston town.

ROBIN S NGANGOM

ROBIN S NGANGOM (b. 1959) a bilingual poet who writes in English and Manipuri, was born in Imphal (the "forgotten theatre" of World War II), Manipur. He studied literature at Shillong's St. Edmund's College, and received an MA from the North-Eastern Hill University, where he currently teaches literature. His three books of poetry are: *Words and the Silence*, *Time's Crossroads*, and *The Desire of Roots.* His poems have appeared in magazines and journals like *The New Statesman*, *Verse*, *Planet: The Welsh Internationalist*, *Kavya Bharati*, and *Chandrabhaga*. Anthology appearances include *An Anthology of New Indian English Poetry* (Rupa), *Khasia in Gwalia* (Alun Books, Wales), *Confronting Love* (Penguin India), *Where the Sun Rises When Shadows Fall: The North-East* (OUP), *The Other Side of Terror: An Anthology of Writings on Terrorism in South Asia* (OUP), and *The Literary Review Indian Poetry* (New Jersey: Fairleigh Dickinson University) edited by Sudeep Sen. With Kynpham Sing Nongkynrih, he co-edited the *Anthology of Contemporary Poetry from the Northeast* (NEHU), and *Dancing Earth: An Anthology of Poetry from the Northeast* (Penguin).

HOUSES

after Cavafy

We believe we own them but
In the evening of a street not a soul will be found.
Only a few stars shuffling in the oily sky and
Orange trees for neighbours.
Here, they've lain huddled in December waiting
For Christmas to rock them on its pinewood floors
And in blue afternoons
You can see them drowsing in the barber sun.

Relentlessly, a dream has hemmed me in these hills
While the future has cast me as a bleak interpreter of signs.
And so many things to finish
That I did not pay any attention to their birth,
There were no labour pains,
And they have shut me off from their hearths.

AFTER 'JASHN-E-AZADI'

a film on Kashmir by Sanjay Kak

The kite transforming into smoke lacing
The *chinars* is not a symbol.
The rose has migrated from the garden of paradise.
Freedom will never come
Poured into goblets waiting to be raised,
Martyrdom is a handout from god the hagiographer.
Only poetry of ruins is real.
The incoherent rose still blooms
From some beloved breast torn open.

SEPTEMBER

after Zagajewski

Things get longer to finish now
even as the pen grows heavier.
Far from the glitterati, I read the daily
without assurance it will arrive each morning,
only the reliability of news-breaking power,
the glum predictability of miscarriage.
I see evening sinking,
cherry leaves sailing somewhere,
the same watchman appearing a little ashamed now
of lowering the nation's flag every twilight.
Birds become forgetful of their chatter
in the frail melody of rain
preparing to conduct the night.
I need a second opening to my shut life
allayed by little mercies
and you within touching distance.
I can hear a lone truck now
well past midnight
pondering at a speed breaker.
Not everything sleeps.

GHAZAL

Am I another you, and you, another I?
— MAHMOUD DARWISH

None waits for nightfall in these mountains
it's got past us and the lamps are misty-eyed.

I have a stale dream which no more bewitches,
it is this seasonal malady that mortifies.

It still hurts nonetheless to shut out the wind which didn't arrive
laden with her voice even at this hour after midnight.

Fearful about my fate as a victim of your indifference
I try to find resemblances of your character in miscellaneous pages.

I had promised I'll not raise the subject twice
even though you spent loveless nights with men.

Your lovers invaded every dominion of yours and left no spoils
I say it's priceless gazing into your eyes of dark honey.

Those who cannot fathom the irrationality of love
are doomed to assassinate our characters an entire lifetime.

When you demeaned yourself to embrace me today
I forsook the horrifying news of my native land.

O how I wish I could transform this unmanly weakness for you,
in love, sometimes, I feel our sexes changing.

Tomorrow's another day and I'm determined to expose you
all suspicions of you will vanish like dew in the flush of dawn.

Robin, when your eyes no more burn from her graven image
earth will be liberated from human taint in enlightenment.

MY INVENTED LAND

after Mario Meléndez

My native soil was created from tiny sparks
that clung to grandmother's earthen pot
which conjured savoury dishes
I've been looking for
all my life in vain.

My homeland has no boundaries.
At cockcrow one day it found itself
inside a country to its west,
(on rainy days it dreams looking east
when its seditionists fight to liberate it from truth.)

My people have disinterred their alphabet,
burnt down decrepit libraries
in a last puff of nationalism
even as a hairstyle of native women
have been allowed to become extinct.

My native place has not been christened yet
my homeland, a travelogue without end,
a plate that will always be greedy
(but got rice mixed with stones)

My home has young people
who found their dreams in a white substance
and the old that transplanted their eyes,
it has leaders who have disappeared
into their caricatures.

My home is a gun
pressed against both temples
a knock on a night that has not ended
a torch lit long after the theft
a sonnet about body counts
undoubtedly raped
definitely abandoned
in a "tryst with destiny".

RUKMINI BHAYA NAIR

RUKMINI BHAYA NAIR (b. 1952) was educated in Calcutta and then went on to receive a PhD from Cambridge University. Nair specializes in cognitive linguistics and critical theory, and her books in these areas include *Narrative Gravity*, *Technobrat*, and, *Lying on the Postcolonial Couch*. Winner of numerous awards and honours, she has published three collections of poetry: *The Hyoid Bone, The Ayodhya Cantos,* and *Yellow Hibiscus.* Anthology appearances (among others) include *Midnight's Grandchildren: Post Independence Poetry from India* (Macedonia: Struga Poetry Evenings), and *World Literature Today Writing from Modern India* (Norman: University of Oklahoma), both edited by Sudeep Sen. She is on the editorial boards of the *International Journal of Literary Semantics,* and *Biblio;* as well as the advisory panel of the Macmillan Essential Dictionary. Nair is professor of Linguistics and English at the Department of Humanities and Social Sciences, Indian Institute of Technology, New Delhi.

THREE

Blood in autumn
One single leaf
A variorum of grief

Colon: isation
When the gut spills
Onto a page of history

Muted, mutilated
Writing is speech made silent
The sound of one hand clapping

LOVE'S LANGUAGE LOST

She ***thinks***

She thinks that he ***knows***

She thinks that he knows that you ***believe***

She thinks that he knows that you believe that I ***feel***

She thinks that he knows that you believe that I feel that they ***imagine***

She thinks that he knows that you believe that I feel that they imagine that we ***sense***

She senses that he imagines that you feel that I believe that they ***think***

She imagines that he feels that you believe that they ***know***

She feels that he imagines that I ***believe***

She believes that he ***feels***

She ***imagines***

LOVE'S LANGUAGE LOST

SHATAKA
MOURNING THE MUMBAI MASSACRE

AUTHOR NOTE

Towards the end of 2008, I completed a book rather dramatically entitled *Poetry in a Time of Terror: Essays in the Postcolonial Preternatural* and handed it over with the usual – and usually unwarranted! – self-satisfied feeling to my publishers. I then settled down to work on an project I imagined was far less troubling: This was to try to read, in keeping with my obscure interests as an workday linguist, the work of the Sanskrit grammarian Bhartrhari. An extract from the Internet on this remote figure:

> Bhartrhari: (born 570?, Ujjain, Malwa, India—died 651?, Ujjain) Indian Hindu philosopher, poet, and grammarian.... *Vakyapadiya* is his major work on the philosophy of language. Also ascribed to him are three collections of poetry, each containing 100 verses: *Shrngara-shataka* (on love), *Niti-shataka* (on ethics and polity), and *Vairagya-shataka* (on dispassion). <www.servinghistory.com/topics/Bhartrhari>

What could be more innocuous than the enterprise of reading a sixth century poet-grammarian, one might have thought. But no sooner had I embarked on my quest, that events contrived to decisively knock me off my smug academic pedestal. For, between the nights of 26 and 29 November, 2008, India and the world witnessed scenes of terror more spectacular than any I'd discussed in my just-written book, forcing me to reconsider some of the theses I'd outlined there.

How, I now asked myself, could I ever explain to someone like Bhartrhari - who lived in an age before mobile phones, automatic weapons and RDX, not to mention academic women with spectacles perched on their noses earnestly typing away at luminous computer screens - what modern terrorism amounted to? In the process of this confused questioning, I discovered, too, that Bhartrhari was a near contemporary of the Prophet Muhammad, also born in the sixth century. How would these wise erudite figures from the past have conversed with each other? What thoughts on mankind's obsessive violence would they have exchanged? It was out of these counterfactual questions that my present, quite unanticipated inspiration, emerged. I wanted to write a collection of Bhartrhari-style 'shataka' (the word means 'one hundred') that attempted to convey to the sharpest of pre-modern minds some of the most intractable of the dilemmas confronting us in the fraught 21st century. Below, following introductory quotations from the Holy Koran and Bhartrhari's verse, are the first nine poems of this - not sonnet but shataka – sequence.

THE CALAMITY
In the name of Allah, the Beneficent, the Merciful

[101.1] The terrible calamity!
[101.2] What is the terrible calamity!
[101.3] And what will make you comprehend what the terrible calamity is?
[101.4] The day on which men shall be as scattered moths,
[101.5] And the mountains shall be as loosened wool.
[101.6] Then as for him whose measure of good deeds is heavy,
[101.7] He shall live a pleasant life.
[101.8] And as for him whose measure of good deeds is light,
[101.9] His abode shall be the abyss.
[101.10] And what will make you know what it is?
[101.11] A burning fire.
— from the *Holy Koran*, 6th CENTURY AD

In the name of Shiva, Dispeller of Darkness

Just as the great Mount Meru will be in the end destroyed by fire
And the oceans that shelter so many crocodiles will one day run dry
And the evidence is that earthquakes shake even this great earth
Held down by the weight of mountains
Can we really expect human life, waveringly delicate
As a baby elephant's earlobe, to survive?
— from the *Vairagya-shatakam* by Bhartrhari, circa 6th CENTURY AD

I. THE TERRIBLE CALAMITY

No invocation, this, but terror's end foretold…

Listen, Bhartrhari, let me be whorish frank with you – those fine
Sanskrit words of yours, *niti sringara vairagya* whatnot - they
Mean damn all when ten boys with guns come blasting through
No, not at pheasants, their brown, cocked heads drooping
And the bejewelled azure of the sky vanishing in a mini-second
From the round-bead droplets of their startled eyes, the feathers
A corona of tiny fireworks illuminating death at noonday
That bow-and-arrows murder would be bad enough but what we saw
After the world's recent burning, Bhartrhari, could your 6th century wit
Encompass? I think not, somehow. I think rain. I just *think rain*, desperate.

When a stranger walks into the rain-forest's glisten, should a madwoman follow?

Another thing, Bhartrhari, I'll have to keep this short, no more than
Ten lines per poem, because it's obvious I'm losing it. My saris hang
Unwashed, hair falls in my cold tea in clumps and nobody knocks *ever*
Which surely is not *vairagya* as you conceived it – that dignified walk
Into a forest glade, renouncing the world's sparkling medallions
Venison banquets, silken robes and that sudden tumescence when you spotted
The vermillion in her adulterous tresses, how could this ascetic role
Be mine? Who am I to mourn, to expiate, who has given up nothing, but
Whom everyone else has given up on entirely, which is not surprising –
My so-called poetry is such bilious trash. Here, judge for yourself!

I wore my clothes

as a woman should

— like a shroud

I combed my hair

as a woman should

— like a cloud

I spoke my words

as a woman should

— soft, not loud

But now I know

that a woman would

gain that world

She never could

if she did the things

she never should

And let those clouds

come down in rain

again, again, *again*...

and even if this stubborn type will not allow these slipslop lines
to dip and curl and blow away, o let me *think rain*
O damn those shoulds and muted coulds
let me think thunderstorms think hail
think words coursing down
think rain…

First, that's not a poem, you say, it's a dirge and second, it's ungrammatical

Ah, Bhartrhari, woe is me! You spot the glitch so blistering fast
I see you're not a grammarian for nothing – the verb 'think'
Can hardly take the object 'rain'. You can think that the world
Full of sorrow or a woman unclean when she monthly bleeds
Or that civilisation would fall apart without safety-pins and cello-tape
And blue-tack to hold it firm – but you can't *think rain* and pass it off
As poetry! Besides, if that was supposed to be some sort of sentimental
Tribute to *niti* just because some pinched, unfortunate creature
Spent her witless life following witless rules, forget it
That's not what *niti* means – anymore than you're a poet!

❧

My *point is, this is neither about poetry nor noble conduct – it's about tragedy*

We grieve, Bharthari, we grieve. So, do you think it matters one
Sodding bit to me what *niti* meant to you, whose fragrant kitchens
Served up mustard lentils and sweet cardamom milk but who could never
Imagine the taste of potato or chilly-hot tomato chutney because these
Items came to us via the warlike Portuguese ten centuries after
You were dust. *After,* that's the operative word! Let's face it, Brat –
May I call you that? Our tastes are different. You knew nothing of America,
Prozac, cement-mixers or Picasso's break-neck assaults on the human frame
Bollywood, now – what would you make of it or a rock-band called Atom-Bomb-
Pocket-Knife? O Bhartrhari, how would your *niti* handle Aamer Kasab?

❧

Anyway, like it or not, I am to tell you Kasab's tale – and of the sad 21st century
Why, you ask. You haven't even heard of this Aamer from God knows where
And you cannot stand my whining womanish verse, so why should *you*
Be the victim? It's a fair question, Bratislava, but ask yourself why
You wrote poetry, wrestled with grammar all your life, why you compared
The hidden lustre of a word to the peacock's egg, containing within it
The monsoon beauty of the *mayura's* dance and shaped
Like the starry universe without. You knew better than most the ache
To know, the urge to speak – anyone will do to talk to then – a mirror
A cat, a friend lurking in the lamplight, but the problem is: I can't bear
To look in the mirror, have no cat and no friends, so *who but you, Bhratrhari?*

❧

There was this terrible thing that happened and no one can figure out why
Kasab from Faridkot, now – he looks such a *baccha*, but there it is on TV
In the newspapers, on SMS, emblazoned on virtual screens in virtual skies
For all to see, the black disaster he caused. *Dis-astra* – bad stars, Bharthari
Read here the Latinate truth: On this night the stars fell into a fetid void
And great dragon-licks of flame and holocaust smoke assailed our sights
And we saw snaking down from a menacing cold, metallic pre-dawn sky
The cat-men we call the NSG, hardly ever visible in daylight but now our
Saviours - how chopper after droning chopper disgorged these cool, secret
Warriors and as they swung free from their huge hovering birds, flung
From their sleepy crannies a myriad tiny fleets of crows – uncannily displaced.

❧

When I mention the disturbance of the crows, you nod, thinking it a bad omen – but…
The rest seems barbarous Greek to you! O Bhartrhari, my guru, I sense
The logician's annoyance rising in you – as if it is Ujjaini's holy river pierced
By a million August spikes of rain and bleeding copious onto its banks
A caulked stag in the King's brutal hunt – and yet this same Ganga returns
Healed, each miraculous spring! It is immortal, men are not, that's
The pity of it, Bharati, as you say. *The silence of a river salves its wounds*
But the words of men destroy, they are a guide to foolishness, so how can I
Possibly explain to you my bludgeoning Anglo-Saxon words, my battering rams
Of acronyms - TV, NSG, SMS, WMDs and others still lurking perfidious
Behind an enemy arras, such as VIP and VOIP - oh innocent Polonius-Bharata…

❧

How can I ever transmit to you the unspeakable lexicon of my century?
Faridkot then – let's begin easy with Faridkot, although the odd
Thing is that they disown Aamir Kasab entirely there – but, being mortal
He has to come from somewhere – so let's say he comes from this small
Green village far from your own arid domain, the black stony soil of Malwa
Where only bajra and sorghum grew – *what, what did you say?* I didn't quite
Catch it. Oh, you're saying I've got things wrong! Do I mean *Sialkot*, not
Faridkot? You've not heard of this Aamer or of his obscure village
But Sialkot now – it was famous, almost as famous as your own Ujjaini
Sialkot stood where Menander ruled, rich Greek satrapy of second century
Outer limit of Alexander's great Bactrian state… But before that *rain*…

❧

SAMPURNA CHATTARJI

SAMPURNA CHATTARJI (b. 1970) is a poet, novelist and translator. She was born in Dessie, Ethiopia; grew up in Darjeeling; and graduated from Lady Shri Ram College in New Delhi. Sampurna's debut poetry collection, *Sight May Strike You Blind*, was published by the Sahitya Akademi (National Academy of Letters) in 2007 and reprinted in 2008. Her poetry has featured in Indian and international journals such as *Atlas, Wasafiri, nthposition, Stand Magazine, Drunken Boat, The Little Magazine, Chandrabhaga, Kritya, Talking Poetry, Dhauli Review, New Quest, Carapace* and *Wespennest*. Anthology appearances (among others) include *The Literary Review Indian Poetry* (New Jersey: Fairleigh Dickinson University) edited by Sudeep Sen. Her translation of Sukumar Ray's poetry and prose, *Abol Tabol: The Nonsense World of Sukumar Ray*, is now a Puffin Classic titled *Wordygurdyboom!*. She is also the author of several books for young people. Sampurna's second poetry collection is *Absent Muses* (Poetrywala, 2010). Her two novels are *Rupture* (2009) and *Land of the Well* (2012), both published by HarperCollins India. She lives in Mumbai.

GAME WITH THREE PAINTINGS

thank you, Georgia O'Keeffe

Black Iris is brooding
On her next step

Will she open to the lick of a tongue?
Or the probe of a look

That may enter
Deeper than she may desire?

Flower-girl, vulva-esque,
She wears a pearly iridescence

And still your eye is drawn
To the cleft below.

What's left to know
Is this: Black Iris is contemplating

"The universe through the portal of a bone"
Looking at the sky-blue blue through

The bone-white white of Pelvis II.
Could be the cross-section of the moon

For all you care about anatomy
Except that it hurts when you dislocate

A hip. This is the door Black Iris
Will slip through one day, soon

Simply for that picked-clean feeling
Of being a bone on a porcelain plate.

She is tired of all the fuss, of the fuzz that grows
In private places. She prefers for now

A world without flesh
Hanging like a Cow's Skull: on a post

She's ready, Black Iris is, to swap her pearls and purples
For the less enticing Red White and Blue.

NON SEQUITURS

A mailbox with a balloon
Means a baby has been born

In washrooms at gas stations
'Employees must wash hands'

This morning I ate madeleines
Waiting for Proust to happen

SO THIS IS SUNDAY IN SUBURBIA

Jethro Tull on iTunes
Shrubs hiding road
A white porch on which a woman in white shorts puts up her tin blond hair

Slate sky through slats
Burglar-proofed from weather
All doors shut windows sealed alarms on not even the slightest breeze can steal in

No one I know up and down the road
I hear nothing see no one
I could get used to living like this forgetting slowly the sound of my name

TRAVEL ADVISORY

Leave the city and learn to lose your way.
Be trustful of a guiding stranger on a motorbike,

Hat pulled hard over his eyes, hitting the rutted road
With the speed of one who is unafraid of accidents.

Remember everything, the bulrushes,
The underpass, the twisted morning.

Glen, marsh, landfill. Mustard flowers.
Through the cloud fields, the wreckage of a new town.

WOULD | NOT | NEED

If we saw each other every day, I would not need your teeth.
Would not need dream, catapult, would not need the alibi of a god.
Would not need ability to replay, second by second, the sequence
of a brushing kiss, an arm slowly unwrapping itself from around
my silent shoulders. Would not need remorse.

If we saw each other every other day, I would need new skin.
Would need the gut of a Trojan horse, the crystal of a cocktail stirrer,
the unnumbered periodic hope. Would need basalt, the shape
of a naked head, mouth open to the sky, breasts pointed to the wind,
the bump of belly and mound, a giant mountain in which you move.

SANDEEP PARMAR

SANDEEP PARMAR (b. 1979) was born in Nottingham and raised in Southern California. She received her PhD in English Literature from University College London in 2008. The subject of her research was the unpublished autobiographies of the modernist poet Mina Loy. She received an MA in Creative Writing (poetry) from the University of East Anglia and BA at the University of California, Los Angeles. She is the Reviews Editor for *The Wolf* magazine and edited the work of the modernist poet Hope Mirrlees. Mirrlees's *Collected Poems* was published by Carcanet Press in September 2011. Her poetry appears in the anthology of emerging British poets, *Voice Recognition: 21 Poets for the 21st Century* (eds. James Byrne & Clare Pollard). Her poetry has been published in various journals in the UK and the US, such as *The Wolf*, *Cimarron Review*, *The Manhattan Review*, *Stand* and *World Literature Today*. She has taught Literature and Creative Writing at the University of Hertfordshire, New York University, the Open University, Wagner College and the University of Cambridge. She is currently a Research Fellow at Clare Hall, Cambridge where she is writing a biography of Hope Mirrlees. Sandeep Parmar's first full collection of poems, *The Marble Orchard*, appeared from Shearsman in 2012.

INVOCATION

for James Byrne

A little bloodstained clockwork in a puddle of blood.
—PETER REDGROVE and PENELOPE SHUTTLE, *The Hermaphrodite Album*

To be of use, but nothing will decant. Perilous consonant, seized as jewel, betrothed as fire is to the ordinary. A spell; a note. Combatant of will and engraver of sighs. Poultice to the hush, to the whispers of women in corded rooms and to the glows beneath doorways. Purchaser of anointments, slatherer of knives and spoons. Rind of merciless ends and clothier of borrowed aliases. Trenchant penurist, hoarder of silvered lakes. Post chaise bending on the whim of royal deliverance. Coin to whom there is no weight to match the fruit of emptied forest. Animal to cistern, face to coda, god to neither me to neither them, to she. To whom one is infinitely married, and yet cannot be affixed. Enter. All that spills over from my able palm is you.

COUNSEL

for Anna Smaill

Looking to ward off danger, I browse the eighth floor of the Bobst Library
for some composite rite,
a wrist-length of red thread,
éblouissements to blind intervening shadows.

❦

It is good luck to dream of your wedding day,
to feed a cat from an old shoe (so long as the cat does not sneeze).
Do not marry a man born in the same month as you,
or eat while dressing. Tear your veil (at the altar by accident).
Wear earrings. Not pearls. Carry salt. Drink water.

Beware a woman carrying an empty bucket.
Turn away from the mothers of stillborn sons, monks, pigs and lizards.
Under no circumstances should you marry on a Tuesday. Or Thursday.
And once you start from home, don't dare to look back.

❦

How to coin the finest and most singular antidote—to dance against possible risk?
From PR6003.U64—the fair-weather lesbians of Dorothy Bussy's *Olivia*—
to the *Diary of Virginia Woolf: 1915–1919* [PR6045.072]
we plunge straight into Lily the 'simple-hearted' servant, her indiscretions.
A married Miss Stephen keeps schtum in her tremorous florals two sizes too big.

Zigzagging to PR4863.A33 *The Letters of Charles and Mary Lamb*:
'Your goose found her way into our larder with infinite discretion.
Judging by her Giblets which we have sacrificed first, she is a most sensible Bird.'
[C.L. to John Rickman, 30 December 1816]

At PR4231.A43: *Robert Browning and Elizabeth Barrett: the courtship correspondence*—
Nuances of love and outrage elongate a shortened life.
I drift towards one leaning oversize *Wandering of the Soul* [PJ1551.E3];

Egyptian Papyri transmuted into spells for safe passage in the afterlife.
'Do not stop to play draughts with the dead lest you be trapped for eternity.'

To the Brothers Grimm [PT921.K56]—
Three women turned into identical flowers in a field.
Only one returned home every night. At dawn she said to her husband:
'If you come this morning and pick me, I shall be set free and stay with you forever.'
Imperative chance. He chose correctly.

Dearest one, the riddle of marriage admits no luck.
What it recognises is pure—
it fires the dew from sleeping grasses.

Only know that he will not err (and nor will you) where love
has paused in an evening's silence to light the unlit road.

TANIWHA AT WHATIPU

'…I remember the bay that never was
And stand like stone and cannot turn away.'
— JAMES K BAXTER, 'The Bay'

Fiesome and button-gunny   the awed tailors
chew their needles   to see you borne out, weathering for beauty.

This is hard-earned sibilance.
The earthly mantle that comes with a hero's death.

The chorus mares its black singing.   From the shore
white-hearted celibates   line up like tall breakers

crown for the pearls you hang in each ear.
The moon as celebrant divides the remaining hours into loaves,

makes oaths of stone as women do.

THE WHITE SISTER

The white sister   tithes her purloined sainthoods
And orders her chalk menagerie into face supplanting face

They are   that is
umbilical favours   discoloured by debt   transposed onto
  your name
Family   to whom one is infinitely wived

Sea-house on a molten shore   where always
you age in half-life   live   as a child might

without dowry or brother   husband or defect   the sister

Floats farther into that silvered catacomb that avowed promontory
between daughter and daughter

AFTER LEE MILLER'S *EXPLODING HAND*

Baleful and proud, the vanity of all that is hers.
    The modern woman   a hand explodes
Do not touch that which is rumoured to prolonged suffering.
High-wire disembark   coolly suspicious she trades each paranoia
On the prelude of undoing.   The hand would be perfect if not
For the herald   poled to her fourth digit   abortive in its roundness.
Would it surprise you to know that on reaching the door she had thought
  to open it.

Mixing curatives, withed and wide-eyed
Knowing that only when the moment has come, has it passed.

DADA AT THE POMPIDOU

Wo ist Dada? Ist da, da, da. In Paris,
a child's hobbyhorse spins in the air,
lonely, amateurish,
extending its ego in autistic egressions.

Die Ausstellung—
Le moment à venir—

O Mother of the World,
you sit cross-legged with your mandolin
and a brown scarf tied about the chin.

Your noise invites coins;
the rain flecks oracles
into daring pronouncements.

At the entrance
under umbrellas, we listen to your Montenegrin fingers
bow strings as if you were grating nutmeg,

food of prophets.
The brasseries are *Vendredi*-ing,
our *cahiers* sigh at the sight.
In minutes we are all as black as you.

RINCONIA

'brackets imply a free space of imaginal adventure'
— ANNE CARSON, Introduction to *Fragments of Sappho*

Thought persists toward language

fledge-heeled harmonics glare and punctuate:

Fragment 87b

]anxiety
]ground

Fragment 87c

]
]daring

600 BC, a brave millisecond.

Mnemosyne cuts out her lashes from the same tree

that spokes the torture wheels of hell.

You blush redcurrant and descend as you must

Artillerist, barren woman

Turning, and then turning to again.

SHANTA ACHARYA

SHANTA ACHARYA (b. 1953) was born and educated in Orissa, India. In 1979, she won a scholarship to Oxford University where she completed her doctoral dissertation. From 1983 to 1985, she was a Visiting Scholar at Harvard University. In 1985, she moved to London where she has lived and worked ever since. Her doctoral study, *The Influence of Indian Thought on Ralph Waldo Emerson*, was published by The Edwin Mellen Press, USA, in 2001. Her five books of poetry are *Dreams That Spell The Light* (Arc Publications, 2010), *Shringara* (Shoestring Press, 2006), *Looking In, Looking Out* (Headland Publications, 2005), *Numbering Our Days' Illusions* (Rockingham Press, 1995), and *Not This, Not That* (Rupa & Co, 1994). Anthology appearances (among others) include *Wasafiri India South Asia & the Diaspora* (London: QMW University), and *The Literary Review Indian Poetry* (New Jersey: Fairleigh Dickinson University), both edited by Sudeep Sen. She is the Founder Director of 'Poetry in the House' at Lauderdale House, Highgate in London, where she has been hosting monthly international poetry readings since 1996. [www.shantaacharya.com]

LESS IS MORE

Less is more is more or less the case,
a true poet will swear by such a hypothesis;

Weed out adjectives, embrace
the energy of verbs, the wholesomeness

Of nouns. Even homeopathy teaches
the power of diluted doses;

More exercise, eating less
are paths to health and physical grace.

We do not need experts to tell us
the world's resources are scarce;

Or that if we consumed less
the earth might be a better place?

IMAGINE

The song of humpbacked whales –
sound air makes when you blow through conch shells –

Their uniquely decorated flukes fall on waves,
huge white flippers slapping the water.

Forests, canyons, rivers, waterfalls,
vast double rainbows that hold us in thrall.

Imagine a grizzly bear on its haunches
in the bend of the river scooping up silver slivers,
tossing minnows into its yawning mouth.

Blush of a bride in the sky at sun rise, sun set
spread in ever widening abandonment.

A smoking volcano blowing spectacular hoops
of fire, molten lava flowing for days,
depositing ash on the tray of land.

Imagine cloud formations of all configurations,
dove white to crow black, altocumulus to tornado chasers.

The smile of a camel filling the desert;
a cheetah in motion, dance of cobras coupling,

The sighing of leaves when the wind gives them a shake.
Hawks rising on tides of wind soaring on wild wings streamlined.

Imagine a colony of bats meditating upside down
on an ancient tree grown big like a grandparent –
branches, trunk, roots jostling together for space.

The beauty of a snow leopard living in recluse
at the feet of majestic Mount Everest.

Imagine the wings of a butterfly hovering;
their translucency in moonlight revealing…

Now open your eyes wide open and imagine
our rich world bereft of nature's blessing.

GRAFFITI

Graffiti on walls spout anger, ridicule, desperation,
the tower block is no Banksy exhibition
only reflects the foul mouth of a beast breathing poison.

Guerrilla art in public spaces do not transform lives.

On a hill nearby female, blue butterflies, *maculinea arion*,
lay their eggs on buds of thyme; young larvae born

Are nurtured by ants that carry them to underground nests
where the larvae feed on ant grubs, emerging as butterflies.

With such a vast intelligence in operation
human beings must fare no less by comparison?

NASA finds traces of amino acid in tail of comet.

Extra-terrestrial life may have evolved in space,
arriving on earth accidentally, the possibilities are immense –

We determine how far we wish to go, what horizons to scan,
but fail to conquer ourselves – our limitations.

The last time this young man saw the moonlight dance
in these streets, he witnessed his friend bleed to death.

A knife for a knife leaves every one wounded,
A gun for a gun leaves none alive to bear witness.

He told me it was his turn now. Turn for what? I asked.
How was I to know he'd been fatally injured
that it would take so long for help to arrive;

He'd be forced to make the ultimate sacrifice?
I couldn't pursue his attackers, thought only of saving him.

I sat here holding his hand as he lay dying.

SHARMILA VOORAKKARA

SHARMILA VOORAKKARA's (b. 1968) first full-length collection of poetry, *Fire Wheel*, was published by the University of Akron Press in 2005. She was awarded a Pushcart Prize for her poem 'The Eternal Immigrant' which first appeared in *Ninth Letter*. Her work has also appeared in *The Virginia Quarterly Review, Ploughshares, Prairie Schooner, Hayden's Ferry Review, The Cincinnati Review, Nightsun, The Carolina Quarterly,* and other journals. Anthology appearances (among others) include *The Literary Review Indian Poetry* (New Jersey: Fairleigh Dickinson University) edited by Sudeep Sen. A non-fiction essay, 'Fairy', appears in *The Normal School.*

PHOENIX

There's only just so much hustle and spit
you can give it, burning down one life to rise
to a new one. Like this, you live
life after life: rubble ruin rise, rubble ruin rise.

One day, you come to the last life,
too old broke crazy to go on.

You douse the place with gasoline,
you light the match yourself. You do up your hair
in the square of the mirror but
you don't budge from that burning down house.

COCA-COLA GOA

Here I learn you don't come to marry Holland woman then run antique business then own guest house in Goa by scrubbing toilets like the man from Varanasi told me he'd done. Oh no. You do not do that. Holland woman mummydaddy die — leave Holland woman ALL their money. No more scrubbing toilets. No more hustling tour groups in Varanasi. No more scrounging scorched-earth Afghanistan, shot-up Pakistan, prying gold and old idols from the hands of the dead. No more filthy middlemen, sliming and conniving. Get real. No one gets to anyplace by scrubbing toilets no-how, not in Goa not in Holland, not in America USofA. Holland woman mummydaddy die and bam! Guesthouse in Goa bought and paid for! Goodbye greasy middlemen, goodbye crooked procurers, goodbye Ganges tour groups, goodbye squat toilets; hello satellite TV, hello once-yearly ticket out of monsoon, hello Coca-Cola, hello!

TAMIL

1. SPAGHETTI WESTERN, NEW JERSEY

I talked bangbang and cowboy and gringo
growing up.
I hacked down a jungle
of a tongue from myself.

I burned its little mudhuts.
I pledged allegiance, practiced
a twang, not knowing what
that would mean. *Not your people*

became my people, and I drifted
all over the place.

2. PILGRIM

Tamil is a crumbling house
inside my mother's mouth:
her *Forgetting Words* turning to dust:
Amma, servant, long, oiled plaits,
dirt that feels beneath
her feet.

The *Forgetting Words* go up
like smoke; some fell to the floor
like thick, black curls.

1963: America America. Pilgrim,
bowed and bareheaded,
you enter.

3. THE WELL

Come live with me, said the well.
And my aunt did.

4. PENNY-CANDY ENGLISH

gone sticky in my hands:
Bazooka, rootbeer barrels, Sugar Daddy,

red hots, jawbreaker,
bubblegum cigar,

sugar-buzz English, also

Bensonhurst, Fort Greene, Red Hook.
Armand the Elevator Operator.
Shit-end, short straw, hot damn, and

Garden State, Black Horse Pike.
A.C.,
dumpster, Hare Krishna Hare Hare.

Waste you.

Roadhouse, gunning
your engine, going
noplace.

I been thisplacethatplace, every
place is one Big No Place.

5. TAMIL FOR BEGINNERS (LESSON ONE)
Fetch the fallen woman
from the well.

Servant's hard dark feet wading
snake- swirled waters.

6. HOW DO YOU SAY?
Language that looks like
knit purl knit purl
knot knot knot.

A Not Person.

I done left that world;
there's no going back.

SIDDHARTHA BOSE

SIDDHARTHA BOSE (b. 1979) is a poet, playwright, and performer based in London. Siddhartha's work has appeared internationally in magazines and anthologies including *Fulcrum* (USA), *The Literary Review* (USA), *City State: New London Poetry* (Penned in the Margins, UK), and *Voice Recognition: 21 Poets for the 21st Century* (Bloodaxe, UK). Siddhartha's debut collection of poems, *Kalagora*, appeared in 2010 (Penned in the Margins, UK). He has been featured on BBC World Service (TV), BBC Radio 3 and was included as one of the 'ten rising stars of British poetry' by *The Times*. He has performed at numerous festivals and venues including Latitude, Alchemy, DSC South Asian Literature Festival, New York University, Southbank Centre, Ronnie Scott's, and the Royal College of Art. Siddhartha has written, performed, and toured a one-man play, also entitled *Kalagora*, which was developed with funding from Arts Council England. After its sell-out premier at London's Rich Mix in October 2010, the play toured the UK and Berlin and completed a critically acclaimed run at Edinburgh Festival Fringe 2011. Siddhartha's follow-up theatre show, *London's Perverted Children*, will premier in July 2012 in London. Siddhartha is a Leverhulme Fellow in Drama at the University of London and is developing a play on migration and diaspora with WhyNotTheatre, Toronto.

Mamallapuram—

In rock,
God sleeps on a ten-head snake, black in iron.

Sighs, wakes, lifts in curls of smoke,
Rattles—

(apsaras drench the sky with laughs,
sadhus fling flowers —rosepetal, saffronstain, lilyweb—
from a cloud).

Manhattan—

A woman spread on 4th street.

Grain of sand in white hair,
Eyes blank, tear-swell,
As she hikes her skirt, nonchalant, to
Piss on the sidewalk—

Eaten by sirens,
Marched upon by clean, shined feet.

ARRANGED MARRIAGE

Outside—
Sexless infant,
Hacked violin voice,
Hands clutching
Strawberries and Chinese bowl
Wails for sky to crack—

Bits of cloud fall
Light as snowflakes, which
Glow the
Ash of cries in
Alley beside
Steaming railway station
Where labourers last night,
With dust brick shovel spade,
Dug out dreams of
Married couples, and boiled them on
Slow waspeaten fires.

Inside—
Hideous laughter
From television talk show—
Thick with sweat.

My fingers bleed with dread,
Dead with manic mosquitoes
Chewing bone-marrow of lung,
Divebombing.

Your hair wet with onions,
Your chin heavy with
Smell of burnt garlic—

The words you speak,
As you conduct concerto in
Cauldron of
Dead tasteless meat

Stream out your mouth
Like ants from peeling black

Hole in wall in
Shabby stale Goa room
I'd once slept in,

Dreaming of tea,
My
Bones
Sharp
As
Knives.

STILL LIFE: ARTICHOKE

Inside an art—
i—choke:
cave of mirrors,
creased petals,
vulva.

EPITHALAMIUM

for Anurag Jain and Hannah Wilson

I dream them in food—

Sautéed like onions in the scaped
Rock of east London. Oysters humid, pork chops bled,
Smell of cheese, dewy, sunburnt.

In this land of cloud, they met with
Stems of colour in their eyes,
Shafted in the wood of an ale house.

He drank the ribs of the sea from her
Eye, she sank in the fog of his cheer,
Pressed like bookpages, embered.

When they laugh as one, they
Wheel.

The play of child's face
Skims on the skin of their joy,
Lit as the green lizard of a
Match fired to sky.

What is said is bronzed—
Eyebrows plucked in iron,
Statues of words breathborn, stoned in
Relief.

Memoried in mist, he recalls the
Strength of a marble palace, etched in the
Bank of pond, graven in an emperor's wealth.

His head plattered, his heart rubied.

These stories grew in the
Country that swallows all others, from
Where he comes, he grows.

She speaks in suncoins, drifts in beauty,
Like woodsmoke, elmed.

In this opening of marriage door, they slip in
Eel, majestic. A garden grows in their
Palms of cup.

They circulate, spreading wonder in
breath of rain.

May you both dream in forms.
This world moves too fast. Take your time...

Let the corners of love
Shade you.

PORTRAIT, LITTLE LANE, CALCUTTA

Cricket on a
Small black and white radio
In a chai shop—

I buy cheap cigarettes,
Five for ten, filters ribbed in red,
Shake hands of oil,

(The owner has a broken
Black hole of tooth,
Swallowing flies,
Atoms of fogfilled winter air)

Noticing a minuscule merchant
On the spat-on sidewalk,
Legs crossed in a lotus,
Selling among other things—

A painting of a Royal Bengal tiger.

An etching of Krishna in wood.

A postcard picture of the
Sidney opera house.

She joyed me with striped shirts cause her father wore them,
my love in the afternoon. Blue and white stripe Calcutta—
enter her parlour shocked with revolving wooden chandelier
darting spots of light, dust in light.
She maps me in her web, spinning limbs.
—Give give, I'll do, she groans in that salt tone, as
she grips me of skin that bubbles in sores. Some like galaxies
sweat pus, not stars. Room is wet with rain that never comes.
Floor heaves under us, instinctive as nitrate.
A Tom Waits razor growl chops me up.
I lie on her single bed the clay of hash in my hair. Black and
wet like Kali, she plays the piston.
I am stung on a rack, flayed.
We go to a play by a temple, and as the blackyellow
cab turns to Ballygunge by the kebab shop with men wrapped
in loincloth cream as milk, who pass the day watching smoke
gather on tram tracks, we see two stray dogs doing what is
natural with an insistence that frightens, as we hike up our
reserve in a giddy laughter.
Not in London— dogs fucking, fleas on backs, stone as my
pocket of alley in the east end, which is home more or less
than home. Sometimes, on a late Saturday when the gods
crawl outta their holes, I see a man taking the piss by a bin,
and the smell, not the trickle—a branch of veins—reminds
me of where I'm from, and I glow like a lantern,
holy.

SMITA AGARWAL

SMITA AGARWAL (b. 1958) is the author of two collections of poems, *Wish-granting Words* (Ravi Dayal, New Delhi), 2002 and *Mofussil Notebook. Poems of Small Town India* (Cooperjal, London), 2011. Her poems have been published in magazines and anthologies such as *Literature Alive: New Writing from India and Britain* (British Council), *Nine Indian Women Poets* (OUP), *Verse: Indian Poetry Feature* (UK/USA), *Confronting Love* (Penguin, 2005), *Quote poet Unquote: Contemporary Quotations on Poets and Poetry* (Copper Canyon Press, USA, 2008), *Indian English Women Poets* (New Delhi, 2009), *Wasafiri: India South Asia & the Diaspora* (London: QMW University), *Midnight's Grandchildren: Post Independence Poetry from India* (Macedonia: Struga Poetry Evenings), and *The Literary Review: Indian Poetry* (New Jersey: Fairleigh Dickinson University), the last three edited by Sudeep Sen. Her critical articles have appeared in *Poetry Review* (UK) and *Journal of Commonwealth Literature* (UK). She is currently engaged in editing a collection of essays on Indian Poetry in English (Rodopi: The Netherlands). Smita is an editor for *Plath Profiles*, an online journal, (Indiana University). She is professor of English at the University of Allahabad, India. Her hobby is Indian music and her songs are available on 'www.beatofindia.com' and You Tube.

AFTER MEERA

Your eyes, what do they search in this pile of ash?
In this ash-pile, neither ember nor spark ....

No longer that love, nor its memory;
The heart set ablaze, nothing remains ....

This ash of devastation I have hoarded;
If you poke around, it may flare again ....

CICATRIX

Rhythm gone astray
I shall keep you.
Off rhyme that jarred
I shall remember you
As a fine line oscillating
Between desire and renunciation.
One cannot possess love.
Shall I preserve it in the
Juices of hate? And always,
After the symphony, recall
The *glissando* when finger
Slipped and the string
Cut through the skin?

MY BINDI

All said and done, at fifty,
dear bindi, you brighten up
the day …

Each morning, I've something
to look forward to in the mirror,
and a game to play …
Which one of you
shall I use today?

A full-stop of red
to keep the ardent lover at bay?
An asterisk of gold
for the one I wish to amuse?
The black exclamation mark
for those curious to learn
how I juggle
fidelity with occasional flings?

Mark of the Hindu; fashion-statement
ever since Madonna took to you;
symbol of wedlock or mere
facial embellishment, dumb bindi,
eloquent in your shapes …

My Morse code of dots and dashes,
bindi, that flashes
the one I wish to invite …

GHAZAL

Civil Lines, Allahabad

Driving through the crush almost every other day,
Why does it always feel like the first time, Civil Lines?

My granddad recalled a for-the-British-only, Civil Lines;
New money from the Saudi now owns most of Civil Lines.

The mom 'n' pop shops were once sprawling bungalows …
At every step, malls are the rage now in Civil Lines.

On the patio of the posh Big Bazaar, a beggar on his mat,
The small change glinting in the sun; high life with the low in Civil Lines.

Mr. Sanwal Das wouldn't hesitate in donning a *sari*, to help his female customer choose …
Uniformed twenty-year-old now point to self-service, in MacDonald's, in Civil Lines.

How long, Palace Theatre, before you succumb to avarice in Civil Lines?
Universal Book Depot, vivisected into four poky shops in Civil Lines.

An event in Mom's family, was an evening stroll down Albert Road to Guzder's for Tutti-frutti.
We, spaced out by the evening, simply call for home delivery from Hotstuff in Civil Lines.

SRIDALA SWAMI

SRIDALA SWAMI'S (b. 1971) poetry and fiction has appeared or is forthcoming in various journals including *Chandrabhaga, The Little Magazine, New Quest, Wasafiri, Pratilipi, Asian Cha, Desilit* and the Creative Writing Issue of *The South Asian Review* (28:3, 2007). Her work also features in *The Bloodaxe Book of Contemporary Indian Poets* (ed. Jeet Thayil, UK: Bloodaxe, 2008); in *Not A Muse,* Anthology (ed. Katie Rogers and Viki Holmes, Hong Kong: Haven Books, 2009) and in *First Proof: 4* (India: Penguin Books, 2009). Swami's first collection of poems, *A Reluctant Survivor* (India: Sahitya Akademi, 2007, rp 2008), was short-listed for The Shakti Bhatt First Book Award in 2008. She has written three books for very young children, which were published by Pratham in 2009. Swami recently had an exhibition of her photographs, titled *Posting the Light: Dispatches from Hamburg*, at Kalakriti Art Gallery, Hyderabad, in November 2009. She lives in Hyderabad, India.

PARAPHRASE

'The soul in paraphrase, heart in pilgrimage'
— GEORGE HERBERT

Say it now, say it again,
at least to yourself.
There must be so many ways to describe
what we are so afraid to name.

Demonstrate. Say it with
what speaks louder. Call me
with a touch and I will answer
with a shiver.

Exchange doubt
for faith. It is not as hard
as you think –
the two are inseparable.

I refuse to be stained
with the ink
of my failures
or of yours.

Find a way
to listen.
Can you hear it:

the soul in paraphrase,
the heart in transit,
the precise moment
when you and I become

tuning forks
making diagrams
of our merging selves?

RED CHILLIES

113° Fahrenheit on
the third day of May.
In Guntur,
every red chilli in the market
as if by concert
bursts
into sharp-tongued flames

and

the air breaks
into loud
applause.

CHROMATOGRAPHY

SOLVENT

Give sleep a chance and know while you do
that very little separates it from death. Rent
your language by the night. Pay your dues:

FILTER

plant your dreams and watch them grow. Consent
to their eventual departure and separate view
of you from where they stand. Discard resentment:

DIFFUSIONS

wear your vocabulary like a badge. Few
dreams can survive their naming. Fragments
of your days dissolve and separate into

SEPARATIONS

impossibilities. Try not to prevent
whatever happens. What happens is, you
will find, your days and nights are never congruent.

REVISIONS

Before the poet was a poet
nothing was reworked:

not the smudge of ink on twelve sets of clothes
not the fearsome top berth on the train
not a room full of boxes and dull windows
not the cat that left its kittens and afterbirth in a pair of jeans
not doubt.

Before the poet was a poet
everything had a place:

six years were six years parallel lines followed rules like obedient children
[the Dewey Decimal System]
homes remained where they'd been left.

Before the poet was a poet
many things went unseen:

clouds sometimes wheedled a ray out of the sun| parents kept photographs under their pillows| letters never said everything they wanted to| lectures were interrupted by a commotion of leaves | | every step was upon a blind spot.

SRIKANTH REDDY

SRIKANTH REDDY's (b. 1973) first collection of poetry, *Facts for Visitors*, received the Asian American Literary Award for Poetry in 2005. His work has appeared in numerous literary journals, including *American Poetry Review, Grand Street,* and *Ploughshares.* Anthology appearances (among others) include *The Literary Review Indian Poetry* (New Jersey: Fairleigh Dickinson University) edited by Sudeep Sen. A graduate of the Iowa Writers' Workshop and the doctoral program in English Literature at Harvard University, Reddy is currently an assistant professor at the University of Chicago.

'VOYAGER'

from a sequence of poems

He wrote formally in private.

Vote for a.

Make wings of straw.

Vote for the.

Everybody say *servant in the cross.*

Thanks be to the university research professor for diplomacy.

Diplomacy is a symbol of the living.

The war became a number.

To enter into the world write *home.*

Neutrality works.

East West North South.

One coin is the kingdom.

Develop proposals for the government of a country beyond ideology.

On a cold winter's day a pack of porcupines huddled close together seeking refuge from the frost.

Soon they had to move apart again as their quills struck home.

Need drew them together.

They found themselves repelled by stabs of pain.

Thus in his fable the philosopher describes an unending *rapprochement* between emotions and the need for peace.

Approach the pendulum.

In the final analysis reason has little to do with the real.

Some believe that the world is governed by economic forces.

Some that everything is a battle against darkness.

Good and evil bound the world. Exploitation and war are engendered by capitalism.

These perceptions must be adequately tested.

The framework of perceptions is deeply rooted in the psychology of peoples.

Unusual or strange perceptions tend to shape wisdom.

By contrast philosophy deals with establishing relations between different sympathies.

Say *objective world.*

He wanted to put an end to history.

The abstract is a way to make the visible divisible.

Human means *weakening vehicle.*

His countrymen have forgiven him his mistakes of course.

He considers evil in the world.

He has convinced himself that the devil is a number.

There is a school of thought that sees constraint as the basis of relations with other people.

Believe facts not myths.

Facts may be formally demonstrated by every citizen.

The book of *the* is taken apart and put together again with relation to *a.*

Over the centuries the oceans have remained unshattered.

The good interpreter shifts ever on.

Lie in the machinery.

Peace. Peace.

One.

The sovereign subject thinking of time reasons accordingly.

One. One. Two. One.

Constraint fathers compulsion.

Do the dead work beyond sense?

Say *creature* into the mirror.

In the mirror is a blueprint of creation.

Regard the world as it appears on both sides.

Peace. Peace.

The world would be the worse for its disappearance.

Brush in the deep sea bed.

Space is attention to the field of concepts.

But is the sea crafted by the will to believe?

The enlightened believe.

They live together in a village in history.

Seven. Six. Five.

Making contains provisions relating to the tenure of fact itself.

The flames continued until a world appeared.

SRILATA K

SRILATA K (b. 1968) is a poet, fiction writer, and translator. She is Associate Professor of English at the Department of Humanities and Social Sciences at the Indian Institute of Technology in Madras. Her debut novel *Table for Four* was long-listed recently for the Man Asian literary prize and was published by Penguin India in 2011. Her books include *The Other Half of the Coconut: Women Writing Self-Respect History* (Zubaan/Kali for Women, 2003), *Short Fiction from South India* (co-edited with Subashree Krishnaswamy; New Delhi: OUP, 2007), *The Rapids of a Great River: The Penguin Book of Tamil Poetry* (co-edited with Lakshmi Holmstrom and Subashree Krishnaswamy; New Delhi: Viking, 2009) and an anthology of poetry titled *Seablue Child* (Brown Critique, Kolkata, 2000). Her poems have won various awards and have been featured in several anthologies and magazines. Srilata K was a Charles Wallace writer-in-residence at the University of Stirling, Scotland (2010). She was also a Sangam House writer-in-residence in Pondicherry.

FOR JEANNE MUKUNINWA[1]

This, my friend, is the question I have:
Just what can you bake into a poem?
Sky blue skies, bouncy clouds of cotton, vanilla milk-shake moons,
red-bottomed robins and other creatures with wings
that visit you on mornings choked with the emptiness of work,
and lines from forgotten sources;
the sea rising in a whisper of piano notes…
these things and others
are easy.
Their batter flows freely
into the moulds of lyrics, sonnets and free verse.
But what of Jeanne Mukuninwa
who slid off sky blue skies and clouds of cotton and milk-shake moons
when she was raped over and over
by soldiers
till inside her fistulas erupted,
till she stopped noticing red-bottomed robins and other creatures with wings,
stopped wishing for seas rising in whispers of piano notes?
There must be a way, surely,
of baking fistulas into a poem?
Of gathering body wastes
and pouring them into moulds newly created
so other worlds can rise?

[1] Congolese war-crime victim

GOMATI

No need to get up, madam,
says Gomati with a smile
that is a hula hoop twirl,
as she swishes her mermaid mop
past my feet.

A drudgery of four houses fold into her days.
Mine is her third and the fourth is —
"a small house where there's just vessels and not much work,
madam".

Gomati isn't in this for roses
and yet, in her wake, wild flowers blossom
and every living creature lives a little more.

Inside her
lies
the delicious yolk of an egg
you will never have the heart to eat.

WHAT FATHER LEFT US

Father left us when we were children,
betraying our innocence
which, mother claimed,
trickled down our faces
like milk.
He left us each other -
two brothers and three sisters,
like so many Russian dolls,
our giggly yearnings
for rough play and stubble,
and blank spaces in five report cards
requesting “Father’s Signature”.
And then of course father left us mother,
with her soft saree
and taken for granted lap,
her voice cracking half-way through
that bed-time story about Ram and his monogamy.

Father left us a couple of unpaid debts
and this vacuum in my children’s lives
marked maternal grandfather.

SUBHASHINI KALIGOTLA

SUBHASHINI KALIGOTLA (b. 1969) grew up in India, the Middle East and the United States. She trained in electrical engineering and gave up a decade-long career in the telecommunications industry to pursue an MFA. A graduate of Columbia University's MFA program in poetry and a 2006–07 Fulbright fellow to India for literary translation, her poems have appeared in such journals as *The Collagist, Catamaran, Crab Orchard Review, New England Review*, and *Western Humanities Review*. Anthology appearances *(among others) include The Bloodaxe Book of Contemporary Indian Poets* and *Indivisible: An Anthology of Contemporary South Asian American Poetry*. At present, she is a PhD candidate in South Asian art at Columbia University.

VESSANTARA

First to go was the talisman—
The elephant who carried rain clouds.

Then brocades and bolsters and millefleur carpets.
Next the girl and boy who served cocktails and zinnias.

After the woman nothing was left. Though still to go: sounds
Overheard through shuttered windows. When his voice grew strange

Like vowels in another language, he reclaimed her: a pitch,
In the mewl of a hinge, and lost that too—body, voice, the keening.

MORNING IN A CITY

after Edward Hopper

Not beautiful, a species
        of beautiful perhaps, composed
of well-made parts, but not
        beautiful; Not erotic either
or arousing:
        There's no quiver, no thrum
in the groin, no blood-rush,
        though the picture
has all the makings
        of desire:
part pinup, part porn,
        part girlie show;
Femme fatale
        with none of the flourishes:
quietly upright,
        white terry cloth towel
raised to her chest,
        in profile,
far from the room's blue
        enclosure, yet standing stolid
by the window.
        The city resuming its business
beneath her.

She doesn't answer the gaze
        from a sumptuous bed, no pillows
plumped behind her, servant
        and feline in attendance, a slipper
dangled provocatively,
        out of pique;
There is no invitation here, no transaction
        to be entered into.
For the bed is abandoned.
        For the room's cool light,
the bed's narrow proportions
        are too small

for the kind of desire she feels,
        for the ambitions she savors
before taking off her hat,
        folding her dress, and letting it rest
for the night
        on the back of the chair.

REFUSING RÂMA

Mother gave birth to a crop
of root vegetables. Like a clay pot
she swelled, leaking me

to him who tilled the land
with blood and everything of mine.

Mother, quick, sow me back—
My husband is calling.

MONOLOGUE

When the idealism goes and the resignation sets in, when ambition makes you snicker and drive becomes a dirty word, when you understand apathy and practice it wholeheartedly, when you want to represent all the deadly sins, starting with sloth, when you feel betrayed by love, of every type, when all the things you have aspired for sound fatuous, it's time to play. It's time to occupy that barstool in the East Village and go home with the first guy who offers. It's time to throw the condoms away. It's time to start eating meat and littering the streets, it's time to cause an oil spill and wrap yourself in seal. It's time to burn all books, especially poetry. It's time to stop saying no, and just say yes. Yes, yes, and yes to ménages, à trois, à quatre or quatorze, what does it matter. You're done for anyway. It's time to burn fossil fuels and expand the hole; it's time to melt icebergs and sink a few villages; it's time to kill. Because whether the world is going to hell or not, you certainly are.

I think I've inherited my mother's
aversion for the *mot juste*. Why say

"pregnant" when "expecting" or "carrying"
will do just as well, and bloodlessly?

Even speaking Telugu she shifts
to English and back to forego the word.

One afternoon when I was twelve
I stole to the kitchen, careful to avoid

my brother: his incomprehension
of taboo and disregard for circumlocution.

I'm dying, I'm dying, like the Uncle
whose duodenal ulcer had burst,

the one the Doctor and Daddy couldn't
save with litres and litres of blood.

She was not alarmed, my mother.
"Here, put this in your panties," she said

handing me a plump, plastic packet, and
sending me back to my books without

a word, a name, not even a stand-in
for the body's change. Why words? What lies

in them? "Bed" is not the physical thing
of spokes and springs, not even a picture of it.

Lips meet, throat hums, tongue touches tooth,
then a final breath—thrice removed from truth.

SUDEEP SEN

SUDEEP SEN (b. 1964) [www.sudeepsen.net] read English Literature at the University of Delhi and as an Inlaks Scholar received an MS from the Journalism School at Columbia University (New York). He was international writer-in-residence at the Scottish Poetry Library (Edinburgh) and visiting scholar at Harvard University. Sen's many books include *The Lunar Visitations*, *New York Times*, *Dali's Twisted Hands*, *Postmarked India: New & Selected Poems* (HarperCollins), *Distracted Geographies*, *Prayer Flag, Rain*, *Aria* (A.K. Ramanujan Translation Award), *Ladakh* and *Letters of Glass: New and Selected Poems | Translations 1977–2012*, and *Blue Nude* (Jorge Zalamea International Poetry Prize). He has also edited several important anthologies, including *The HarperCollins Book of English Poetry*, and *Midnight's Grandchildren: Post-Independence English Poetry from India*. His poems, translated into twenty-five languages, have featured in major international and national anthologies. His words have appeared in the *Times Literary Supplement*, *Newsweek*, *Guardian*, *Observer*, *Independent*, *Telegraph*, *London Magazine*, *Poetry Review*, *Literary Review*, *Harvard Review*, *Hindu*, *Hindustan Times*, *Times of India*, *Outlook*, *India Today*, and broadcast on BBC, PBS, CNN IBN, NDTV & AIR. Sen's newer work appears in *New Writing 15* (Granta), *Language for a New Century* (Norton), *Leela* (Collins), *Indian Love Poems* (Knopf/Random House/Everyman), *Out of Bounds* (Bloodaxe) and *New Oxford Writing* (Blackwell). He is the editorial director of AARK ARTS and the editor of *Atlas*. [www.atlasaarkarts.net]

MEDITERRANEAN

1

A bright red boat
Yellow capsicums

Blue fishing nets
Ochre fort walls

2

Sahar's silk blouse
gold and sheer

Her dark black
kohl-lined lashes

3

A street child's
brown fists

holding the rainbow
in his small grasp

4

My lost memory
white and frozen

now melts colour
ready to refract

BANYAN

for Jane Draycott

As winter secrets
melt

with the purple
sun,

what is revealed
is electric —

notes tune
unknown scales,

syntax alters
tongues,

terracotta melts
white,

banyan ribbons
into armatures

as branch-roots
twist, meeting

soil in a circle.
Circuits

glazed
under cloth

carry
alphabets

for a calligrapher's
nib

italicised
in invisible ink,

letters never
posted,

cartographer's
map, uncharted —

as phrases fold
so do veils.

DESIRE

Under the soft translucent linen,
the ridges around your nipples

harden at the thought of my tongue.
You — lying inverted like the letter 'c' —

arch yourself deliberately
wanting the warm press of my lips,

it's wet to coat the skin
that is bristling, burning,

breaking into sweats of desire —
sweet juices of imagination.

But in fact, I haven't even touched
you. At least, not yet.

BHARATANATYAM DANCER

for Leela Samson

Spaces in the electric air divide themselves
in circular rhythms, as the slender
grace of your arms and bell-tied ankles
describe a geometric topography, real, cosmic,
one that once reverberated continually in
a prescribed courtyard of an ancient temple

in South India. As your eyelids flit and flirt, and
match the subtle *abhinaya* in a flutter
of eye-lashes, the pupils create an
unusual focus, a sight only ciliary muscles
blessed and cloaked in celestial *kaajal*
could possibly enact.

The raw brightness of *kanjeevaram* silk, of
your breath, and the nobility of antique silver
adorns you and your dance, reminding us of
the treasure chest that is only
half-exposed, disclosed just enough, barely —
for art in its purest form never reveals all.

Even after the arc-lights have long faded,
the audience, now invisible, have stayed over.
Here, I can still see your pirouettes, frozen
as time-lapse exposures, feel
the murmuring shadow of an accompanist's
intricate *raag* in this theatre of darkness,

a darkness where oblique memories of my
quiet Kalakshetra days filter,
matching your very own of another time,
where darkness itself is sleeping light,
light that merges, reshapes, and ignites,
dancing delicately in the half-light.

But it is this sacred darkness that endures,
melting light with desire, desire that simmers
and sparks the radiance of your
quiet femininity, as the female dancer
now illuminates everything visible: clear,
poetic, passionate, and ice-pure.

NOTE: The line-end rhyme-scheme —
a b a c c a ... d b d e e d ... f b f g g f ...
— maps and mirrors the actual classical dance
step-pattern and beat — *ta dhin ta thaye thaye ta.*
Left-hand margin indentations match the
same scheme and form.

KARGIL

Ten years on, I came searching for
war signs of the past
expecting remnants — magazine debris,
unexploded shells,
shrapnel
that mark bomb wounds.

I came looking for
ghosts —
people past, skeletons charred,
abandoned
brick-wood-cement
that once housed them.

I could only find whispers —
whispers among the clamour
of a small town outpost
in full throttle —
everyday chores
sketching outward signs
of normality and life.

In that bustle
I spot war-lines of a decade ago,
though the storylines
are kept buried, wrapped
in old newsprint.

There is order amid uneasiness —
the muezzin's cry,
the monk's chant —
baritones
merging in their separateness.

At the bus station
black coughs of exhaust
smoke-screens everything.
The roads meet
and after the crossroad ritual
diverge,

skating along the undotted lines
                    of control.
A porous garland
          with cracked beads
adorns Tiger Hill.
          Beyond the mountains
                    are dark memories,
and beyond them
          no one knows,
                              and beyond them
no one wants to know.

Even the flight of birds
                    that wing over their crests
don't know which feathers to down.
     Chameleon-like
they fly, tracing perfect parabolas.

I look up
     and calculate their exact arc
and find instead,   a flawed theorem.

CHOICE

drawing a breath between each
sentence, trailing closely every word.
— JAMES HOCH, 'Draft' in *Miscreants*

1.

some things, I knew,
were beyond choosing:

didu — grandmother — wilting
under cancer's terminal care.

mama — my uncle's — mysterious disappearance —
ventilator vibrating, severed
silently, in the hospital's unkempt dark.

an old friend's biting silence — unexplained —
promised loyalties melting for profit
abandoning long familial presences of trust.

devi's jealous heart misreading emails
hacked carefully under cover,
her fingernails ripping
unformed poems, bloodied, scarred —
my diary pages weeping wordlessly —
my children aborted, my poetry breathless forever.

2.

these are acts that enact themselves, regardless —
helpless, as I am,
torn asunder permanently, drugged, numbed.

strange love, this is —
a salving: what medics and nurses do.

i live buddha-like, unblinking, a painted vacant smile —
one that stores pain and painlessness —
someone else's nirvana thrust upon me.

some things I once believed in
are *beyond* my *choosing* —
choosing is a choice unavailable to me.

A BLANK LETTER

An envelope arrives unannounced from overseas
containing stark white sheets,

perfect in their presentation of absence.
Only a bold logo on top

revealed its origin, but absolutely nothing else.
I examined the sheets,

peered through their grains —
heavy cotton-laid striations —

concealing text, *in white ink*, postmarked India.
Even the watermark's translucence

made the script's invisibility transparent.
Buried among the involute contours, lay sheets

of sophisticated pulp, paper containing
scattered metaphors — uncoded, unadorned,

untouched — virgin lines that spill, populate
and circulate to keep alive its breathings.

Corpuscles of a very different kind —
hieroglyphics, unsolved, but crystal-clear.

WINTER

Couched on crimson cushions,
  pink bleeds gold

and red spills into one's heart.
  Broad leather keeps time,

calibrating different hours
  in different zones

unaware of the grammar
  that makes sense.

Only random woofs and snores
  of two distant dogs

on a very cold night
  clears fog that is unresolved.

New plants wait for new heat —
  to grow, to mature.

An old cane recliner contains
  poetry for peace — woven

text keeping comfort in place.
  But it is the impatience of want

that keeps equations unsolved.
  Heavy, translucent, vaporous,

split red by mother tongues —
  winter's breath is pink.

VARIATIONS ON WAKA: STILLS FROM SANSKRITI

1. TRIPTYCH

three haiku

STAR GLASS

tiny-star-flecked grass —
scattered mirrors cut-pasted
to reflect the sky —

LEAF ON WATER

slate-edged lotus pond —
mosaic-leaves fanning water
blooms, refract white light —

ARCH

red sandstone arches —
gateway to beyond, through which
everything passes —

NOTE: This poem-sequence using the classical Japanese waka-form was initially written as a site-specific piece of creative work mapping the geographical terrain of Mr O P Jain's Sanskriti Foundation on the outskirts of Delhi. The overall production includes collaborative work by British artists — Jenny Lewis and Frances Kiernan — involving innovative theatre, composed original music, art, collographs, book sculpture, experimental photography, digital video projection, and performance.

MUSTARD
tanka

mustard blooms swaying
under the sharp winter sun —
shed pollen — yellow

rain. banyan tree hides butter
cups for Krishna — Radha waits.

BARAHKHAMBA
haiku

a lone teak rises
in the square of 'twelve pillars' —
uncapped, free-spirit

3. QUARTET

four katauta

CENTRE

the wild beds around
Barahkhamba and Banyan —
flowers for your room centre

GAON

in Gaon's courtyard,
a *tulsi* sapling — in the
village centre, sacred tree —

IRIS

red-eye and iris
focus, sight locking axis —
diagonals dove-tail light —

SHAPE

silhouette, a form —
artist alone centre stage
poet alone studio space

4. TRIPTYCH

AMALTAS
choka

broken pillars lie
defeated, scattered around

aimlessly in mud —
different lengths retelling

different stories.
huddled in a heap amid

a weathered concrete
grave, Amaltas germinates
bringing life to the ruins.

HAVELI
bussokusekika

yellow jasmine floats
on still water — an *urli.*
a Buddha-like head
disengaged from its body
sits patiently at tree's feet —
petals, grass, path, haveli.

INSTALLATION
sedoka

seven marble slates
large, rectangular, cut white —
leaning as three triangles
anchored tight, live-earthed —
another on top, like a
table-top, lifeless, brooding —

SUDESH MISHRA

SUDESH MISHRA (b. 1962) is a descendant of Indian indentured workers in Fiji. He was born in Suva, and educated in Fiji and Australia. He has taught at various universities in Australia, Fiji and Britain. He is the author of four books of poetry: *Rahu, Memoirs of a Reluctant Traveller, Tandava,* and *Diaspora and the Difficult Art of Dying*; a couple of critical monographs, *Preparing Faces: Modernism and Indian Poetry in English* and *Diaspora Criticism*; two plays *Ferringhi* and *The International Dateline*; and several short stories. He is also (with Seona Smiles) the editor of *Trapped,* an anthology of writing from Fiji. He has contributed articles to *Social Text, Subaltern Studies X, Meanjin, Journal of Postcolonial Writing, Borderlands, New Literary History,* and *Emergences.* Anthology appearances (among others) include *Twelve Modern Young Indian Poets* (Edinburgh: Lines Review), and *The Literary Review Indian Poetry* (New Jersey: Fairleigh Dickinson University), all edited by Sudeep Sen. Sudesh Mishra is presently professor of Literature, Languages and Linguistics at the University of the South Pacific, Fiji.

RED BUTTON

take time out
to watch the sun go down
on an evening
not like a coin
slid nonchalantly
into a pocket
but like a button
come off
a favorite shirt
and found
implausibly
on the windowsill
the very next day

HANUMAN

when pressed
for proof of his allegiance,
the langur
tore into his breast
as if tearing
into a despised fruit
and drew aside
burst ribs and ligaments
that his lord
might see an example
of what he lacked.

MUSTARD SEEDS

O
bottled
droppings
of a sly grammarian
without your blessing
this verse
(spare as it is)
must outshoot
the point of itself…

X

In her eyes a sky so intense
It presages storm
Which, when it breaks,
Breaks fabulously
In a chiasma of wings
Before crossing over
To flock in her lover's iris.

AN EPICURE

no allusions,
the sea needs no allusions.
it lives in itself
like the cockle and the clam
and needs no metaphor
to impearl it.
but here comes the poet
with his swag
of tokens and tropes
which he rams down her throat
whereupon
like a fine diner
she turns green as gangrene
and throws up.

lines conceived
in the cool
of innuendos,
in the heat
of non sequiturs

may be likened to
a gust of sparrows
inside a red guitar

TRIMURTI

to master
(through all the mist
and miasma)
a being
tumultuous as the word itself,
the sufi must see only 3
of the 222 swans
tacking across the bay
a minute
into foreshadowing
while blinding himself
to the after-
shadow
of boobs and buttocks.

SUJATA BHATT

SUJATA BHATT (b. 1956) was born in Ahmedabad. She grew up in Pune and in the United States. She received her MFA from the Writers' Workshop at the University of Iowa. She has published seven collections of poetry with Carcanet Press, UK. She received the Commonwealth Poetry Prize (Asia) and the Alice Hunt Bartlett Award for her first collection, *Brunizem* (1988). Subsequent collections include *Monkey Shadows* (PBS recommendation, 1991), *The Stinking Rose* (short-listed for the Forward Poetry Prize, 1995), *Point No Point* (1997), *Augatora* (PBS recommendation, 2000), *A Colour for Solitude* (2002), and *Pure Lizard* (short-listed for the Forward Poetry Prize, 2008). She received a Cholmondeley Award in 1991, the Italian Tratti Poetry Prize in 2000, and the German Literature Prize, *Das neue Buch*, in 2008. Sujata Bhatt's work has been widely anthologized, broadcast on radio and television, and has been translated into more than twenty languages. She lives in Germany with her family.

GREGOR'S SISTER SPEAKS

Gregor, dear brother,
why didn't you think of wings?

Why didn't you turn into a butterfly instead?

I would have joined you, and mother and father too—
if only you had told us how.

We could have all grown huge orange wings,
you could have added tiger stripes
to be different—

We could have made the sky
orange and gold with black tiger lines
brushing against the clouds.

We could have inspired lilies to grow as tall as trees—

And the neighbours would have called us the new angels—

We could have flown far away
migrating to India or Costa Rica—

We could have escaped our fate,
our ordinary deaths—
truly escaped what History expected from us.

A WORD SPOKEN ON LAND

A word spoken on land
    is worth nothing at sea—

It's a meaningless, dangerous sound,
    he's told.

So the sailor turns mute
    as the ship sails south—

Then, in a new land he has never seen,
    he watches butterflies;
catches two of them to bring back
    to his treeless island—

Little nymphs he won't set free.

"What shall I name you?"
    He asks—

"What shall I name you?"

OBLIQUE

Oblique, gentle—
a fluttering near your peripheral vision—

First, she powdered her eyelids
until they shimmered like butterflies—

Butterflies in the sun,
early in the morning.

The story you tell defines you—

Will you add lilacs, will there be butterflies?

How many birds will be allowed
to interrupt your voice?

Will the butterflies be white or blue,
orange or yellow?

Plain white, or just orange and ordinary?

Can a butterfly be ordinary?

The story you tell defines you—
Will there be butterflies?

And if there are butterflies,
who will be the first to see them?

TRUTH IS MUTE

Truth is mute, she says,
but you need words to find it.

A bull's head in water, a mermaid's split tail—
centuries in silt, and the words that came down to us:
a blue spell of longing, now translucent on paper.

Is *filigrane* the sound you want
or is it *watermark*?

How many dictionaries
do you need for the words you seek?

Remember, she says,
instinct is wordless
even as it lives within words.

Remember, she says,
love will be silent with love.

Mother tongue, father tongue—
when the child started to speak
she used all her words at once,
at once in a rush: *pani*, *water*, *Wasser*.
When the child started to speak
she meant *fish* and *Fisch*.

How many languages must you learn
before you can understand your own?

When she lived on a mountain
amongst people whose language
she did not know, her own language turned
into a festival of fruits, and a festival of birds.

When she lived on a mountain
oxygen-deprived, near ice-covered rocks,
she only dreamed of the sea
night after night— algae and seaweed.

Will oxygen determine the meaning of your words?

Remember, she says,
love will be silent with salt.

Remember, she says,
truth is mute, and love will be silent.

ALWAYS CHOOSE THE JACK OF HEARTS

Always choose the jack of hearts, my friend.

The king is blind, the queen is cold,
and the ace is full of lies.

But the jack of hearts
knows the way.

The jack of hearts can speak
with worm-light
and crushed butterflies.

Does your soul have chromosomes too?

And a few broken cells?

What colour? What colour?

You'll never know.

Can your soul really be
a butterfly?

SUMMI KAIPA

SUMMI KAIPA (b. 1975) received her MFA in Poetry from the Iowa Writers' Workshop. She has authored three chapbooks: *The Epics* (Leroy Press), *I Beg You Be Still* (Belladonna), and *The Language Parable* (Corollary Press). Anthology appearances (among others) include *The Literary Review Indian Poetry* (New Jersey: Fairleigh Dickinson University), and *World Literature Today: Writing from Modern India* (Norman: University of Oklahoma), both edited by Sudeep Sen. Kaipa was the recipient of the Holmes Award from *Fourteen Hills Review* and the Potrero Nuevo Fund Prize in 2002 for her first play. *Interlope*, a magazine devoted to innovative writing by Asian Americans, was founded and edited by Kaipa from 1998 to 2003. She is a co-editor of *Indivisible,* the first anthology of South Asian American poetry (University of Arkansas Press, 2010), and is also working on her first full-length collection of poems. She lives in Oakland, California.

the slip underneath my dress her valedictory address is showing the future for the overeducated english major is living in a flop house buying chips and beer on your father's gas card until he cuts you off folding perfect t-shirts in a go-nowhere retail job documenting the apathy and fear of your friends as they roll in and out of bed with a long list of anonymous lovers terrified they might die of aids i was going to class forgetting class watching my roommate a korean baptist who covered a hole in the wall next to her bed with a poster of jesus fall messily in love the fiddlestick of hedonism unfurled for the both of us i reeked of clove cigarettes of the transient thrill of breaking up with your first love before he beats you to it everything was excess rip it out damn it get rid of it damn it courtney love ditched her dress stripped to the underslip so the boys fueled by cisco and testosterone launched the furniture out of the seventh floor window we were one part teen spirit one part american spirits in my pocket everyone was smoking themselves silly i was getting hard i was getting soft my mouth burned like a stranger to my mother's food i grew a sailor's tongue salty and swollen a thriving and invasive new colony of individualism and irony while the language of childhood atrophied the untranslatable bits faded into a was-i-ever-there home movie could i explain this newly discovered tragi-romance walt whitman singing heartily of himself henry rollins lunging and thrusting into his robust quads body surfing the mosh pit trusting the hands that buoy you until you fall nikki giovanni talking black arts black revolution litwack quoting public enemy don't don't don't believe the hype clutching foucault to my chest deconstructing everything to smithereens the naked man in a loin cloth imagined feathers in his hair like a statue of quetzalcoatl if you look closely you'll see everything in my bloodshot eyes

QURBANI

"Hi, Lollipop!" catcalls the horny matron. As Firoz Khan turns around to look at her, we witness his winsome profile. He's a cross between the bumbling Mr. Bean and the unswervingly suave Pierce Brosnan. His Solid Gold girlfriend sports shimmery floor length dresses and sings lounge songs with backup girls like Abba in space-age silver go-go boots. I wished I was Zeenat Aman, the Indian Bo Derek "10," and dreamed of her white feather boas to wrap around my shoulders while I mimicked her shaking hips. The dulcet voices of my family sadly skipped past me like a tooth fairy forgetting a kid on her rounds. A motorcycle helmet in hand, Firoz Khan embodies cool and watches on. They are in love, or they are in love without kisses, which led most of us down a path of wonder and confusion. Were passionate "French" ones, ever swapped by Indians? Or did they just dance and sing and fight, in jeans that were too snug or a sweater a decade too ripe? But the curve of Zeenat's belly is precise, and her red sequined number all fever. Large circles of fabric missing where the hips of her dress should be. A hundred times, I pressed rewind, a carrot as my microphone, belting off-key "Aap Jaisa Koi . . . " with the disco sound of falling stars nevertheless egging me on. "Arre, Zeenat!" My father winked at the uncles, and Firoz, listening, drunk on a cocktail of lust, knows he's a lucky man.

You're always smiling like a ventriloquist's dummy. Underneath the silly impulse of love-at-first sight, I know the rubble has begun to fall. The glass curtain of your world is not illusory. You just can't see it through a cloud of love. Let me tell you, then, what I know. My father is a bumbling recent immigrant, who could never compete—the jewelry drips from your chin like an old man's jowls—but he is still my father. Before you, I loved a cab driver's son. My home in a motel along Highway 99 coursing through strip malls, farms, and desert. "We're all the same," you'll say. You'll say it for awhile until the naiveté rubs thin. The loss of your mother's hand on your cheek and your father's fail-safe business is enough to break you. You will see, then, that we don't dance alone. And I'm only a public school girl.

MERA NAAM JOKER

It was that opening scene. You are the centre of the circus, the sublime moving force of this farce with baggy pants, suspenders and comically large shoes. The clown face which so purposefully betrays suffering that it epitomizes it. It was that opening scene. The characters of your past blot dew from their eyes as they turn the corners of their mouth upward to meet yours. You are lying on an operation table. Even as a child, I knew the scene was staged to tap the essence of dark humor. Another clown performs surgery to remove your heart. "I no longer need it," you say, flippantly. You say it because you don't mean it. Because you have chosen solitude. Or, as you scan the audience's attentive eyes, hoping for comedy, because it has chosen you. The red glass heart, as big as a candy box, belongs to no one. It's free for all. It's the most difficult thing you have ever encountered. You toss it carelessly into the air. I watch my father watch the scene, gazing at the television with a sadness I have rarely seen. As the heart shatters to shards, I exit the room.

After Jassbir, almost blind, loses her glasses, it's all downhill. Daddy's flirtations unzip the family unit. In a swift and untenable fork in the story, Mom and Prashant are gone. Dead? Something like that. Back then, the distance between continents like the suspension of disbelief in this story was insurmountable. The bold girl flips her hurt into a Kerouac karmic love and trades coke bottle glasses for glamorously large pink frames. I ditched mine, too, and got hip after slipping on the word "rhetoric" and losing the 8th grade spelling bee. A beaten up copy of *The Dharma Bums*, the one she later borrowed from me, on her bedside table next to the painkillers and poppers. "What does the world care about us?" she sings, as she puffs at a pipe and raises her arm to the sky. When I first lost my religion, I sullenly dreamt of the rooftop parties on Rose Street and wondered, punch-drunk, if The Beats might help me find it. Flubbing chemistry and fingering poetry like a new charm, I hummed "Dum Maro Dum," with the image of Zeenat's backside like an hourglass ticking at the hip. Descent into hell, we're supposed to believe, is made easier by her corrupted Canadian background. Only the West can beget such exquisite womanly decadence, and I am filled with admiration and autobiography.

TABISH KHAIR

TABISH KHAIR (b. 1966) was born and educated mostly in Gaya, India. He is the author of five collections of poetry: *My World, A Reporter's Diary, The Book of Heroes* (all Rupa), *Where Parallel Lines Meet* (Penguin India), and *Man of Glass* (HarperCollins); and five novels: *An Angel in Pyjamas* (HarperCollins India), *The Bus Stopped* (Picador), *Filming: A Love Story* (Picador), *The Thing About Thugs* (HarperCollins/Fourth Estate), and *How To Fight Islamist Terror From The Missionary Position* (HarperCollins/Fourth Estate); and a number of academic studies: *Babu Fictions: Alienation in Contemporary Indian English Novels* (OUP); *Amitav Ghosh: A Critical Companion* (Permanent Black); and *Other Routes:1500 Years of African and Asian Travel Writing* (co-editor / Signal Books & Indiana University Press). He has won the All India Poetry Prize and other awards for his prose and poetry. Anthology appearances (among others) include *Twelve Modern Young Indian Poets* (Edinburgh: Lines Review), *Wasafiri India South Asia & the Diaspora* (London: QMW University), *Midnight's Grandchildren: Post Independence Poetry from India* (Macedonia: Struga Poetry Evenings), and *The Literary Review Indian Poetry* (New Jersey: Fairleigh Dickinson University), all edited by Sudeep Sen. Tabish Khair currently teaches in the Department of English at Aarhus University in Denmark. [www.tabishkhair.co.uk]

ALMOST SONNET

At one instant it seemed to be within my grasp:
Your love was a jewel I could reach out and feel.
It made me come alive as nothing had before;
I felt no need to keep it in a selfish clasp.
I knew it was something no one could ever steal,
It had no need for locks; it was a magic door.

I sit here now and think of what I would have found
If I had walked the way my heart still bids me go
(The closest word I know is "paradise"),
But here my body's tied to a stake in the ground
Of many yesterdays and not one tomorrow,
And though it may implore and struggle, still it lies

In all the mud of language that turns doors to walls
And makes the best of truths, despite us, false.

THE SOLDIER HOME FROM IRAQ

(*The Tinder Box*)

What could I do being what I was:
Saviour of old women, their killer too.
On my chest there sat a big dog;
Trained to get answers, move it, jump jump jump,
I picked up my M16A2 and shot her.
There she lay. There they lay.

Back home I was rich like anyone else,
Princesses clutched my dog hairs
In fantasy, in ecstasy.
Later we slept.

I had my will
Until

The shades of a prison-house closed upon me
And I remembered I had forgotten
Something.
It eludes me still.
Was it a candle, a wick, a tinderbox?
Something to do with light surely.
Something that would have set me free.

WAR REPORTER

(*Elder-Tree Mother*)

Everything he looks at turns story:
He makes a tale of all he touches.

Embedded with the boys, he slowly pours
Stories out of regimental teapots.

But will he tell of the girl who worried
About the next knock on the door?

Will he tell of the boy who lay
Drenched in a dry dry land?

Will he tell of children who fly
Always always through the sky?

Will he tell why their parents roam
Slowly slowly towards your home?

MECHANICAL

(*The Nightingale*)

It does not sound like glass bells.
It sounds like guns.

What art has gone into the manufacture
Of this mighty machine!

If it had feathers, it would also fly.
If it had a tongue, it could also tell.

But it sings the same song over and over again:
Won't we ever get tired of listening to it?

COUPLETS IN ICE

(*The Snow Queen*)

1.
The walls of your palace are made of snow.
The game of reason is cold and slow.

2.
You cannot tell your love apart:
The Queen of Ice sits in your heart.

3.
How well we understand in tongues unknown
The word that in English is pronounced 'alone.'

4.
Always the crow knows where your love went,
Though he speaks harshly and with an accent.

5.
How soon it happened: just a while ago
You held my hands and walked in sand or snow.

6.
The last story cannot be told:
Its words were patented and sold.

REFUGEE

(*The Princess on the Pea*)

Who can tell her identity?
The gold, the silk mattress, such stuff
Are noble and yet not enough:
Where is the blasted pea?

Note: Except for the first poem, all the others are based on stories by H C Andersen. The titles of the stories in italics are given in parenthesis.

THACHOM POYIL RAJEEVAN

THACHOM POYIL RAJEEVAN (b. 1959) was born in Paleri, a rural hilly village in the district of Calicut, Kerala, the southernmost state in India. He writes both in Malayalam, the regional language of his home state, and in English. He has published five poetry collections, a collection of essays, a travelogue and a novel in Malayalam. His published works in English include a chapbook (*Kannaki*, The Crux Publishers, USA, 2002), a poetry volume titled *He Who Was Gone Thus* (Yeti Book, India/Six Gallery Press, USA, 2003) and an anthology (*Third Word: Post Socialist Poetry*, Monsoon Editions, India, 2007), co-edited with Croatian poet, Lana Derkac. His poetry is represented in various anthologies such as *The Brink*, *Bruised Memories*, *The Green Dragon*, *Midnight's Grandchildren*, and *Promise of the Rest* and has been translated into eleven languages. Rajeevan works as advisor to the Minister for Culture, Government of Kerala, and an editor for Monsoon Editions/ Yeti Books. [www.thachompoyilrajeevan.com]

PROLOGUE TO AUTOBIOGRAPHY

I had a dream
The day before I was born

In it, my father was sculpting a sun image in stone
By the banks of a river that the mountains had called back
In an island not known in which sea it was

Mother was dancing in the streets of a city
Which is a dense forest now

Father was burnt alive in the forest fire
Sparked off from the stone chisel,
Mother was drowned to death
In the deluge spread out from a water drop
Scattered from her anklet

God had kept me in a Chinese jar
Which we used pickle in tender mangoes
In our house now non-existent by the paddy field

Along with a grain of paddy
A measure of darkness, a centipede
And a star

The granny who killed herself swallowing a diamond
Scared of Tippu Sultan's onslaught told me stories
And a butterfly that caught in spider web
The day the Simon Commission came to India
Drew me pictures

It was that dream my mother gave birth to
The next morning.

VASCO DA GAMA
(*1460–1524*)

The harbour I set sail from
May not be there now.

The grey granite-laid alleys
The old streets smelling of pickled radish
The tall arched doors opening to them
The thin, endless frills
The midnight's music and dance behind them too.

The temples I have prayed in
Might have turned into cemeteries
My prayers there might be growing as cactus
My gods will not understand my sorrows anymore.

My children are orphans in nameless countries
In their eyes, are depths
Deep enough to drown me to death.

I have to set off on another voyage
To discover my own country.

I am not scared of giant sharks and pirates
I have no fear of killer waves and sea-ghosts
My compass never errs
My ship will never hit any rock.

But I can't stand
That solitary star following me from the very start
This candle that no wind can put out
This mast standing as always
This sail reluctant to drop down
And this silence the sea heaps up at the bottom.

When I step in
Sand grains rise like virgins
The sea enters my blood
The night anchors in my flesh
And the cavalry of desires

Walk me blindfolded
Through the bottomless marshes.

I never land in the continents
I want to discover.

I am a mariner
Who died in a shipwreck that didn't happen
Who prefers to believe he is not born yet.

Between the ends of peninsulas
Unmarked in history,
And the fingertips
Absent in life;

I remain
The remains of innumerable shipwrecks
No one knows about.

NEELAKURINJI

We don't have a common goal
nor our destination is same.

There isn't a colour, smell
tune or taste
we agree on.

Though we talk all the time
I can't make out what you're saying
nor you what I am.

We are in two coaches
running in opposite directions.

The tress that fade away against us
lampposts
the faces that speed rolls out
streets villages
the hills that chase us, watching persistently
rocks towers
the fields that lie on waiting
crops
the bordering horizon
and the cloudlet in it,
all are different.

But
Hardly had we passed the eleventh curve
Stopped for a while
For someone to get off or in
And through the slit of the door or window
Neelakurinjis made their way in

Dozed
You leaned onto my shoulder

I was lying
Head on your lap
In a coach that goes to a city
That none had ever been in till then, then.

This is not a green leaf;
This is your tongue
You forgot in my mouth
When we kissed in the field

This is not a ripe areacunut;
This is your heart
You misplaced in my body
When we embraced in the valley.

The is not *chunna*;
This is your breath
You abandoned in my blood
When we killed each other in the sea.

This is not tobacco;
This is your hair
Flung when we danced
In the crematorium.

I'm sleeping in you
Like in a coffin
Listening to the festive drums of
The immaculate nature,

Shooting my red

TISHANI DOSHI (b. 1975) was born in Madras. She received her master's in writing from the Johns Hopkins University and worked in London in advertising before returning to India in 2001 to work with the late choreographer, Chandralekha, with whom she performed on many national and international stages. Her first poetry collection, *Countries of the Body* (Aark Arts), won the Forward Poetry Prize for best first collection in 2006. She also won the All-India Poetry Competition in 2005, and is a recipient of an Eric Gregory Award. She has worked as a journalist, contributing to such publications as the *Hindu*, *The New York Times*, *Outlook*, *India Today*, *Vogue*, and *the Guardian*. Her first novel, *The Pleasure Seekers* (Bloomsbury), was published in 2010, and has been translated into several languages. Her latest book is a collection of poems, *Everything Begins Elsewhere* (HarperCollins India).

BRIDGE-BUILDING

The road is long. So do not mind the smallness of the present.
— PRAJNAVEDA in a letter to Xuanzang, circa 645 AD

I. SAMSARA: THE WORLD

'Journey long,' the teacher says,
so we go down, deep and deeper,
till we see ankles first, then feet.
And only after touching our heads
to the diamond back of the earth,
do we rise again, arched like curls
of river silk, emptying our souls
into the sky, forgetting the world.

II. DHAMMA: THE MEANS

We meet as lovers do, through births
and deaths, worn-down nubs of thigh
and breast, silent spaces of inadequacy.
'Come through the gates of drowning,'
the teacher says, so we cross with lotus
rafts and abandon them at the water's edge
where love's refrain is whispering: *The world*
begins and then it ends. Begins and ends again.

THE ADULTEROUS CITIZEN

I am an adulterous resident;
when I am in one city, I am dreaming of the other.
I am an exile; citizen of the country of longing
— SUKETU MEHTA, *Maximum City*

When it comes to it,
there's only the long, paved road
that leads to a house
with a burning light.
A house you can never own,
but allows you
to sleep in its bed
without demanding sex,
eat from its cupboards
without paying,
lie in the granite cool of its tub
without drowning.
And only when the first shards
of day slice through
the blinds
of the basement windows
nudging you
with something of a whisper,
something like, *Maybe it's time to go* —
do you finally drag
your suitcases
up the carpeted stairs,
out the front door,
on to the summer pavements.

It is nothing
like losing a lover,
or leaving behind
the lanes of childhood.
Nothing like scaling
the winged walls of memory
to discover your friends
have packed up their boxes
and vanished.
More like stumbling

into a scene from the future,
where the ghost
of a husband
beckons with pictures
of a family
you no longer recognize,
and other peoples' children
race across the grass,
lulling you into belief
that you can always return like this —
without key in hand,
to lie in the folds of one city,
while listening to the jagged,
carnal breaths of another.

LESSON IN STILLNESS

All morning I try to hold it —
the desperation of a fly
beating against glass,
a dog's distant bark,
the dull throb of a lorry
winding its way up the hills.
By afternoon I think I've mastered it.
Nothing the world offers me
can be as complete or as full as this.
When I step in to the light,
I have no song for the stones,
no thought for the grass.
I only want to remember
this long road,
this steady pulse,
which feels like love.
So when evening
feeds itself to night,
clearing the way
for frost or flood,
I'll still be left with this —
the bright suffocation of flowers,
the weight of the day's hours.

MADRAS MORNING

It is early in Madras
and the temple priests are busy
with their morning prayers
like the walkers and the joggers
and the coffee-makers at *Hi-Cool*
and *Re-Lax* and *Maheshwari Snacks*
and the bus drivers and taxi drivers
who've left their dreams in bed
and the vegetable sellers
and the call centre boys and girls
who are practising their accents
on their way to work
and the construction workers
with thermometer-shaped legs
and the airhostesses in green
comparing heels
and the stewards and the clerks
in brass buttoned coats
and the Air India pilots
sneaking their last smoke
and we who've kissed
the children goodbye
and left instructions
with the maid
we who don't know how easily
the world moves without us
we are sitting upright in chairs
balancing trays on our knees
eating the air

LEARNING MUDRAS IN BHUTAN

Here, in this room of Bhutanese elders,
I learn to catch my breath again, allow my fingers
to be shaped into lotus-flowered offerings
to the sky. And when I can do this 108 times without
guidance, the woman behind me — cataract-beset,
toothless, wrinkled – who's been picking stray flecks
of fleece off my back, touches me in a way you can't;
gives me the food she hasn't eaten all day, the words
she hasn't spoken. So afterwards, it is almost easy.
To walk outside where the young monks are chewing
gum in the sun, listen to them scatter down stairways
like sparrows, point to the opening of space through
which I mean to escape. I want it to be graceful,
as she was, feather touches on your jacket and a jewel
in your hands. But when the light hits us from behind
the granite cliffs, all I can muster is to lie with you
on the monastery floor, guide your fingers to the door-
ways of my shattered heart, so you can feel it too —
the ocean that travels with me; how it gathers and breaks,
gathers and breaks; like love, how it stills, then parts.

USHA AKELLA

USHA AKELLA (b. 1967) is the author of three books of poetry: *Kali Dances, So Do I*, and *A Face That Does Not Bear the Footprints of the World*. Most recently she published and produced her first musical *Ek*, an English musical on the life of Shri Shirdi Sai Baba (Sterling Publishers) that premiered in Austin in February 2012. Becoming a multi city tour, *Ek* is gaining wide attention and recognition. She has edited *En(compass): The Poetry Caravan Anthology*, *Borderlands issue on contemporary Macedonian poets*, and a yearly section on Diaspora Poets in www.museindia.com. She has been interviewed widely and has read at many international poetry festivals including Siir Festival, Turkey; Struga poetry evenings, Macedonia; poetry festival in Medellin, Colombia; Granada international poetry festival, Nicaragua; Festival de la Palabra, Mexico City; Days of poetry and wine, Medana, Slovenia, and others. She is the founder of a community service poetry project in White Plains, New York and Austin, called 'The Poetry Caravan' that provides free readings and workshops to the disadvantaged. She also writes travel articles. She lives in Austin, Texas.

NICARAGUA

Nicaragua, in the wrinkles of your face lies
the lost poem of your meaning I try to retrieve,

In the poem is another poem, always at least two faces,
alligator-human, two coasts, two anthems, two dances, two skins,

Like a recipe on a page it unfolds, ingredient by ingredient
couplets it was, I believe, like your trade in two currencies,

your arm in arm with the beguiling harlot,
a parade of your anthem like a glittering belt buckle,

The proud fuck of your steeples, the warm
chants of your womb still whispering in the back alleys.

Anthropomorphic, you remain half civilized, vitalized by a
volcano's breath, prehistoric rumbles, shambles of

demonic rock and polluted lakes corseted in the jean clad.
You came to me in sound first: *masaya, sandina, pora pora,*

the juice of language sticky sweet on the tongue,
Meaning, secondary like the second course of a meal,

To me who comes from the country that says
The final marrow is unity, sees it enacted

on your yawning plazas- the long lineage of
faces stacked like dominoes in arrays of equations lost in time,

On your wrists dangle the bloodied bangles of your history,
encircling your melted song, a lagoon of breath.

THIS IS JUST TO SAY TO WILLIAM CARLOS WILLIAMS

I have not eaten the plums
nor has my daughter,

the mangoes win, plump-bellies, down,
pregnant with juice and yellow flesh,
the fresh taste of scathing summers,
and childhood's innocence,

and the moist memories
of dead grandmothers,
bellowing grandfathers,
the sweet homesickness,
sticky dribble on the chin,

The plums are prudish,
slow to ripen, a bit stiff,
in the back of the fridge,
they are not delicious or sweet
though cold,

Your plums Carlos,
Where do they come from?

THE POST OFFICE WITH MANY COUNTRIES

for Agha Shahid Ali

You whispered truths. Your songs floated down the valley to Amherst,
Echoed in Manhattan. The streets followed you like incense.
You who could not go home, hear now, "It is here. It is here."

Kahmir your bangles are broken

The children are in plastic bags clear as grapes plucked from the vine.
Are they mine? Did you write your poems with ink clear as plastic
Or tears. Shall we mourn in rhyme? Refrain. Refrain. Refrain. Refrain.

Kashmir your borders are open

Build a church within a mosque within a temple within a heart within a poem,
You found your home. Is it mine? To whom shall we leave our lines instead
of LOCs? Whom shall we bribe for air? The children are harvested in our time.

Kashmir your lines are on our palm

You never named the enemy or the Beloved. You knew the nameless horror.
To whom will you post your letters now? To whom shall we be faithful?
You've crossed the river. Kashmir is upon us as rain. We are stained.

Kashmir your heart has no borders

USHA KISHORE

USHA KISHORE (b. 1962) was born and brought up in Thiruvananthapuram, Kerala. Usha Kishore now lives on the Isle of Man, UK. Usha was educated at the University of Kerala (India), Sheffield Hallam University (UK) and Canterbury Christ Church University College (UK). After having taught for some time in the British Secondary and Tertiary Sector, Usha now teaches English at a Secondary School on the Isle of Man. Usha's poetry has been published in international magazines and anthologies, including *Atlas* and *Kavya Bharati*. Some of her poems have been translated into German, Spanish and Gujurati. She also writes critical articles for international magazines. Usha's poetry has won prizes in UK competitions and has been part of national and international projects. Her short story "Dowry" was shortlisted for a major UK literary award, the Asham Award (UK) in 2005. Usha's translates from Sanskrit and her translations of Sankara have been published internationally.

ATHYARMADOM TEMPLE

Prayers light up-
incense pours out
into the mystic air…

The inner temple
is shut – dreams squint
from the chinks…

The doors open
to a vision in red –
Woman, mother incarnate…

Ringing bells ululate,
conch shells blow -
Grant me three boons, mother:

Emerald sea and palm fronds,
singing desert sands,
a dark eternity…

I ask for a fourth boon
the doors shut and I
am left a wandering

soul in penance for
another life – an exile
in search of a homeland…

A priest sprinkles holy
water as lamp light
masquerades with shadows…

A life spent living a dream…

SITA

Who are you woman,
waiting on Saryu's banks,
water pot in hand?

You are the earth,
waiting for the sky.

You wait in vain,
on Saryu's banks,
for the lost rhythm

of your heart - you have
a heart of gold, chained
to the Kingdom of the Sun.

You are the earth,
waiting for the sky.

What sun will gather your
tears in *asoka* flowers?

What fire burn your chastity?
What Monkey God, your messenger?

What cuckoo bird will coo your
grief in classic rhymes?

What poet turn into woman
to know your soul?

Unplant your eyes from
the sky, Sita - your Lord
sits on a silver pavilion -

He performs his *yagna*, wedded
to a woman of gold; his eyes
are set on conquering the world -

Kingdoms for a horse -
The saviour of the world
is now its destroyer -

The horizons of an empire
have swallowed love in
Rama's Ayodhya -

The arrows of power
have pierced man's
heart and bled it to stone –

Crawl back into your
dark womb, Sita!
Back to your mother earth -

Banish him, as he banished you…

AMULETS

I wore amulets of gold
to ward off the *Yakshis*
dancing under the *pala* tree…

I wore amulets of silver
to keep the laughing
Brahmarakshas at bay…

What do I wear now?
Life's demons have
cast their eyes on me…

What do I wear to ward
off the bad will, the
stars throw on my path?

You wear a smile on
your lips, a prayer in
your soul and hope
in your heart…

Yakshi – female vampire
Pala (Alstonia scholaris) – An Indian tree with fragrant flowers. According to Kerala legend, the *yakshis* reside on the Pala tree.
Brahmarakshas – ghost of a Brahmin

VIJAY NAMBISAN

VIJAY NAMBISAN (b. 1963) was born in Neyveli, Tamil Nadu. He started studying engineering at the Indian Institute of Technology in New Delhi, dropped out and went into journalism. He has worked as a journalist for various magazines and newspapers including *City Scan, Debonair,* and *The Hindu.* His poems have appeared in various journals such as the *London Magazine, Poetry Review,* and others. Anthology appearances (among others) include *Twelve Modern Young Indian Poets* (Edinburgh: Lines Review), and *Wasafiri India South Asia & the Diaspora* (London: QMW University), both edited by Sudeep Sen, as well as *60 Indian Poets* (Penguin), edited by Jeet Thayil. He was the winner of the first All India Poetry Competition organised by the British Council and the Poetry Society of India in 1988, and the *Gentleman* poetry prize in 1997. Some of Nambisan's early poetry is available in *Gemini.* He is also the author of two non-fiction books, *Bihar is in the Eye of the Beholder,* and *Language as an Ethic,* as well as of a book of translation, *Two Measures of Bhakti* (all published by Penguin India). He lives in Kodagu (Coorg) in Karnataka.

MIND THE GAP

Mind the gap. The seasons toil and change
But the gap is to be minded. Not mended, mind;
For each to each must forever be strange:
Mind the gap. There, that's a splendid chap.
Please mind the gap.

We may look ahead or read *The Daily Mail*,
We may study the ads and even find
The perfect holiday; but on this tunnelled trail
We mind the gap. That's a splendid chap.
Please mind the gap.

Stiffly we sit; our Empires are within
And must not touch each other. Behind
In some holey station, musicians swing.
But we Mind the Gap. We are splendid chaps.
Please mind the gap.

We travel each to a peculiar end,
Rock with the rock, grind with metallic grind
And will not recognise enemy nor friend.
Mind the Gap. Yes, that's a splendid chap.
Please mind the gap.

I mind my business and watch the seasons mend.

MAHASHIVARATRI

Crisply burning up the sky
Tails of fire come to try
Domination. Lord with hair
Aflame do you unlock your lair
And summon death made at creation
For once for all end the nations

Watching seas of spirit burning
In your cradle endless turning
Whose end no earth can hold whose mouth
Shrieks forth always an unquenched drought
Settle dear friend I seek a stern
Unwinking arbitration an end

KALKI

Difficult now, to predicate order.
The wheel spins without weight at a careless touch.
Those who stand alone are always alone
And the mobs assemble at every border.
Who remains to guide me, how or how much
Shall I give of my gifts. Coming unknown
In other ages I brought a great prize
To my seekers in unconfounded peace.
Elsewhere I returned fire with fire, ice with ice
And bore a sword to those who would not fight.
Now I am welcomed in hourly agonies.
My foolish news of the conclusive war
Comes to the inconsequential dead. My might
Is lonely: An unpeopled avatar.

SANGAM

a translation from the ancient Tamil for Gowri

Parrot,
caged parrot,
sweet parrot in a cage,

whisper to me

and I will give you milk
and honey
to sweeten your tongue:

whisper one word to me.

Moon, hornèd moon,
Lord of the hornèd moon,
Lord of the city of the hornèd moon

by the refulgent sea:

Parrot,
sweet parrot,
sweet parrot in a cage

whisper His name to me.

THE DESERTED TEMPLE

Sravanabelagola

The god is gone. His cave is bare.
	In shadow from the sun
The clotted bats hang from the roof.
	Below, the scorpions run
And pious folk no longer come
	Lest evil should be done.

Ruins of flowers on the floor
	Bear imprints of his feet.
They point through the door into
	The many-miraged heat.
His voice was heard. His fragrance kept
	This prisoned air once sweet.

His voice was heard: It told his tribe
	To leave this sun-cursed hill.
They went, and left his dwelling here.
	They went; it was his will.
Who piled these stones knows when he comes
	And where he stays until.

CHYAVANA

When the great sage immured his narrow law
Within the anthill, that his confined eye
Might open inward, and stare upon the truth,
His sacrifice was vain; for he little thought
That human innocence would interfere,
The silly girl would poke the thorn within,
Convert metaphor into fact, and show
What he deemed illusion was really so.

That was the test: to see if he would smile
And thank the princess, and say, "Now this anthill
Is quite unnecessary, and all my life
I'm freed of temptation"; and so grow wise
And the three worlds would shake to see the Man.
But he, blind fool, only roared in rage
(Which quite tickled Fate) like an overgrown boy
Whose toy's broken, and wants another's to keep.

So satisfied, the primal fancy curled
Within the actions of the living world
Winked its broad eye, and went back to sleep.

GROWN-UP

When I was a child I'd sometimes lie at night
Awake, and hear my parents talk in bed:
I could make little out of what they said
But I could tell, their stern surrations light
Today's events to rest. So comforted,
I'd fall asleep, wishing to be a man,
To lie thus in the matrimonial bed,
To talk today away, and make a plan
For tomorrow.
                    But now that forty years
Have made me half a man at least, my wife
And I exchange good-nights, then fall asleep:
It's surely not because we have no fears
To cherish, or we know we have lived life
One golden day; but that our clay will keep.

LINT

Those who sweep beneath beds know the smell of lint.
It is something like musk, murmuring of age
And wickedness: something less than ashes, more than dust,
Lighter than the air which wafts above the bed,
Yet heavy as that which weighs upon your head at night
When you want sleep and it will not come.
                                        Lint is light
Captured in windows, kept captive against the dark:
It is all of yesterday that we wished to forget,
Creeping silently back when we thought it was gone.

Lint is power, wicked only in its weakness. Lock
It in cupboards and it triumphs; sweep it aside
And it owns no master.
                              The smell of lint is thus
The smell of waking to the very ill, who need
No compassion, but it smothers them. Yet those
Who sweep beneath beds are also sometimes wise,
And they know enough to leave the lint alone.

VIJAY SESHADRI

VIJAY SESHADRI (b. 1954) was born in Bangalore, India, but moved to the USA at age five. He grew up in Columbus, Ohio. His work has appeared *in Threepenny Review, The New Yorker, Shenandoah, Antaeus, AGNI, The Paris Review* (which awarded him the 1995 Bernard F. Connors Long Poem Prize for 'Lifeline'), and *The American Scholar*. Anthology appearances (among others) include *Under 35: The New Generation of American Poets* (New York: Anchor Books) edited by Nicholas Christopher, *The Yellow Nib Modern English Poetry by Indians* (Belfast: Queens University), and *World Literature Today Writing from Modern India* (Norman: University of Oklahoma), both edited by Sudeep Sen. His three collections of poetry are *Wild Kingdom, The Long Meadow,* and *The Disappearances.* He teaches poetry and is the director of the graduate non-fiction writing programme at Sarah Lawrence College, and lives in Brooklyn, New York.

VISITING PARIS

They were in the scullery talking.
The meadow had to be sold to pay their riotous expenses;
then the woods by the river,
with its tangled banks and snags elbowing out of the water,
had to go; and then the summer house where they talked—
all that was left of an estate once so big
a man riding fast on a fast horse
couldn't cross it in a day. Genevieve. Hortense. Mémé.
The family's last born, whose pale name is inscribed on the rolls
of the Field of the Cloth of Gold. As in the fresco of the Virgin,
where the copper in the pigment oxidizes to trace a thin green cicatrix
along a seam of Her red tunic,
a suspicion of one another furrowed their
consanguine, averted faces.
Why go anywhere at all when it rains like this,
when the trees are sloppy and hooded
and the foot sinks to the ankle in the muddy lane?
I didn't stay for the end of the conversation.
I was wanted in Paris. Paris, astounded by my splendor
and charmed by my excitable manner,
waited to open its arms to me.

MEMOIR

Orwell says somewhere that no one ever writes
    the real story of their life.
The real story of a life is the story of its humiliations.
If I wrote that story now—
radioactive to the end of time—
people, I swear, your eyes would fall out, you couldn't peel
the gloves fast enough
from your hands scorched by the firestorms of that shame.
Your poor hands. Your poor eyes
to see me weeping in my room
or boring the tall blonde to death.
Once I accused the innocent.
Once I bowed and prayed to the guilty.
I still wince at what I once said to the devastated widow.
And one October afternoon, under a locust tree
whose blackened pods were falling and making
illuminating patterns on the pathway,
I was seized by joy,
and someone saw me there,
and that was the worst of all,
lacerating and unforgettable.

The bedroom slippers' silk linings.
The dressing gown of brocade, stitched with the zodiac.
The pajamas underneath also made out of silk,
for which how many individuals of the species *B. mori*,
having munched the succulent, pale-green mulberry leaves
and insinuated a sack wherein to magnify themselves,
were steamed to death from the inside out?
The delicate fibres are intact.
He feels their ripeness on his skin.
He listens deeply into the night, which listens back.
The birch log pops in the fireplace.
The fetishes brood on the mantelpiece.
The ice melts in the gin.
And yellower and deeper than dandelion yellow,
yellower and stronger than Moroccan yellow,
the color, almost, of a yellow marigold, is
the yellow silk kimono she wears to greet the floating world.
Moths on the wing clutter the starlight.
Ghosts of dead moths are on the windowpane and
knee deep in the ballroom,
in social clubs and places of worship.
They are proof, if anyone still needs proof, that
awesome are the powers of humankind,
who have taken this selfsame moth
and endowed it with a gene from the jellyfish
so as to produce fluorescent silk!
And all in the interests of beauty!
(I shall spare you, by the way,
my exhaustive researches into the history
of the Silk Road.)

FAMILY HAPPINESS

On our first date, I told my wife
I was a lesbian trapped in the body of a man.
Everybody says that now, of course,
on TV and radio, alternative media outlets,
tattoos and bumper stickers, but this was long ago, when
none but the brave (who deserve the fair)
would come up with something like that.
She smiled the pleased and goofy smile that flowers in her big eyes,
and I thought I had her.
Looking back now, though,
I can see her appraisal of me rounding to completeness.
I can hear her cognition firing.
She knew it. She knew even then
the truth it has cost me the aeons to acquire,
climbing and climbing the broken stairs:
I'm a man trapped in the body of a man.
I clutch the smooth walls and see through his eyes
the oil fires and containment units,
the huge clawed gantries strung out on the twilit polar horizon.
Through his alloyed ears, I hear
the objects of his scorn, his compassion, his hatred, his love
crying out and crying out.
Half my arms are his arms.
Half my face is welded to his face.
The other half mouths his clumsy ironies.
"Life is war," he says.
"Tragic," he says. "Tragic."
The simulacra are marching everywhere,
and deep in the caves the chimeras are breathing.

ELEGY

I've been asked to instruct you about the town you've gone to,
where I've never been.
The cathedral is worth looking at,
but the streets are narrow, uneven, and a little grim.
The river is sluggish in the summer and muddy in the spring.
The cottage industries are obsolete.
The population numbers one.

The population numbers one fugitive
who slips into the shadows and haunts the belfries.
His half-eaten meals are cold on the empty café tables.
His page of unsolved equations is blowing down the cobblestones.
His death was so unjust that he can't forgive himself.
He waits for his life to catch up to him.

He is you and you and you.
You will look to him for your expiation,
face him in the revolving door, sit with him in the plaza
and soothe his fears and sympathize with his story
and accustom him to the overwhelming sun
until his death becomes your death.
You will restore his confiscated minutes to him one by one.

THOUGHT PROBLEM

How strange would it be if you met yourself on the street?
How strange if you liked yourself,
took yourself in your arms, married your own self,
propagated by techniques known only to you,
and then populated the world? Replicas of you are everywhere.
Some are Arabs. Some are Jews. Some live in yurts. It is
an abomination, but better that your
sweet and scrupulously neat self
emerges at many points on the earth to watch the horned moon rise
than all those dolts out there,
turning into pillars of salt wherever we look.
If we have to have people, let them be you,
spritzing your geraniums, driving yourself to the haberdashery,
killing your supper with a blowgun.
Yes, only in the forest do you feel at peace,
up in the branches and down in the terrific gorges,
but you've seen through everything else.
You've fled in terror across the frozen lake,
you've found yourself in the sand, the palace,
the prison, the dockside stews;
and long ago, on this same planet, you came home
to an empty house, poured a Scotch-and-soda,
and sat in a recliner in the unlit rumpus room,
puzzled at what became of you.

I woke up on the stainless-steel autopsy table.
My chest was weighted down.
Bodily fluids stained my paper hospital gown.
My life readings were stable,

though. They were, in fact, decisive—
one round number and one simple line.
A cop gave the coroner a form to sign,
but he lingered undecided over me,

murmuring to himself,
"That must have been a dream, or was it a vision?"
I felt along my length his long riverine incision.
Outside it was Chicago—

city of world-class museums,
handsome architecture, marvellous elevated trains—
rising from the plains
by the impossibly flat lake.

VIKAS K MENON

VIKAS K MENON (b. 1969) is a poet and playwright whose poems have appeared or are forthcoming in publications such as *Lantern Review*, *Burntdistrict*, and *Diode*, among others. His poetry manuscript *godflesh* was a finalist for the 2010 Kinereth Gensler Award and semi-finalist for the Beatrice Hawley award, as well as a semi-finalist for the 12th Annual Elixir Press Poetry Awards. He is a board member of Kundiman, the first organization of its kind dedicated to supporting Asian-American poetry and is the Resident Playwright of Ruffled Feathers Theater company. Anthology appearances (among others) include: *Indivisible: An Anthology of Contemporary South Asian American Poetry* (University of Arkansas), edited by Neelanjana Banerjee, Summi Kaipa and Pireeni Sundaralingam; and *The Literary Review Indian Poetry* (New Jersey: Fairleigh Dickinson University), edited by Sudeep Sen. His play written in collaboration with the members of Ruffled Feathers Theater Company was staged in New York in 2010. He received his MFA in Poetry from Brooklyn College, and his MA in Literature from St. Louis University. He lives in New York City.

PYRE

Have you ever watched a man burn?

The scaffold of his flesh
falls away.

He will burn down to a few handfuls

of ash,
and an awkward stick of bone.

His skull.

Did they crack
his skull? I did not hear.

I did not see.

They poured water over my
half-naked body

to make me pure for him.

It was me—

half-kneeling, staring away
from him—

it was me—

I lit my father aflame.

As smoke rose into the humid air

men talked
and we waited.

I knew not what for.

FATHERTONGUE

Forranners kalpikyana, he'd snarl in Malayalam
when he felt he was being ripped off—
They're teasing the foreigner.
At work, he was full-on a malarkey alert:
Golf—who has time to play games
with these jimokes?
Boilermakers had burned bourbon
into his English, but his otherkiltered
rhythms laid bare his roots,
an American Banyan tree.
Always respect your elders,
he said, *but question everything.*

Only once did an alien
sound come between us—
when I said to him, *I love you.*
My drawled hosannah on the altar of us
was so paltry an offering
that we both laughed,
poured more drinks,
sat down to eat with our hands.

THIRUNAAVAYA, 2005

Here we are sons or daughters, mothers
or fathers of the dead. Here, we are all kin

in the rictus that stoops our shoulders,
pales our breath. Kin in the quick grimace

as we mimic the priests,
between our gestures and theirs

an impossible distance.
Fling flowers onto water,

touch your fingers
to grains of rice. Pray.

Bharathapuzha river
spills with dawn flame

cattail spears like sentries in the distance.
We wait, tree-quiet.

The sun's halo frames us,
the bewildered living,

our postures struck with gold.

ELEGY

for Kottiazth Rugmini Thirumulpad

Maker of my history,
rose of roses,

how can I praise her?
From her lap

my horizon limitless
I watched gods and demons

arrive and depart—
if Gopala's mouth held the universe

then she spun the cosmos on her tongue
with stories like cradles,

like thrones.
From even her little loves

sunflowers blossomed,
ate light and wagged their heads

over mine. For she whose hands
hovered over needlework,

lips moving silently,
eyes cast back in time;

for she who whispered
Men propose, god disposes

as I wiped her mouth,
cleaned her dentures

combed the thin white
hairs on her scalp;

today I pour milk through flowers onto her ashes
my limit,

my overflowing—

words cannot
wash the dust from her feet.

VIKRAM SETH

VIKRAM SETH (b. 1952) was born in Kolkata. He studied and lived for several years each in India, England, USA, and China. Winner of innumerable national and international awards, his genre-spanning works include — [travelogue] *From Heaven Lake,* [novel-in-verse] *The Golden Gate,* [poetry] *Mappings, The Humble Administrator's Garden, All You Who Sleep Tonight, The Poems: 1981–1994,* [children's verse] *Beastly Tales,* [poetry translation] *Three Chinese Poets,* [prose novels] *A Suitable Boy* and *An Equal Music,* [libretto] *Arion and the Dolphin,* and *The Rivered Earth;* [non-fiction/memoir] *Two Lives.* His work has been translated into many international languages and anthologized widely. Seth lives in New Delhi and London.

'Why
do
you
cry?'
'I flew
too
high.
Un-
done,
all
see
me
fall.'

THE FEVER BIRD

The fever bird sang out last night.
I could not sleep, try as I might.

My brain was split, my spirit raw.
I looked into the garden, saw

The shadow of the amaltas
Shake slightly on the moonlit grass.

Unseen, the bird cried out its grief,
Its lunacy, without relief:

Three notes repeated closer, higher,
Soaring, then sinking down like fire

Only to breathe the night and soar,
As crazed, as desperate, as before.

I shivered in the midnight heat
And smelt the sweat that soaked my sheet.

And now tonight I hear again
The call that skewers through my brain,

The call, the brain-sick triple note —
A bone of pain stuck in its throat.

I am so tired I could weep.
Mad bird, for God's sake let me sleep.

Why do you cry like one possessed?
When will you rest? When will you rest?

Why wait each night till all but I
Lie sleeping in the house, then cry?

Why do you scream into my ear
What no one else but I can hear?

ACROSS THE TREELESS STREET

Across the treeless street
A moist breeze blows.
I re-arrange my sheet,
Wiggle my cold toes,
Stare at the sky, and toss,
Insomniac. A train
Screams through wide plains across
The scent of desert rain.

I am too tired tonight
To sleep. I lie
Companionless. The white
Clouds gut the sky.
Orion, Pleiads, Plough,
All signs and certainties
Are lost to vision now.
The willow trees

That name the town are gone.
The freight-trains go.
The loaded trucks move on.
This is the great depot
Where nothing stays.
The hours move towards light.
Sleep: in the tall-skied days
You will forget tonight.

A MODEST PROPOSAL

As you've asked for black and white,
May I send these lines to you
In the tacit hope you might
Take my type at least as true.

Let this distance disappear
And our hearts approach from far
Till we come to be as near
As acrostically we are.

FOR PHILIPPE HONORÉ

Perhaps this could have stayed unstated.
Had our words turned to other things
In the grey park, the rain abated,
Life would have quickened other strings.
I list your gifts in this creation:
Pen, paper, ink and inspiration,
Peace to the heart with touch or word,
Ease to the soul with note and chord.

How did that walk, those winter hours,
Occasion this? No lightning came;
Nor did I sense, when touched by flame,
Our story lit with borrowed powers —
Rather, by what our spirits burned,
Embered in words, to us returned.

GILES GORDON

Gone though you have, I heard your voice today.
I tried to make out what the words might mean,
Like something seen half-clearly on a screen:
Each savoured reference, each laughing bark,
Sage comment, bad pun, indiscreet remark.

Gone since you have, grief too in time will go,
Or share space with old joy; it must be so.
Rest then in peace, but spare us some elation.
Death cannot put down every conversation.
Over and out, as you once used to say?
Not on your life. You're on this line to stay.

DUBIOUS

Some men like Jack
and some like Jill;
I'm glad I like
them both; but still

I wonder if
this freewheeling
really is an
enlightened thing —

or is its greater
scope a sign
of deviance from
some party line?

In the strict ranks
of Gay and Straight
what is my status?
Stray? or Great?

DISTRESSFUL HOMONYMS

Since for me now you have no warmth to spare
I sense I must adopt a sane and spare

Philosophy to ease a restless state
Fuelled by this uncaring. It will state

A very meagre truth: love like the rest
Of our emotions, sometimes needs a rest.

Happiness, too, no doubt; and so, why even
Hope that 'the course of true love' could run even?

UNCLAIMED

To make love with a stranger is the best.
There is no riddle and there is no test. —

To lie and love, not aching to make sense
Of this night in the mesh of reference.

To touch, unclaimed by fear of imminent day,
And understand, as only strangers may.

To feel the beat of foreign heart to heart
Preferring neither to prolong nor part.

To rest within the unknown arms and know
That this is all there is; that this is so.

from THE GOLDEN GATE

1.6

It's Friday night. The unfettered city
Resounds with hedonistic glee.
John feels a cold cast of self-pity
Envelop him. No family
Cushions his solitude, or rather,
His mother's dead, his English father,
Retired in his native Kent,
Rarely responds to letters sent
(If rarely) by his transatlantic
Offspring. In letters to *The Times*
He rails against the nameless crimes
Of the post office. Waxing frantic
About delays from coast to coast,
He hones his wit and damns the post.

2.44

John looks downwards, as if admonished,
Then slowly lifts his head, and sighs.
Half fearfully and half astonished
They look into each other's eyes.
The waiter, bearded, burly, macho,
Says, "Madam, though it's cold, gazpacho
Is what I'd recommend. Noisettes
Of lamp, perhaps, or mignonettes
Of veal to follow...." Unavailing
Are his suggestions. Nothing sinks
Into their ears. "Ah, well," he thinks,
"They're moonstruck. It'll be plain sailing.
Lovers, despite delays and slips
And rotten service, leave large tips."

5.4

Why, asks a friend, attempt tetrameter?
Because it once was noble, yet
Capers before the proud pentameter,
Tyrant of English. I regret
To see this marvelous swift meter
Demean its heritage, and peter
Into mere Hudibrastic tricks,
Unapostolic knacks and knicks.
But why take all this quite so badly?
I would not, had I world and time
To wait for reason, rhythm, rhyme
To reassert themselves, but sadly
The time is not remote when I
Will not be here to wait. That's why.

6.1

How beautiful it is, when waking,
To find one's lover at one's side;
The delicate slow light is breaking
Irresolutely through the wide
Bay windows of their bedroom, falling
On Liz's hair, and John's recalling
How last night she untied it, how
It flowed between his hands; but now
She lies asleep, unswiftly breathing;
Her thoughts are not with him, her dreams
Traverse the solitary streams
Of inward lands, yet her hair, wreathing
The pillow in a mesh of light,
Returns to him the fugitive night.

13.51

He hesitates a minute, eyeing
The script; then reads on. When he's done,
His chest is tight, and he is crying.
It says, *Dear John, We have a son.*
We hope that you'll be his godfather.
We've called him John. We would far rather
Have you than any other friend.
Please speak to us, John. In the end,
We'll all be old or dead or dying.
My mother died two weeks ago.
We thought perhaps you might not know.
Phil and I send our love. Liz. Sighing,
A harsh, prolonged, exhausted breath,
John feels his heart revisit death.

13.52

Depleted by his pain, he slowly
Walks to Jan's desk. What did not last
In life has now possessed him wholly.
Nothing can mitigate the past.
He gently touches Jan's sand dollar.
It soothes him in the ache, the squalor
That is his life, and she seems near
Him once again, and he can hear
Her voice, can almost hear her saying,
"I'm with you, John. You're not alone.
Trust me, my friend; there is the phone.
It isn't me you are obeying.
Pay what are your own heart's arrears.
Now clear your throat; and dry those tears."

THE HERMIT ON THE ICE

The hermit sits upon the ice.
The bluish light burns all around,
Immune to flame and sacrifice,
To breath and death and scent and sound.

The scent of pine, the river's roar
Are muted in his breath and pace.
The blue earth with its iron core
Spins on through time, spins on through space.

VIVEK NARAYANAN

VIVEK NARAYANAN (b. 1972) was born in Ranchi, Jharkhand to Tamil-speaking parents; since then, he has lived, worked and studied in a number of countries, including Zambia, South Africa, and the US. His books of poetry include *Universal Beach* (2006) and *Life and Times of Mr S* (HarperCollins, 2012). Recent anthologies in which his work has appeared include *The Bloodaxe Book of Contemporary Indian Poetry* (Bloodaxe, 2008) and *Language for a New Century: Contemporary Poetry from the Middle East, Asia, and Beyond* (W.W. Norton, 2008). Narayanan is currently based in New Delhi, where he works at Sarai-CSDS and is Co-editor for the journal *Almost Island*. He has also been an Associate Editor for the poetry annual *Fulcrum*.

IN THE EARLY DAYS OF THE DELHI METRO
(2005)

1. CHAWRI BAZAAR

In the early days
of the Delhi metro, a thin susurrus and a burr spoke
of a new sound to come, for the roads above, yoked
to another destiny's praise

had snapped
and coiled and split in strands; and turned us
below, mining that older darkness for room. Then consciousness,
that was still as rapt

a contest as one had
ever had in common, filled a cabin we could each
enter from our hidden place, when feet
bloomed from that flux

into bogeys and
a man lay himself flat on the moving floor
with the hope of moving in before
the inspectors and

the magistrates
could. But things had changed. Now little girls with pursed lips read the story
of an already given land, learning a journey
that none escaped:

it had chosen
us, there was nowhere to go but *into*: a thrill
and below that, utter powerlessness, and below that, the will of contrapuntal
continental

plates, an alluvial
shift. Still, in the early days of
the Delhi metro, the only explosions we saw
were of men in orange shirts,

ladies with purple
    lips, a hunchback in a spotless unrippling
    white suit he wore with so much style
                    I thought I would cry;

for each stop
    had its merits, as the doors parted and enormous containing
    tubular blobs of light offered the long view
                    to the naked eye,

new notions
    of freedom gesticulating and circulating up to the libation of
    crossing wires carelessly outside. It was each self's lay
                    salvation on display,

it was hope so vast
    it had to devour us. And while the day could still reveal the measure
    of a kid who ran to his mother's wrist-flicking gesture,
                    or, up top, a man

with a gas cylinder
    on his bicycle; these very sights
    now made us tremble, as if they might
                    dissolve into the hinterland

where also bull-
    -dozers blazed and the plots parceled themselves sparsely out,
    and the new resorts arrived to hoist their multi-coloured
                    pink and green

and red little
    triangular flags. And as the smear of sacrifice dried
    on the tarmac, speed was the state the new state wanted,
                    speed was the glass goblet

we downed, that picture
    in our window: that indefinite garrulous grey pasture
    that thin and continous bar pretending
                    to be the moving thing:

and we could not resist
pressing our faces to that glass,
and we made our own time pass
in our vanishment.

2. KASHMERE GATE

And we were so young
then. Young enough to faintly perceive
our own ageing. There wasn't much money
but almost enough

and more of it
was conjured day by day. We bitched about each other
a little less than before or after
and we wore

our weight when
it fit us. We sunbathed in the everywhere view and
though the bulbs seemed to disappear
the world penumbral

of pimps
and hookers and good-time gigolos who had lived
in the crannies of a fantastic, dwarfing, suddenly ancient
architecture,

there were virtues
to each other in the open. In the early days of the Delhi metro
a man looked right at me as if to show
dark shades of blue

on his face,
a code: he was alone. There was a sly
charge in that contained air, and when our eyes met
for the fourth

time he
smiled a stranger's gift. This was
a brighter danger of the heart; when the intercom began
to announce

each stop arrived
with the words, "This station is your station,
my lovely human," we knew we were to be joined
by the end of the ride.

3. RAJIV CHOWK

Such good fortune
it was then that spoiled us, when the moon,
crusty satellite, rose on mended circles abuzz
with twinkling toys

beating with the red
flashing-light core, pulsing concentric
in outward embrace, as if with cathartic
reclamation wed

to the reinvented
thorn-shaved borrowed rose, the fist in which it was held.
Yes: we were nearly one at last, it seemed, for the brief
years before grief

like delayed
melody returned—but no one until the husk
could be cured into whole. The ribbon cutting fussed
us over good, enjoined

us to its familial, familiar, fairground roar,
then mowed us in its mobs
of policemen. I'm having problems remembering what happened
next: no reasons

now remaindered but these
left spinning, like reborn galaxies in the brains
of our architects, our necromancers and meter-readers.
But I remember the koel's refrain

somehow returned
on a summer morning. And the lost birds
arrived in the newer boulevards too, unangered
as improvisers:

the wood-
-pecker, the mynah, the starling,
even the house crow with its shade undying,
I recognized

them all, whom
I had never really known. I saw that trees
could still stand their ground, frozen, as if in the midst
of orison

and an old
man, broken, but with his white hair neatly oiled
and parted in the previous style, onced
me over

on a side
street and, looking straight into my eyes, just laughed. Our
destinations one by one arrived. We
rose on

escalators into
the dazzling, auroral, consuming play
of the sky at night, O for the early days, for the early, early days,
for the early days of the Delhi metro.

THE FINAL ASANA

The *Smriti-sthana*, now lost to us, was a 4th century Sanskrit practical manual and commentary on Patanjali's *Yoga Sutras* that, according to the accounts we have available, contained a detailed classification of several aspects of memory (relating to the memory of both texts and life experiences) as well as a series of asanas graded to train the practitioner's skills in each of the enumerated categories.

In the 7th century writer and literary scholar Dandin's account of this book, he notes that there is one asana in particular that should be considered the most dangerous and the most powerful. The details of this exercise, presented in the very first pages of the work, were apparently not obvious on the page, but instead encoded in a series of word and letter games, including but not restricted to puns, similes, extended metaphors and symbolic tales, in such a manner that they appeared to be nonsensical until one had finished the book and returned to them. The authors of the *Smriti-sthana* believed that this was the best way to protect their last exercise from inadvertent or inexperienced practitioners.

Dandin, however, does provide a gloss on the final asana, which is simply this: if, in each of the previous sets of asanas, the student is asked to receive information, either by instruction or in the rawer state of sensory input, imprint it on the structures of the brain and recall it in various forms, this last set asks the student to *resist*, that is, actively push away any kind of sensory input or data (first from the forebrain). The principal metaphor used here is *push away the sea waves with your bare hands.*

Read all day yesterday, mostly on the net, distractedly: this and that. Bits and pieces of the self-anointed American avant-garde, most of it so damn quiet, in spite of its own polemic. Another of Rodefer's *Four Lectures*; again, the trepidation at the start of the lecture, viz., where is this heading, etc., but once more ends after having passed through such wisdom, such fury. The poet, returning home from Hell, lifts up his can of vegetable juice and smiles at the man next to him. Then Brian Somebody's essay on the *Poetry* website, 'Poetry and the Problem of Taste', which addresses an ennui as old as ancient Berryman heavy bored: subjective vs. objective taste. Roared towards an intervention but never got round to it. More restlessness. Mouni Sadhu was a Nazi? Investigations on his site reveal a whole world of occultists, including the Eastern European contingent, unique to itself. What exactly was Gurdieff's Fourth Way. Approaching night, slouching towards neuroscience, the brain as understood by one's own anatomy. Longing for Geoffrey Hill. What does it all mean, this ricocheting around the by-ways of human knowledge and human self-conception (in the blurred border between the two lies the rub)? Wrote to G. on Facebook: 'In the new literary space, no one can hear you scream.'

THREE STEREOGRAMS

If I wake up with a headache,
I might die with a headache.

The magazines that spoil hearts are
not the ones who break them.

A rust-coloured spear tip
of light on my accelerator pedal:
even when I move my hand over
to disappear it, it refuses to divulge
or give up its materiality.

A HORSE STUMBLED IN THE WAVES

to Bahauddin Dagar

A horse stumbled
unsteady
in the waves. He
was a small horse and
his pelt
was wet
up to his haunches. The beach
was shallow
but the waves were strong,
the pull was strong.

A horse stumbled
in the waves. He
lost his footing on
his forelegs — and his entire body seemed
to carry
an expression
of panic —
though clearly he
was happy enough
to be wet
in the morning sun.

Stumbled
in the waves. Then
— regaining cautious hold —
looked towards the hand
— tacit submission, faith in instruction —
that showed its palm
to turn his face
away.

PERMISSIONS & ACKNOWLEDGEMENTS

All the poems that appear in this anthology (except those that are listed below) are new and unpublished in individual book form. Permission to print the originals and reprint the ones listed below has been granted by the individual poets, publishers, or their literary executors. Grateful acknowledgments are due to all of them.

Aditi Machado
'Surrealistic film-making' first appeared in *Mayday* magazine.

Amit Chaudhuri
'Insomniac', 'Cordless', 'Education', 'Education' and 'The Fall of Baghdad' first appeared in *Insomniac* (Aark Arts) and *St Cyril Road* (Viking Penguin). All poems reprinted with written-email permission of the author.

Anita Nair
'An Ostrich's Love Song', 'Love for a Cat Man' and 'Transgressions' first appeared in *Malabar Mind* (Yeti Books/HarperCollins). All poems reprinted with written-email permission of the author.

C P Surendran
'Malabari: Inspiration', 'Milk Still Boils', 'A Cold Feeling', 'Offspring' first appeared in *Gemini II* (Viking Penguin), *Posthumous Poems* (Viking Penguin), *Canaries on the Moon* (Yeti), and *Portraits of the Space We Occupy* (HarperCollins). All poems reprinted with written-email permission of the author.

Chitra Banerjee Divakaruni
'After: A Landscape', 'The River', 'Arjun', 'The World Tree', and 'On Opening a Box My Mother Left in My House' first appeared in *Leaving Yuba City: Selected Poems* (Harcourt). All these poems are reprinted with written-email of the author.

David Dabydeen
Selections from 'Turner', 'Slave Song', 'For Ma', and 'Two Cultures' first appeared in *Turner* (Jonathan Cape / Peepal Tree). All poems reprinted with written-email permission of the author and Peepal Tree publishers.

Jeet Thayil
'Fool and Flea' first appeared in *English* (Ratapallax/Penguin), and 'The Heroin Sestina', 'The Sonneteer', 'Letter from a Mughal Emperor, 2006', '2007' in *These Error Are Correct* (Tranquebar). All poems reprinted with email-written permission of the author.

Kynpham Sing Nongkynrih
'Winter Weeds' and 'Beloved Is Thy Name' are part of a long poem 'Lita, Thy Name is Beloved'.

Maya Khosla
'Sychronicity' was first published in *Prairie Schooner* and 'A Poet's Keystone' in *Byline* magazine.

THANK YOU

A massive book project like this one ultimately has to be a labour of passion. And for that passion and love to be fulfilled, many along the way have lent their quiet support over the last few decades. Thank you to:

— Karthika V K, Shantanu Ray Chaudhuri and Shuka Jain of HarperCollins for their constant enthusiasm, valuable suggestions and inputs, and for their utter belief in this book as a whole. Also to Antony Thomas, Maitreya Nair, Girija Padmanabhan, Lipika Bhushan, Mallika Roy, Ratna Joshi, and Neha Punj at HarperCollins. — M E H Haider, Sourabh Sangam and Ashutosh Kumar Jha of InoSoft for unflinchingly translating my master book and cover design into elegant typeset pages.

— the literary editors and publishers who have commissioned me to edit or curate special issues/portfolios of Indian literature/poetry or anthologies. All those projects, ideal preparatory work for this book, have helped this anthology to be a better one. I'd like to put on record the names of the following editors: Peter Forbes and Fiona Sampson (*Poetry Review*, UK), Djelal Kadir, William Riggan and Daniel Simon (*World Literature Today*, USA), Ciaran Carson and Ed Larissy (*Yellow Nib*, Seamus Heaney Centre for Poetry at Queens University, Belfast), Ilya Kaminsky, Christian Wiman, Don Share & Beth Allen (Poetry Foundation, Chicago / *Poetry* magazine), Tessa Ransford (*Lines Review*, Edinburgh), David & Helen Constantine (*Modern Poetry in Translation*, UK), Ursula Owen and Judith Vidal-Hall (*Index for Censorship*, UK), Susheila Nasta (*Wasafiri*, UK), Zoran Anchevski (commissioning editor & translator, *Midnight's Grandchildren*, Struga Macedonia), Walter Cummins, Thomas Kennedy and Minna Proctor (*The Literary Review*, USA), Adonis [Ali Ahmad Said Asbar] and Osama Esber (*The Other*, Damascus/Paris), David Shook (*Molossus*, USA), James Byrne (*The Wolf*, London/New York), Kavita Jindal (*Writer's Hub*, London), Brinda Datta (*Biblio*, New Delhi), and others.

— the judges of various committees who awarded me fellowships, visitorships and residencies (and others who helped in that process) where parts of this book was worked upon: late Sir Stephen Spender, Christopher Reid [Faber & Faber poetry editor], Jonathan Galassi [Farrar Strauss Giroux literary editor], John Casey, Caroline Moore, The Lord Briggs, The Earl of Perth, The Lord Quinton, The Lord Weidenfeld, Sir Steven Runciman, Adam Czernawski, and Drue Heinz [*The Paris Review* publisher] for the Hawthornden Fellowship (UK); Pat Donlon, Janet Pierce and Patrick MacCabe (Tyrone Guthrie Centre, Ireland); D W Gibson (Ledig House, New York); Prabhu Guptara (Wolfsberg UBS, Switzerland); Chandrika Grover (Pro Helvetia Swiss Arts Council, New Delhi); Henk Propper and Thomas Mohlmann (NLPVF Dutch Foundation for Literature, Amsterdam); O P Jain (Sanskriti, New Delhi); Wang Anyi and Hu Peihua (Shanghai Writers Programme, China); Clare Morgan and Jane Draycott (Oxford University); John Kinsella (Cambridge University); Douglas Dunn and Robert Crawford (St Andrews University); John Thieme (University of Hull); Susheila Nasta (Queen Mary & Westfield College); Dennis Walder (Open University); George Szirtes (East Anglia University); William Radice

Reetika Vazirani
'Grievance' first appeared in *Manoa*. 'What a Fisher Girl Said in Defence of her Absence' first appeared *Meridians*. 'Luxor' first appeared in *New England Review* and *Callaloo*. All poems are printed with email-written permission from Heea Vazirani, the poet's mother. Acknowledgements are also due to Ravi Shankar and Leslie McGrath for sourcing these poems that were left out of Vazirani's posthumous collection, *Radha Says*.

Rishma Dunlop
'Saudade' and 'Radio New Mexico' were first published in *The Literary Review Indian Poetry*, edited by Sudeep Sen. 'Testament' appeared in an earlier version in *Metropolis*, Mansfield Press and 'Elegy' in *White Album*, Innana Publications.

Sridala Swami
'Paraphrase' appeared first in *Wasafiri* and 'Red Chillies' in *Pratilipi*.

Srilata K
'What Father Left Us' was first published in *Winners* (Vol. 3), co-published by the British Council and Unisun, Bangalore.

Subhashini Kaligotla
'Vessantara' and 'Morning in a City' were first published in *The Collagist*.

Sudeep Sen
'Mediteranean' first appeared in *New Writing 15* (Granta). 'A Blank Letter' first appeared in *Language for a New Century* (Norton) and *Postmarked India: New & Selected Poems* (HarperCollins). 'Banyan' first appeared in *Initiate: Oxford New Writing* (Blackwell). 'Desire' first appeared in *Indian Love Poems* (Knopf/Random House/Everyman). 'Winter' and 'Choice' first appeared in *The Literary Review* and *Yellow Nib*. 'Kargil' first appeared in *Platform, Yellow Nib, Caravan, Australian Poetry Journal* and *Ladakh* (Tyrone Guthrie Centre / Gallerie). All poems reprinted with email-written permission of the author.

Vijay Sheshadri
'Visiting Paris', 'Memoir', 'Thought Problem', and 'Family Happiness' first appeared in *The New Yorker*. 'Guide for the Perplexed' first appeared in *Ploughshares*. 'Elegy' first appeared in *Epiphany*. All poems reprinted with written-email permission of the author.

Vikram Seth
'Sampati' first appeared in *Granta*. 'The Fever Bird' and 'A Modest Proposal' first appeared in *A Suitable Boy*. 'For Philippe Honoré' first appeared in *An Equal Music*. 'Giles Gordon' first appeared in *The Guardian*. 'Dubious', 'Distressful Homonyms' and 'Unclaimed' first appeared in *Mappings*. 'Across the treeless street' first appeared in *From Heaven Lake*. '1.6', '2.44', '5.4', '6.1', '13.51', '13.52' first appeared in *The Golden Gate*. 'The Hermit on the Ice' first appeared in *The Rivered Earth*. All poems reprinted with written-email permission of the author.

(SOAS London University); Linda Hess (Stanford University); Graham Huggan and Sharmila Sen (Harvard University); and others.

— my publishers/editors/readers: Jon Philips, John Welch, Jeremy Poynting, Bryce Milligan, Leona Medlin, R K Mehra, Nirupam Chatterjee, Renuka Chaterjee, Sanjana Roy Choudhury, Chandana Dutta, Bipin Shah, Bina Sarkar Ellias, and all at HarperCollins of course.

— A K Ramanujan, Dom Moraes, Nissim Ezekiel, Jayanta Mahapatra, Adil Jussawalla, Keki Daruwalla, Shiv K Kumar, Agha Shahid Ali, Amitav Ghosh, Vikram Seth, Shashi Tharoor, Amit Chaudhuri, Ravi Shankar, Arundhati Subramaniam, Priya Sarukai Chabria, Tabish Khair, Daljit Nagra, Imtiaz Dharker, Leela Gandhi, Chitra Banerjee Divakaruni, Arshia Sattar, Anamika, Aminur Rahman, Gulzar,

— Peter Porter, Daniel Weissbort, George Szirtes, Alan Jenkins, Carol Ann Duffy, Elaine Feinstein, Jenny Lewis, Lesley Saunders, Kim Morrissey, Paul Nandi, Aamer Hussein, Sunetra Gupta, Stephen Watts, James Byrne, Todd Swift, Bernardine Evaristo, Maggie Gee, Ruth Borthwick, Melanie Abhrams, Michael Walling,

— Joseph Brodsky, Derek Walcott & Sigrid Nama, Les Murray, Donald Hall, William Matthews, David Ignatow, Phillis Levin, Kwame Dawes, Colin Channer, Wendy Barker, Fred D'Aguiar,

— Dan Daor & Gaby Silon, Amir Or, Tsur & Dorit Shezaf, Ya'ir Dalal, Mark & Sara Sofer, Eli & Yael, Sharon Rappaport, Zoran Anchevski, Iztok Osojnik, Hans van der Waarsenburg, Ciaran O' Driscoll, John Davies,

— Malashri & Robey Lal, Leela Samson, Aftab Seth, Pavan Varma, Amal Chatterjee & Susan Ridder, Marlisse Mensink & Bauke Steenstra, Deb & Purobi Mukharji, Pinak & Radha Chakravarty, Riva Ganguly & Proshanto Das, Probir Sen, Gopal & Tara Gandhi, Aftab Seth, Romi Chopra,

— Ma, Baba (who sadly did not live to see the bound finished copy of this book), Didu, Mama, Maj'uncle — and my dearest family, Priti and Aria, for putting up with all the time away from them travelling, researching, pouring over hundreds of slim volumes of poetry, door-stopper anthologies, unpublished manuscripts, and books of criticism. Their support, calm and love have been invaluable. Hey Aria — now we can go golfing, gaming and shooting without interruption, now that this book for you is done.

— and finally, all the poets in this book (and others who did not make it due to technical or other unavoidable reasons), without whose fine work this anthology wouldn't be what it is.

I take responsibility for any unwarranted errors in the book, but all praise should go to the poets for their fine work and to the supporters of this huge endeavour. And apologies if I have inadvertently left out any names in this list.

My gratitude and love to you all.

— Sudeep Sen
New Delhi | May 21, 2012

Poets are poetry, writers are prose — //
Prose can hold anything including
poetry, but in poetry, there's only
room for poetry —
— WISLAWA SZYMBORSKA

The poem is the detour from you to you;
it is the route. It is also the route of language
toward itself, its becoming visible and mortal:
wherewith the poem becomes the *raison d'être*
of language.
— PAUL CELAN